# EVERYDAY PIETY

# EVERYDAY PIETY

## ISLAM AND ECONOMY IN JORDAN

### SARAH A. TOBIN

CORNELL UNIVERSITY PRESS
*Ithaca and London*

First published 2016 by Cornell University Press
First printing, Cornell Paperbacks, 2016

Printed in the United States of America

Library of Congress Cataloging-in-Publication Data
Tobin, Sarah A., author.
    Everyday piety : Islam and economy in Jordan / Sarah
A. Tobin.
        pages cm
    Includes bibliographical references and index.
    ISBN 978-1-5017-0045-3 (cloth : alk. paper)
    ISBN 978-1-5017-0046-0 (pbk. : alk. paper)
    1. Islam—Economic aspects—Jordan.    2. Islam—Social
aspects—Jordan.    3. Islam and civil society—Jordan.
I. Title.
    BP173.75.T63 2016
    297.095695—dc23          2015036026

Cornell University Press strives to use environmentally
responsible suppliers and materials to the fullest extent
possible in the publishing of its books. Such materials
include vegetable-based, low-VOC inks and acid-free
papers that are recycled, totally chlorine-free, or partly
composed of nonwood fibers. For further information,
visit our website at www.cornellpress.cornell.edu.

Cloth printing          10  9  8  7  6  5  4  3  2  1
Paperback printing      10  9  8  7  6  5  4  3  2  1

*For my grandmother Pearl. I miss you.*

Each and every day countless and different prayers
and petitions, some in repetition and others born
anew, are addressed to Him for different requests,
each according to his or her circumstances and needs.

—Qu'ran 55:29

 Yet the dailiness, by breaking coherence and
introducing time, trains our gaze on flux and
contradiction; and the particulars suggest that
others live as we perceive ourselves living—not as
automatons programmed according to "cultural"
rules or acting out social roles, but as people going
through life wondering what they should do, making
mistakes, being opinionated, vacillating, trying to
make themselves look good, enduring tragic personal
losses, enjoying others, and finding moments of
laughter.

—Lila Abu-Lughod, *Writing Women's Worlds: Bedouin
Stories*

# CONTENTS

# ACKNOWLEDGMENTS

Although writing is often a solitary process, one is never truly alone. I conducted this research in Amman from 2007 to 2009, with an additional visit in 2012. In the process I accrued many debts. Many people contributed their time, efforts, resources, and support to help make this research and publication possible. First and foremost, many Jordanians and Palestinians not only gave me windows into their daily lives but also provided years of friendship and support. While the research demands anonymity, this is not an indication of a lack of appreciation. I am forever indebted to them. I can only hope that I have done their lives some measure of justice.

The International Islamic Arab Bank allowed me exceptional access, and I would like to acknowledge the hard work of Akef Hamam, Manar Al-Kisswani, and Alia Ali on my behalf. I know it was not always easy for the employees to give me so much of their time. This research would not have been possible without their help, sitting with me and walking me through day-to-day operations. I am deeply and tremendously grateful. I hope those affiliated with the bank will find my assessments well reasoned and respectable, even if they disagree with them.

The Department of Anthropology at Boston University was steadfast in providing financial, intellectual, and moral support. In particular, thanks to Bob Hefner for a decade of assistance. This project came about only because of a lengthy letter of encouragement that Bob sent my way. I am extraordinarily grateful that he was and is still looking out for me. I was also extremely fortunate to have a wealth of support from Richard Norton, Rob Weller, and Nancy Smith-Hefner. Kimberly Arkin, Charles Lindholm, Parker Shipton, Shahla Haeri and Jenny White also provided feedback over the years. Mark Palmer and Kathy Kwasnica were endlessly patient with me. I am deeply appreciative. I also acknowledge the time and support provided by Wheaton College and its Department of Anthropology. Berlin Graduate School Muslim Cultures and Societies and the Center for Area Studies at the Free University in Berlin provided me with extended periods of support to dig deep into the writing. The book is considerably better for their help.

I am grateful for the years of financial support that I have been awarded. The Institut für die Wissenschaften vom Menschen in Vienna; the American Center for Overseas Research in Amman, Jordan; Philanthropic Educational Opportunities; Alain McNamara at Fulbright and the Institute for International Education all generously funded portions of fieldwork. The Andrew W. Mellon Foundation, through Wheaton College, provided assistance with the 2012 research period.

Other people and institutions also supported this research. Fida Adely, Daromir Rudnyckyj, and Jillian Schwedler were instrumental to its development. I continue to be inspired by their scholarly contributions. The Arabic instructors at the Qasid Institute for Classical and Modern Standard Arabic in Amman endured many painful hours of my developing language skills. The University of Jordan brought me in as an instructor of English and opened the resources of the university to me. Dar al-Tawfiq allowed a non-Muslim through its doors. For all of these people and places, I am grateful.

I offer a very special thank you to the many people who read and commented on the book. Their feedback was vital. I thank Brian Howell, Stephen Mathis, Chloe Mulderig, Claire Oueslati-Porter, Chris Phillips, and Chris Taylor for reading and commenting on various drafts and sections. Special thanks to Jillian Schwedler for the particularly thoughtful comments. The Members of the Unnamed Research Group (MURG) read the draft in its entirety at least once, providing constructive feedback every week during the spring of 2012. Austin Jessie Davidson, Sally Dexter, Savannah Geasey, and Claire Rowell constituted a tremendous editorial team. Their dedication, even at times when it likely conflicted with their own studies, was admired and deeply appreciated. Austin Jessie Davidson, Amira Jaradat, Tamara Maaita, Maise Kattab, and Jessica Tibbets served as research assistants at various points in time. I could not have completed the project without them. A very special thanks goes to Jaime Jarvis for her keen editorial eye and indexing skills. I acknowledge the hard work of the anonymous reviewers whose insights were key to the development of this text. A heartfelt thank you goes especially to Cornell University Press. Peter Potter, Max Richman, Kitty Liu, and others worked very hard to make this manuscript as strong as possible.

Many works here are reproduced in whole or in part by permission. Austin Jessie Davidson provided many of her original pictures, as well as the cover art and French translations used in this text. Osama Hajjaj graciously provided an image, and I would also like to thank the École Biblique, Jerusalem, and acknowledge the importance of Father Jean-Michel de Tarragon's vocational endeavor in the photo library. Their images and contributions are unmatched. I would like to thank the Middle East Policy

Council and its journal *Middle East Policy*, in which portions of chapters 2 and 8 were published in 2012 as "Jordan's Arab Spring: The Middle Class and Anti-Revolution," *Middle East Policy* 19 (1): 96–109. Portions of chapter 3 were published in 2013 as "Ramadan Blues: Debates in Pop Music and Popular Islam in Amman, Jordan," *Digest of Middle East Studies* 22 (2): 292–316. Portions of chapter 7 were published in 2014 as "'Is It *Really* Islamic?': Evaluating the 'Islamicness' of Jordan's Islamic Banks," *Research in Economic Anthropology* 34 (1): 127–56.

I would especially like to thank the people in Amman, Jordan, who took the time to walk with me through this process, educating me and caring for me along the way. The original and latter-day women in *bait al-binaat* and fellow friends and academics—Nora Barakat, Gail Buttorff, Adam Kucharski, and Bozena Welborne—were steadfast compatriots in my journey. Although Becky Chabot was in Boston, she was online with me enough that it was almost as though she were in Amman. Many others, too many to name individually, influenced this work directly and indirectly.

Finally, my parents and siblings stand out for their care, compassion, and encouragement. They tolerated years of missed Thanksgivings and Christmases, birthdays and graduations, and they did so without complaint. I remain immensely grateful that my dad, mom, and Auntie Kate visited me in Jordan. They were endlessly encouraging and loving.

A very special thanks goes to my husband, Stephen, whose support was vital in seeing the book, and me, through from proposal to publication. Thank you for your love, encouragement, and sharp editing eye.

Truly, my experience has been one of an embarrassment of riches. With all of these amazing contributions, it is clear that any outstanding errors are mine alone.

# NOTE ON TRANSLITERATION

Arabic words have been transliterated based on a modified version of the system of the *International Journal of Middle East Studies*. I omitted diacritical marks but retained the 'ayn as ' and *hamza* as '. Occasionally, colloquial words retain their original written spelling based on a localized transliteration system. In those cases the 'ayn is written as a 3 and *Ha* (h) is a 7. A glossary of Arabic terms can be found at the end of the text.

Commonly recognized Arabic words, cities, and towns follow English spellings, so that *Haram* and *Hijab* are rendered *haram* and *hijab*, respectively, and "'Amman" is rendered "Amman." Proper names of informants are all pseudonyms and follow colloquial pronunciation.

# EVERYDAY PIETY

# Chapter 1

# A Muslim Plays the Slot Machines

It was a hot July day when the 19-year-old Jordanian girl walked into the Las Vegas casino. It was 1969, and young Asma was in awe of what she saw: Chandeliers softly illuminated the brown-carpeted walls and floors. Table after table hosted card games of poker and blackjack. Slot machines lined the walls, their flashing lights and bells heralding new fortunes. Showgirls with styled hair and feathered costumes rushed through on the way from performance to performance. Men in tuxedos brought drinks and cigarettes around, while Creedence Clearwater Revival's "Proud Mary" played in the background. The floor was alive with hope and opportunity. The energy was palpable.

Despite her best efforts to blend in, Asma's self-consciousness at being a Muslim in a casino showed through. As though out of habit, she tugged her miniskirt down low on her hips, trying to cover another inch or two of her thighs. She kept pulling her long brown hair over her exposed shoulders, embarrassed by the sunburn's betrayal of her skimpy swimsuit. Asma inched closer to her older brother, her escort and protector on this trip, as he walked confidently through the dimly lit maze of tables and machines, loud bells and cheers from winners and losers alike, a haze of cigarette smoke, odors of spilled drinks and perfume. Surely he knew that this was all so wrong. Didn't he? He led her to a row of slot machines. She looked up at him.

Ahmed leaned down and whispered in her ear, "Go on." He pushed a nickel into her sweaty palm and urged, "It's not going to kill you. Try it." Asma turned slowly toward the slot machine. With trembling fingers she pushed the nickel into the slot. Her

1

*other hand reached up to the lever. She took a breath, uttered the invocation recited before all Islamic prayers,* "Bismillah Al-Rahman Al-Raheem," *and pulled the lever.*

"And I won! I won a lot of money! I still can't believe I won!" Asma laughed and shook her head in lingering disbelief.

I was sitting across from a now middle-aged Asma in the living room of her suburban home in Amman, Jordan. I visited her and her family often, familiar with the softened hues of the couches and chairs in the late afternoon sun, its summer heat bearing down on us. We sipped Turkish coffee and ate the cupcakes I had brought with me, surrounded by three of her five adult children and her husband. Asma sat comfortably in her professional working clothes: a brown-and-white, long-sleeved, button-down shirt and floor-length corduroy skirt. Her head was covered with a matching headscarf, or *hijab*, and her plastic house slippers tapped on the floor from time to time as she chatted. She continued the story:

> But I felt too guilty keeping the money. Even then I knew in Islam that gambling was *haram* [forbidden]. I knew Sura Al-Baqara said, "They ask you about wine and gambling. Say, 'In them is great sin and yet, some benefit for people. But their sin is greater than their benefit'" [Qur'an 2:219]. So it was a sin, and I knew that it was wrong. I had to make it right. I gave the money away to create some good from this and for an eternal reward. I gave some money to family members, and I gave some to charity to purify it. But I couldn't keep it. Even then I knew gambling was a sin and *haram* and forbidden in Islam.
>
> You know, we had so many modern ideas back then. We used to think we were so free and liberated. [Starts chuckling] I used to wear really short skirts, like up to here [signaling her mid-thigh] and low-cut shirts [makes a sweeping motion of the top of her breasts]. Not just women. Men thought this too. My brother was the one who showed me the casino!
>
> Things were really changing then. They called it the "Islamic Resurgence." People were thinking about Islam more and more. Everyone was talking about it all the time. Everyone was becoming more Muslim. I came back to Amman, and I too started to think about this life. I started reading and learning about Islam, and I learned that how I was living was really *haram*. Well, it wasn't really really *haram*; I was a good person. But I wasn't taking every opportunity to be the best Muslim and do the most with Islam in my life. And there were so many different opinions about what to do! So, I went on 'Omrah. You know, the

"mini-Hajj." I did it for spiritual purification and forgiveness. I started wearing the proper *hijab*, showing only my hands and face. I decided to study Islam for myself, and I am so happy that I did.

We don't know our religion. We have this long history and scholarship that we never learn about. We just take it all for granted. But I studied it, and my life is better now. I pray. I fast for Ramadan. I even have my accounts at the Islamic bank. I am enlightened and educated about Islam, and I am now living as a real Muslim. So, *Al-hamdulilah* [Praise God], my sins and my past are forgiven, and now I'm living the real Islam.

I tell the story of Asma to illustrate a certain anxiety that exists today among many Muslims of Amman, Jordan. People like Asma—who is far from atypical among today's Ammanis or those living in Amman—are concerned that they practice an Islam that is authentic or "real."[1] They wonder, "Am I Muslim enough?" and "How can I be a better Muslim?" In my research I focused on one aspect of this desire to be a better Muslim—specifically, the need to reconcile personal piety on the one hand with matters of money and personal finance on the other. Asma and Muslims like her struggle deeply with the challenge of living their daily lives in a modern economy that requires them to purchase goods and services, have a bank account, use a credit card, or perhaps even invest in stocks or business ventures. They are concerned with engaging in economic practices that are "really" Islamic, but they are often uncertain and anxious as to what that should look like because public opinion on this issue varies greatly not only in Amman but throughout the Muslim world. Furthermore, other factors complicate aspirations for the "real" Islam—for instance, whether one is male or female, middle-class or upper-class. Taken together, these uncertainties and anxieties reveal an underlying desire to firmly engage in contemporary economic life and to do so with Islamic authenticity, or "realness."

In this book, I explore these issues in greater depth, drawing on my research, which included twenty-one months of participant observation at sites in and around Amman. The focus on Amman is significant. Economically, the city is a major regional hub and growing at a swift pace. With a population of more than 2.5 million people, Jordan's capital city is both a popular tourist destination and a major business center, with a strong regional economy bolstered by foreign direct investment and U.S. foreign aid. Along with Doha and Dubai, Amman is a favorite location for the regional offices of multinational corporations. One of the Middle East's largest banks, International Islamic Arab Bank, is headquartered in Amman; during my time in Jordan I obtained an internship there. Politically, the country's leader, King

'Abdullah, is known as a close ally of the United States and is well known for quipping that Jordan is a "safe home in a rough neighborhood." And socially, the country maintains peaceful coexistence of millions of Muslim Jordanians and Palestinians with refugees from surrounding countries. Due to this relative economic, political, and social stability in the Middle East, Amman has also seen the emergence of a consumer-oriented and market-friendly Muslim middle class.

Amman also hosts a growing Islamic banking and finance sector. Islamic banking in Amman is a particularly salient lens for understanding the processes described in this book, as it is a technologically and institutionally new space in Jordan's economy, with a history that traces back only to the mid-1980s. Islamic banking and finance is known regionally for its more explicit and conservative expressions of Islam and Islamic law. The field constitutes an important area in which questions of the role of and place for Islamic economic practice are readily debated, challenged, and—at least to some degree—accepted and promoted.

While I was conducting this research in Amman, I also taught English at the University of Jordan and at the United Nations Relief and Works Agency for Palestine Refugees (UNRWA), where I met and had opportunities to talk with students, professionals, and their families. I was a participant observer in the homes of more than a dozen Muslim and two Christian families. I studied Arabic intensively and attained a very high level of proficiency, which made all these connections deep and productive. All told, my time in Amman provided rich opportunities to explore the ways in which middle-class Muslims negotiate their everyday economic and pious practices in this global and Islamic-dominant city.

A major theme in the lives of those who I interviewed—and therefore, in this book—is the role of Islamic Law, or Shari'a, which is the moral code and religious law of Islamic life. In the West Shari'a is often portrayed as a static body of laws meting out punishments for civil and religious crimes. It is associated with the stoning of adulterers, cutting off thieves' hands, and killing of apostates. In the West Shari'a is understood to be medieval: something backward and nonmodern that ought to be feared and abhorred.

In reality, Shari'a is a set of reference points for questions about moral comportment and ethics of everyday life for Muslims. It is highly interpretive and flexible. Shari'a is a process of knowledge cultivation that Muslims use when addressing the challenges of everyday life. Muslims living in Amman put Shari'a to work as a means to engage in their daily economic lives in an authentically or "real" Islamic way and to entrench their religious practices in a globalized world. Shari'a is both a tool and a standard Muslims employ in pious endeavors.

Muslims in urban Amman resolve their moral uncertainties and anxieties for the "real" Islam in economic life in two ways. First, they engage in efforts that mark their economic practices as distinctly "Islamic." Economic practices of all kinds—from gambling at a casino and banking and finance, to dining out during Ramadan and wearing the *hijab*—are subject to scrutiny and Shari'a-based judgments regarding their authenticity or "real Islamicness." Economic practices are subject to all sorts of "Islamizing" or attempts to incorporate religion into them. Second, Muslims in urban Amman are thinking about Islam and acting on it in ways that reflect economic calculations, which include evaluations of value, profit, and risk; rationalization of processes and outcomes; audits of "performance indicators"; or ways of judging and assessing actions in religious life. These calculative agencies make Islamic piety measurable and assessable. There is a simultaneous Islamizing of economic practices and an economizing of Islamic pious practice.

## Neoliberal Piety

The fields of economic action and piety merge when Ammanis fuse neoliberalism and their Islamic practice. This results in what I call "neoliberal piety." Neoliberalism is a political-economic theory asserting that societal and individual well-being is best advanced through private property rights, free markets, and free trade (Harvey 2005, 2). This requires that capitalist arrangements be largely unfettered by governmental regulations, thereby diminishing the role and influence of the state. Individuals are included in neoliberal theory in aims to liberate personal freedoms and skills in market-friendly areas, and by requiring people to rely on and regulate themselves in most areas of life. Neoliberalism asserts the ascendency of the market and the primacy of the individual, and it emphasizes their combination as the solution to complex local and global relationships. The pursuit of these ideas is an ethical endeavor (Oueslati-Porter 2011, 65). Free markets, the position holds, make for more freedoms for individuals and more just societies.

At first blush, this may seem unrelated to one's Islamic piety. Rather, similar to Atia (2012, 2013) I found that the challenges and opportunities between economic life and Islam are pronounced. As Asma experienced, the act of obtaining cash is questioned for its Islamicness, and charitable giving is infused with religious intention. Asma saw her fashion options in skirts and tops as something to be altered and Islamized. Ammanis wrestle with the "Islamicness" of a bank account or a credit card for heightened consumer spending. Neoliberal piety is also social, which creates public pressure to eat certain foods at certain restaurants at certain times during Ramadan and to defend a relationship between the fabric on a woman's head with the moral fabric of her being. These challenges and opportunities are further intensified by the proliferation of compulsory schooling, ubiquitous mass media, and regional and global popular culture. Ammanis are unable to avoid the presence and pressures of neoliberal influences on their lives and lifestyles.

Neoliberal piety also derives from contemporary understandings of Islamic law, or Shari'a. It is considered a truism in the Middle East that more women don the headscarf, more men pray in mosques, and more children are conversant in the Islamic scriptures today than in the twentieth century.[2] This is because the Islamic Resurgence that Asma referenced amplified the expectations for a public and visible Islam in everyday life in Jordan.[3] Today's Ammanis engage neoliberal piety while using Shari'a to claim that they are practicing "the real Islam." The resulting claims are then debated and judged in terms of authenticity, or "realness," emphasizing "correct" religious practice and demanding competency in referencing and utilizing Islamic Law, or Shari'a.

Neoliberal piety emerges because neoliberalism and Islamic piety share similar temporal sensibilities. Both produce a sense of shortcoming and a desire for more—more profit, more gain, and greater expansion into new spaces and new markets (Schielke and Debevec 2012, 142). As this thinking goes, just as one must calculate and work toward ever-elusive higher rates of profit, one can and should work to attain a commensurable spiritual reward. Simply put, there is never enough monetary or spiritual gain, and such pursuits remain unfulfilled even as they prompt further action and new aims. This relentless striving toward profits and blessings and rewards, and the avoidance of punishment and hellfire, is the archetypal reflection of neoliberal piety. Neoliberal piety prompts both Islamized economic practice in the dreams of higher levels of profits and economized Islamic practice in the objective of more rewards. The desire to practice "the real Islam" is equivalent to the pursuit of ever-increasing profit: it is a primary motivator and aim for action. I argue that this is the main reason that Ammanis report an anxiety and need to express "the real Islam" publicly and authentically.[4]

In fact the "commodification of the future" (Appadurai 1996) that has enabled futures markets in financial trading has affected Islam as well. Calculations of sin, forgiveness, and eternal rewards have come to dominate decision-making processes as the influence of neoliberal piety spreads. One can calculate one's own prospects for eternity. By extension, individuals can then make adjustments in worldly practice to be better assured of *jenna*, or paradise. This extends risk management into the afterlife, based on the calculative principles applied to Shari'a in the Qur'an. The successful penetration of calculative agencies in the marketplace, which prove generally predictable and reliable, has lent credence to their use in pious practices.

## Defining the Middle Class

Jordan is an important place for witnessing these calculations in practice with a Muslim middle class. Though the government last conducted an official census in 2010, it did not document the population in terms of ethnicity or religion. While conducting my research, common belief amongst my friends was that the country's demographic majority is ethnic Palestinian (50 percent), followed by ethnic Jordanian (30 percent), refugees and immigrants from wars in Iraq and Syria (nearly 20 percent), and a small number of native Assyrians and Circassians, as well as migrant workers from Egypt, Sri Lanka, and the Philippines. During a visit I made to a United Nations High Commissioner for Refugees processing center in Amman, I witnessed the registration of new residents to the city who were coming daily from areas as far-flung as Sudan and Somalia. Truly, the regional reputation of Jordan as an economically and socially stable and secure home for everyday Muslims of all nationalities and ethnic backgrounds is well known.

Ninety-two percent of Jordan's residents are Muslim, and they are overwhelmingly Sunni. Salafis, particularly serious, often fundamentalist practitioners of Sunni Islam with roots in Saudi Arabia, constitute an important if marginalized group. They underpin a growing interest in public demonstrations of Islam, though their aesthetic austerity is often disregarded by more mainstream Ammanis.

Amman is now a city in which religiously diverse Muslims can and do cohere in an economically and socially dominant middle class. Despite economic diversity in monthly salaries, social and cultural life gives precedence to middle-class values, ethics, and ideas. University students and part-time employees make around 25 Jordanian Dinars (JD) per month ($35 USD). Government employees—typically ethnic Jordanians—make 200 JD ($282 USD) per month, in addition to guaranteed employment and a secure pension, while private sector employees—who are typically ethnic Palestinians—make 250 JD ($352 USD) per month. The highest earners are often landowners and business proprietors (also typically ethnic Palestinians), who make in excess of 1,000 JD ($1,411 USD) per month. Nonetheless, they all overwhelmingly consider themselves middle class. This is because late twentieth and early twenty-first century understandings of the middle class in Amman are less about income and more about a set of social and cultural practices—a "suburban consciousness"—that bring this society into a new kind of re-imagined community (Tobin 2012).

In less than a century, Amman saw tremendous alterations to its demographics and class constructions. As is discussed in chapter 2, the establishment of the Jordanian state in 1946 and especially the voluminous influx of Palestinian refugees defined and redefined the ways by which social class was understood and practiced throughout the second half of the twentieth century. Notably, landowning, commodities trading, and religious professions declined in status and importance. In their stead, neoliberal reforms prompted swift urbanization and injected value into the pursuit of educational and professional skills (Adely 2012; Anderson 2005; Clark 2004; Rueschemeyer, Stephens, and Stephens 1992; Schwedler 2006).

Neoliberal piety is an economic and religious development closely associated with Amman's robust middle class. The symbolic power of a strong and comprehensive middle class lies in its consideration as the most just and equitable societal arrangement, particularly when in its neoliberal formations. As scholars have noted, this conceptualization of society is highly compatible with Islamic ethics, which deem Islam a religion of equity, fairness, and hopeful promise for individuals (see also Davis and Robinson 2006; Hefner 1993a).

Jordan's middle class operates as a dynamic cohort of Islamic consumers and producers who are engaged in everyday practices through which they define themselves and their world. As a result, there is a set of preferences, aesthetics, knowledge, skills, education, and certain advantages—what Pierre Bourdieu calls "cultural capital"—that define the comprehensive Ammani middle class (Bourdieu 1977, 2008, 2013). Cultural capital is the middle class's stock-in-trade. It includes non-financial social assets that promote social mobility beyond economic means, often manifesting as "taste" or "competencies" in fields including art, food, music, film, fashion, and other forms of consumer goods (Bourdieu 2013).

Debates about "the real Islam" are contests about taste, such as *hijab* fashion or expensive venues for Ramadan meals. These are resolved through the wielding of specific competencies to better claim Islamic authenticity, such as by more elaborate or sophisticated references to Shari'a. These contentions are both "real," in some economized sense, and aspirational. In these disputes over what is "really Islamic," the points of reference are meaningful and highly personalized. They are economized in the self-interest of the individual. At the same time, they are aspirational, as their solidification as "really Islamic" is part of potential upward mobility—economic, spiritual, and social. Furthermore, cultural capital is an important means by which new spheres of life become economized and Islamized. Neoliberal piety in urban Jordan's Muslim middle class is powerful symbolically because it mobilizes people most widely in realms of life previously untapped by market logics and pious considerations.

## Authenticity, Modernity, Cosmopolitanism in Piety

In Amman, authenticity and modernity play highly complementary roles. On the one hand, urban Ammanis self-consciously identify a normative and timeless ("real") Islam through a set of beliefs, values, and practices (Hefner and Zaman 2007).[5] They develop and invoke Shari'a-based evidence that they are practicing, as one informant said, "the same Islam of the Prophet Mohammed (Peace Be Upon Him), his Companions, and the true Muslims of our past." Authenticity and truth claims are grounded in one's ability to establish credible and reliable discursive links and references to the past through Shari'a (Salamandra 2004). These assertions are also grounded in a sense of timeless "truth" about Islam, because the references are believed to be divinely enjoined and therefore objectively "real." Authenticity is about developing connections to the divine past.

While authenticity is about connections to the divine past, such connections are made in contemporary moments. Connecting to an imagined Islamic community of history—complete with recorded rituals, social groupings, and moral exhortations—is (re)imagining the community that is being made today (Anderson 1991). Authentic connections to the past are made in the present, making debates about the "real" Islam also about the contemporary world and desires for wider connections across time and place.

Ammanis also invoke modernity. In fact, although the Arabic word they most commonly use for modernity is 'asriya, one of my students indicated, "Let's be realistic, 'Arabeezi[6] has taken over. Everyone just says 'Amman kiteer (very) modern!'" Exerting a modern, stylized Islamic self who is competent, educated, and informed and skilled at wielding such knowledge grants one authority and justifies one's claims of authenticity in the real Islam. Modernity is about connections in the present that are used to legitimate authenticity claims.

Modernity for Ammanis is a style and an aesthetic of consumption, connections, and self-presentation. Being modern in today's Middle East is about "how you spoke, what you ate, what movies you'd seen, what you wore, where you bought it, and where you were seen wearing it" (Peterson 2011, 5–6). Being modern in urban Amman is a mode of performance and way of living that indexes middle class–based notions of taste and education

(Jameson 1984) and other forms of cultural capital. Furthermore, an Islamic modernity is a mode of performance that indexes these notions as well as something identifiable as "Islamic" simultaneously. This integrated Muslim modernity is enacted through contests over authenticity in textual references and in competitive claims of Islamic authority.[7]

Ammanis affirm a Muslim modernity through cosmopolitanism. I define this as economized practices that reference points beyond the local and place oneself in expanded, often global economic and cultural flows (Peterson 2011, 7). Ammanis use cosmopolitanism to transcend localized or regional interests and engage agonistic others[8] in the debates about "the real Islam" (Bayat 2010; Salamandra 2004).

As a case in point, I took several courses at an Islamic Institute in Amman. The courses were gender-segregated and designed for Muslims who were keen to deepen their knowledge of Islamic history, theology, and ethics. During one class on *Seerah*, the life and times of the Prophet Mohammed, we discussed the historical context in which the Prophet had received a command to wage war. According to Shari'a, the last ten years of Mohammed's life saw tense relations between recent converts to Islam who were then located in the city of Medina and the powerful Quraish tribes of Mecca, from whom these new Muslims has escaped persecution. Initially, Mohammed refused to fight the Quraish, despite the pleas and urgings of the Muslims. However, this changed when Mohammed received the revelation, "Permission to fight is given to those who are fought against because they have been wronged, truly Allah has the power to come to their support. They are those who were expelled from their homes without any right, merely for saying, 'Our Lord is Allah' . . ." (Qur'an, 22:39–40)

In this classroom of women, debates and discussion turned to what "the real Islam" meant in this verse. They asked questions such as, what is persecution? Who commits it? Was the verse universal in the sense that Muslims should fight all non-Muslims? Did it mean that Muslims should only fight if persecuted by non-Muslims? What if they were persecuted by a government? What does it mean to "fight back"? What is the role of violence? The discussion was vibrant, even heated, with a wide diversity of opinions.

Eventually the class reached consensus using modern claims and cosmopolitan positioning. My classmates agreed that the "persecution of Muslims" came mainly in the form of large-scale military attacks, such as the then-recent bombings of Gaza, wars in Afghanistan and Iraq, and drone strikes in Pakistan. They also agreed that the verse meant that nonviolent resistance, as exemplified in the traditions of Jesus, Gandhi, Nelson Mandela, and Martin Luther King Jr., should be the first path that Muslims take to "fight back" when persecuted. In this class, an ancient text was believed to speak relevantly and coherently on issues of modern and global warfare to contemporary women in Amman who were seeking "the real Islam." They claimed authenticity through discussions of scriptural intent and historical facts, and exerted modernity through contemporary reference points, which situated them in a global and cosmopolitan community. Furthermore, referencing the four historical nonviolence proponents as *Islamic* examples demonstrates the ways in which knowledge can be Islamized and economized, and stylized as modern and authentic. According to the women, these highly revered figures reflect some inherent truth about the contours of "the real Islam." In the course of the discussion, my classmates came to align their individual beliefs and Islamic perspectives with some agreed-upon variation of practical, relevant, and normative Islamic practice in contemporary society.

Ammanis in this study "believe as they live" more than "live as they believe" (Estruch and Glick 2000). The most important question people debate is rarely "What do you believe?"; instead, it is the two-pronged "What do you do, and how does it align (or not) with consensus?" and "Whose consensus?" In authenticity and modernity debates and cosmopolitan claims, one's beliefs are highly flexible and often of lesser relevance. Altering one's belief in accordance with consensus in public practice is a viable means to lay claims to the real Islam.

To understand this malleability in belief and practice, I utilize a tripartite model. The first part consists of the religious activities and rituals that individuals perform in public. Social scientists' collective term for these is "orthopraxy," a word from the ancient Greek meaning correct actions or practices. The second part of pious practice is doctrine—a set of beliefs, frequently normative, that individuals hold as the essential tenets of Islam. The third element is orthodoxy, or individually held belief.

I realize that construing orthodoxy as such may surprise some readers. For some writers on Islam, orthodoxy is defined in terms of adherence to doctrine (see also Deeb 2006; Mahmood 2005). However, with this tripartite construction, I aim to interject a conceptual space for internal agreement and disagreement, which is consonant with person-centered constructions of neoliberal piety. To define orthodoxy as adherence to doctrine overlooks many of the important ways by which rejection and dismissal of certain doctrinal precepts occurs while these Muslims still consider themselves practitioners of "the real Islam." Multiple verses in the Qur'an emphasize how the interpretation of Shari'a is ultimately a matter of *individual* responsibility and choice (An-Na'im 2009, 10–12). This framework provides such space.

Historically speaking, Islam has insisted more on orthopraxy than ortho-doxy (Kuran 1997a, 1997b). As Wilfred Cantwell Smith points out, "There is no word meaning 'orthodox' in any Islamic language. The word usually translated 'orthodox,' *sunni*, actually means rather 'orthoprax,' if we may use the term. A good Muslim is . . . one whose commitment may be expressed in practical terms that conform to an accepted code" (1957, 28). This is il-lustrated by the fact that the learning and correct recitation of sacred texts in Arabic—even when local populations do not use Arabic as a non-sacred language for everyday life—is considered more important than comprehen-sion of their meaning (Denny 1989a, 1989b; Starrett 1998). Furthermore, parts of Islamic doctrine have changed over time (Bonner 2008). As will be demonstrated later in this book, contemporary Islam in urban Jordan reflects different doctrinal emphases and content in economic practices than were present at the religion's advent.

Ammanis are able to lay claim to practicing "the real Islam" through analytical separation of orthopraxy, doctrine, and orthodoxy. Because there are no assumptions of a preexisting movement, linkage, or even coherence between them, there is great flexibility to disentangle these realms of living one's life as a pious Muslim. The post–Islamic Resurgence context in Amman is one of heightened and ever-increasing public expectations for Islam in economic practices, particularly in terms of fasting for Ramadan, donning the *hijab*, and banking and finance. As a result, fulfilling the mandates of the religion in public norms and ethics does not require one to cultivate an inner, pious self. Orthopraxy does not require orthodoxy, and doctrinal correctness is so highly contested that it demands neither. Fasting for Ramadan, donning the *hijab*, or choosing to open an account at an Islamic bank does not require one to actually believe in the practices' Islamic nature. In fact, many people reported conducting their Islamized economic practices to assert authenticity despite actively believing something very different. The cases of producing and consuming Islamic banking are particularly salient for this. Their Islamic authenticity does not assume a predetermined inward state.

Islamic authenticity carries mandates for orthopraxy as a part of religious sociability. On one hand, Ammanis are subject to the demands of the public. On the other, they constitute the very public who demands highly visible displays of Islamic practice. This generative cycle (Bourdieu 1977), or self-reproducing process, is directly attributable to the Islamic Resurgence. The Islamic Resurgence has often been conceived of in terms that—particularly since the 1970s—closely link the activities of Muslims to a broader reli-gious ethos or moral sense in Middle Eastern societies (Mahmood 2005, 3). In Amman, the religious ethos and new public norms and ethics include "reciting the Qur'an, keeping the fast, wearing the veil, avoiding alcohol, giving alms; not necessarily anything strictly political" (Hefner 2005, 21). These orthopraxic engagements are contested: some people assert that they are a set of historical, timeless norms that align with the first generations of Muslims as revealed by Shari'a with others asserting that they are not convincingly Islamic. The dispute is over whether these key practices are the essential and most crucial elements of Islam or whether they are too narrow and "the real Islam" constitutes something larger and less literal. Simply enacting these pillars, many Ammanis agree, does indicate that someone is a "real Muslim."

Nonetheless, in orthopraxy relatively predictable parameters for claims of Islamic authenticity are now present throughout the Middle East. They include prayer, fasting for Ramadan, and the *hijab*, and have expanded to include Islamic banking and finance, as well as the production and consumption of various religious media and literature, and adherence by intellectuals to a self-described Islamic point of view (Mahmood 2005, 3). These displays, while not necessarily doctrinal, directly reference economic life, particularly those practices that are useful for constructing a life within the demands of contemporary society: comporting oneself "properly" in the economic sphere, purchasing and presenting certain types of clothing, consuming new religious knowledge and cultural forms, and working in the marketplace of religious ideas. When seeking "the real Islam" in economic practice, Muslims find any number of sources able to provide answers.

## Finding "The Real Islam": Conducting Research in Amman

When I began my research in 2007, it did not take long before I began hearing people discuss their economic practices in terms of "the real Islam," *al-Islam al-haqqiqi*. Ammanis debating Islamic authenticity and legitimacy of practice centered around reference to an objectified, singular, and monolithic idea of "an Islam," which resided objectively "out there" and was understood to exist without complication, interpretation, or influence. When I asked a friend about the Arabic translation and etymology of "the real Islam," she replied, "We never refer to Islam as anything else! Islam is Islam. It hasn't changed and it never will. It is the real Islam."

These explanations frustrated me: Where was this "real Islam"? How did you find it? How did you know if it is real? Perhaps most importantly, what forms of Islam were *not* "real"?[9] Furthermore, how could I make sense of public normativity in economic practices when everyone seemed to have something different to say about it? It became clear that "the real Islam" was tied to what people learned about the religion and how they engaged it in their everyday economic practices. Beyond that, I was stumped. I needed to know where and what people learned about Islam.

When I inquired about where religious education and knowledge transmission happened, the most common response I received was "at home." The predominant mode for religious education happened within the confines of the home, whether in front of the television, around the dinner table, with family elders, or among siblings. Ammanis have a reputation for being "family-centered." One friend from the Gulf—a Kuwaiti who had difficulties making friends in Amman—told me, "Jordanians are the least friendly of all the Arabs. They hold you an arm's length away as a 'guest,' and it is really hard to get to know them." As a tall, blonde-haired, blue-eyed, non-Muslim, noticeably Western researcher, I found that this tendency created some difficulties for me. Gaining entrée into homes in a society known for being extremely family-centered and private became a difficult, though vital, method for observing knowledge transmission, vetting its "Islamicness," and witnessing the processes of identifying and developing new economic spheres for religious questioning, negotiating, and action. My most common method for developing close contacts was through mutual acquaintances and a gradual process of spending hours with subjects in a public space such as a coffee shop, then slowly integrating into the domestic spaces of their home. As this developed into a study of economic life, Islamic piety, and public expression, my research population became a rather broad-based collection of otherwise unrelated and unaffiliated people, as is often found in contemporary, urban ethnographies.[10] Though their lives and lifestyles could all be construed as middle class, nothing otherwise tied these families to each other.

One source of Islamic authority that I found in the homes is of an intergenerational nature. Stories like Asma's are quite common among women who came of age during the 1970s and 1980s. They anchor their Islamic authority with their husbands (Mahmood 2005), their children (Adely 2012), and each other (Deeb 2006). These women have become virtuosos of both text and experience (Stadler 2009). Many of them shared their stories of enlightenment and (re)discovery of Islam in an attempt to establish a baseline of practice for the people in their homes and social circles: Asma came to understand *that* she should don the *hijab* and go on pilgrimage, whereas her daughter came to understand *when* she should don the *hijab* and assumed that pilgrimages would occur throughout her life. Women in homes are redefining normative Islamic piety in economic practices.

Outside the home, Jordanians learn about Islam and Islamic teachings, and are inculcated with a sense of moral goodness in a number of formal education centers (Adely 2012, 88), including those registered with the Ministry of Religious Endowments and Islamic Affairs (Wazirat al-Awqaaf wa al-Shu'oon al-Islamiya) as well as the Muslim Brotherhood and its schools, public educational centers, NGOs, and hospitals (Clark 2004). The Jordanian government provides Islamic education to all Muslim public school pupils, which serves to complicate the intergenerational learning in homes. Many times I saw schoolchildren completing homework exercises about Islam, only to turn around and teach their parents. In one instance, a third-grade boy asked his mother if she could read with him the school's text about prayer. As they read a story from Shari'a together, the mother turned to her husband and said, "I've never heard this before. Have you?" After her husband replied that he, too, had never heard this, the mother turned to the son and said, "This is important. Our family should all learn this together." As Fida Adely points out, "Although the textbooks make religious references, the relationship between religious doctrine (in the form of verses from the Qur'an or *ahadith*, or recited stories of the words, actions and teachings of the Prophet Mohammed) and many of these day-to-day matters is less than direct" (Adely 2012, 88–89), requiring additional interpretations and interlocutions in everyday life and beyond one's natal home and primary education. While the state and other external voices make claims and transmit a kind of normative Islam to all citizens via educational efforts and schooling, we should not immediately assume widespread adoption of state-sponsored or schooled Islam. Significant (re)interpretation is still being done in homes and other important spaces that are often economic and social.

Another primary learning space in which I researched is the workplace. Many ethnographies speak to the kinds of information sharing that occur through daily interactions among coworkers and between supervisors and employees.[11] To access the kinds of conversations and knowledge sharing that occur in professional settings, I became a student, teacher, and colleague so that I could more easily gain access to my students, fellow professionals, and their families.

I was also able to obtain an internship and training at a local Islamic bank. The primary means by which I originally gained access was Facebook.[12] Despite the large number of people I had met through acquaintances, Arabic language classes, and my work as an English instructor during my first year of fieldwork, I had been unable to find anyone employed by or affiliated with an Islamic bank. In a last-ditch attempt, I scoured Facebook for anyone in the Jordan network whose profiles mentioned either of the two Islamic banks. I then contacted all of them, and requested assistance in contacting their human resources departments or other employees who could help arrange interviews or an internship. It was through these contacts that I obtained research access and an internship at the International Islamic Arab Bank.

Another location where I spent sizable amounts of time was Aspire, a women's-only gym near the University of Jordan. In the Middle East, the gym is becoming known as a location for social interaction (Salamandra 2004) and associational life (Gifford 2009). Although mixed-sex gyms in Amman are often regarded as public, masculine spaces and Muslim women would normally remain veiled in such settings, Aspire was completely free of men. Women were able to trade their headscarves, *abayas*, and outdoor clothing for tracksuits, spandex pants, and T-shirts and engage in physical motion—on the treadmill, bikes, and Nautilus and in aerobics classes—that would otherwise render their reputations suspect. The gendered seclusion of the rooftop swimming pool allowed them to don bikinis and openly slather on tanning oil, even as the *athaan* (Friday call to prayer) and *khutba* (sermon) were broadcast over loudspeakers from the neighboring mosques. The additional services of the all-women's environment—hairdressing, manicures and pedicures, even full waxing and massages—enabled freedom in the members' movements and manner of conversation. I spent hours as a participant observer with middle-class and upper-middle-class Jordanian and Palestinian women, as well as the migrant Arab, South Asian, and Southeast Asian workers, who engaged each other in conversations about everyday life, Ammani and regional politics, local events and popular culture references, health and the body, and other topics. Aspire was a locus for much of the contextual knowledge I obtained in Amman.

Person-to-person interactions remain most salient for religious education and knowledge transmission (White 2003). However, interpersonal relationships have been supplemented heavily by connections engendered by a prominent feature of advanced capitalism: the media, especially radio and TV. In Amman, the most popular English-language radio station, Play 99.6, along with my favorite Arabic-language station, 91.5, often did not address or debate religious topics explicitly. They were much more likely to invoke Islamic norms, ethics, or ideas in their call-in shows and comments by radio hosts. Titla' min Ra'si (Get Out of My Head), a nightly call-in show on 91.5, featured two hosts, one male and one female, who would often pose questions for discussion such as, "Is love something that happens immediately, as in love at first sight, or does love develop over time?" Call-in responses typically took one side or the other. Some referenced stories from the Qur'an and the time of the Prophet Mohammed. Some cited *hadith* in support of one side of the argument or the other. Still others reported personal stories about how they or their parents, friends, and celebrities had found love through one of these methods. The language of Islam was intermixed with other authoritative, Shari'a-derived references, in addition to popular appeals.

Other radio debates with religious inflections and justifications were framed in terms derived from Shari'a, such as comparisons of mixed-sex interactions in dating and love-marriages and the still relatively common arranged marriages. Explicitly religious programs were widely available on stations such as Hayat FM (Life FM) and some stations that played only Qur'anic recitation were commonly heard in taxis and throughout the city. In fact, taxis and other forms of public transportation are often important sources for daily updates on local and international news events and carry other information ranging from debates about the Palestinian-Israeli conflict to sermons by preachers. The radio and other technologies for enhanced "soundscapes" (cassette tapes, CDs, and now mp3s) is often cited as an important technology throughout the Arab world (Gordon 2003; Racy 2003; Shannon 2003) for the formation of ethical subjectivities (Hirschkind 2006), in contests and debates about popular Islam (Tobin 2013), and in the Islamic world more widely (Qureshi 1986, 2006). The plethora of choices in radio stations and audio transmissions speaks to the diverse Islamic voices that can be heard throughout the city on any given day at any given time.

Knowledge transmission and religious education also happen via television. Although religious programming on TV was commonly found in public spaces—such as a Saudi Arabian sheikh featured on sets displayed for sale in the French hypermarket, Carrefour—in my experience families and individuals rarely turned to them in their homes. Rather, they opted to tune into the daily events reported on Al-Jazeera or watch American programming such as *Friends*, *Grey's Anatomy*, and *American Idol*, which are subtitled in formal Arabic on Gulf-produced stations like MBC4 and carry a decidedly modern aesthetic. Chapter 3 of this book explores the opportunities that these TV shows offer for creating Islamized engagement and economizing practices during Ramadan and chapter 4 the conflicts that invoke the *hijab*.

Emergent cultural and social institutions that were developed in the twentieth century, especially as a result of the Islamic Resurgence, created new struggles for the "commanding heights of public ethics and culture" (Hefner and Zaman 2007, 32). I witnessed several of these in Amman, including postcolonial nation-building projects, nationalism, the rise of mass education, and the emergence of mass media. As Fida Adely (2012, 87) points out, the Hashemite regime has "sought to keep close control over religious public spaces, religious teaching, and preaching in mosques and in Islamic centers." The Jordanian populace has not overwhelmingly responded to this control with a resurgent political agitation and activism, even during the Arab Spring of

2011, which precipitated dramatic political events in neighboring countries (Tobin 2012). Despite the wide range of informants and social settings, my research population shared a general lack of interest in larger Islamic political movements that reference the state, the Hashemite ruling family, local and parliamentary elections, and political party participation. Although a few informants were members of the Muslim Brotherhood and a few advocated boycotts of parliamentary elections, there was a striking absence of wider political activism. Few, if any, of my informants protested during the Arab Spring (Tobin 2012). Contrary to studies in political mobilization in neighboring countries (e.g. Wickham 2002) and the research that has emerged as a result of the Arab Spring (e.g. Byman et al. 2011), this research population was not largely interested in making political statements with their religious practice or projecting it into the public sphere in a way that would mobilize people for some ultimate, political goal. This is discussed in greater detail in chapter 8.

As a result of swift twentieth-century developments, some new religious intellectuals, preachers, and public figures—whose reach includes Amman—both play a part in destabilizing the authority of the traditional ʿulama, or Islamic scholars and clerics, and offer up new and diverse interpretations for religious authority and practice. Amr Khaled, an Egyptian accountant commonly referred to as "the Sheikh of Cool" or "Sheikh of Chic" (Stratton 2006, 181, 262, 273) now leads a popular "Lifemakers" group in Amman. Another example is Sami Yusuf, an Azeri-British singer known for such songs as "Al-Muʿallim" ("The Teacher") and "Supplication," used in the major motion picture *The Kite Runner*. These two are among the most pronounced of the elites bringing an "updated" and modern message to young, Muslim, and middle-class Ammanis. As one informant said to me, "You know, Sami Yusuf is really a singer for the younger people. He's like Amr Khaled. It's for young people. And it's good. He doesn't have one of those creepy beards." "Creepy beards" here symbolizes an Islam understood as a culture "of the past" and of the traditional ʿulama, no longer applicable or practical for daily life. In this case, it is even understood to be "scary" or "threatening."[13] Knowledge that comes from popular preachers and public figures such as Amr Khaled and Sami Yusuf assists Ammanis as they navigate their everyday economic piety, and do so in ways that appeal to a contemporary, modern aesthetic without being "threatening" with a "creepy beard."

The research population represented a wide variety of religious adherence. Some prayed five times per day with ease. Some had difficulty fasting for Ramadan without spending many daytime hours sleeping away the hunger and avoiding the headaches induced by caffeine or nicotine withdrawal.

Some did not. Some embraced Islamic banking exclusively and others called it a "scam." What they held in common, however, was that they invoked, used, and negotiated modern and authentic "real" Islam in their economic practices quite visibly. In fact, there were strong and normative, yet debated and contested, expectations for a public religious life in economic practice, regardless of one's personal piety and beliefs.

Shari'a, an important and traditional source for authority on the issues of "the real Islam," has been given new life through these contemporary voices of Islamic authority, often in the form of "invented traditions" (Hobsbawm and Ranger 1983). This renewal and reinvigoration is possible because Shari'a is a process "shaped through ongoing discussion and debate rather than a fixed content" (Zaman 2002, x). Its religious authority is therefore not a static reference list developed by either the *'ulama* or Amr Khaled that Muslims can turn to for singular and definitive answers to questions about how to invest their money or how late into a pregnancy it is no longer safe to fast for Ramadan. Attempts to construct Shari'a as a kind of monolith, coupled with the inability to find it in an objectified form, simultaneously contribute to the pluralities of "real Islams" in contemporary Amman and continue to raise questions about how Islamic authority is "constructed, argued, put on display, and constantly defended" (Zaman 2002, x).

Throughout this book I examine normative understandings in light of diverse practices, from legal requirements to uphold the Ramadan fast to extra-legal and social requirements for public statements about the *hijab* and public justifications for working in an Islamic banking system. These public expectations prompted by family members, encounters with media messages, and friends and acquaintances in one's place of employment or state-mediated spaces such as neighborhood mosques, also caused Muslims to consider again and anew the implications of their everyday economic practices on their religious life. All were in social positions—entangled with families and friends and coworkers—where they had to both ask and answer questions about what their religious practice in economic life meant and how they knew those things to be true. Shari'a became the anchor that they used in highly contingent and flexible terms to make legitimate their claims to economic practices that reflect an authentic and modern middle class Islamic piety.

## Post-Islamism

The Islamic Resurgence of the mid to late twentieth century, as Asma mentions, pushed for an enhanced public role and space for Islam. The resulting "Islamism" fueled the idea of using Islamically derived ethics and norms, and legal and political extrapolations as the basis for a feasible alternative mode of organizing society (Brown 2000, 124–25). Political Islam is perhaps the most commonly cited result of this movement. Its primary concern was "building an 'ideological community'—establishing an Islamic state or implementing Islamic laws and moral codes" (Bayat 2007, 8).

Looking past Islamism, this book turns to "post-Islamist" movements, which turn away from politics. Rather, post-Islamism aims to fuse religion to notions of freedom, individual choice, liberty, the cultural normalization of an Islamic identity, and modernity (Bayat 2007, 7; Haenni 2005). Other spheres in which compatibilities between Islam and economics emerge include new lifestyles that emphasize options such as Islamized travel, education, or work; the freedom and liberty to produce and consume Islamized goods in food, fashion, and leisure; and the privatization of property and market-friendly avenues for investments and entrepreneurialism pursued through Islamic banks and financial institutions.

Because of post-Islamism's emphasis on modernity, spheres for new compatibilities are informed by a variety of sources for religious knowledge that constitute something relevant, practical, and applicable for daily life. This "modern Islam" includes popular and lay preachers and advocates, plus urban spaces and new usages that utilize Shariʿa to promote market-friendly resolutions to contemporary problems. It also includes social media–based forums that link Muslims who have moral questions to peers who offer up a wide variety of answers. Modern Islam is relevant and engaging, as Muslims in Amman turn away from austerity of life and lifestyles and embrace contemporary market-friendly, consumer-oriented elaborations in economic practices. The diversity of Islamized options and choices available in the quest for "the real Islam" render Shariʿa more useful and germane to everyday life (Kuran 1997a, 1997b).

This ethnography reveals the ways by which neoliberalism holds out distinct and highly attractive promises to Ammanis in the post-Islamist era: all Muslims—even those at the margins—can participate in global economic relationships, find satisfaction in heightened levels and types of consumption, and seek fulfillment in the promises of returns on both economic and Islamic investments. These economizing logics affirm that many, if not most Muslims in urban Amman do not hold a view of economic practices as a menace or as morally corrupt, but rather as the very means by which they can attain happiness, security, and the good life. Further, such economic practices also promise the good *Islamic* life, complete with spiritual happiness and eternal security.

## Overview

Using ethnographic comparisons and case studies drawn from my research in Jordan, the chapters that follow examine how Muslims in Amman engage in calculated processes of identity construction around "the real Islam." They use a variety of forms, through daily choices about what to wear and where to bank, as well as whom to date and to marry, where to work, and how to pray. These everyday actions reveal the complex calculations through which Ammanis Islamize their economic selves and economize their Islamic selves in the public sphere—justifying and showcasing their "everyday piety" through complex constructions of authentic Islamic piety that inform both their professional and personal lives.

Amman's history of relatively rapid transition from a small farming community to a modern Islamic capital city has important implications for the public representations of Islam and the public ethics of its expressions by Muslim residents. The city's swift structural changes in the economic and social realms set the stage for the ways in which Islamic piety is contingent and negotiated. This history also has implications for the Islamization of economic practice and the economization of Islamic practice as they relate to other actions characteristic of a Muslim middle class, such as personal consumerism and economic production, local economic interests and agendas, and nationalism and political mobilization around, for example, the outcomes of the Arab Spring in Jordan. The multifaceted and heavily contested ways Ammanis approach these processes holds out hope for Jordan as a place "branded" by Islamic diversity, moderation, and cohesion.

# CHAPTER 2

# The History of Amman

*"I Don't Recognize It Anymore"*

Two strikingly different pictures show a century's worth of change. Figure 1 is the Roman Amphitheater and surrounding area of downtown Amman in 1925, and figure 2 is the same area today, nearly a century later. The pictures depict two very different cities: one barren and rural, the other urban and densely populated. Examining these photos together, the development of today's Amman is striking: a desolate village has become a metropolitan city of durable limestone buildings, public spaces and parks for shared interactions and leisure time, and wide concrete roads. The urban history of Amman is one of swift development, change, and population growth, and constitutes a distinctive twentieth-century story. Within one hundred years, the city unfolds from a barren, desolate farming community of refugees to a bustling, globally connected capital. The remarkable speed of change has rendered it something significant from something small (Potter et al. 2009). This carries implications for social and religious life as it has fomented new and at times unprecedented ways for people to understand themselves as modern and authentic, economized Muslims, which underpins their Islamized economic practices. Despite an ancient Islamic history often referenced in debates about authenticity and modernity, much of Amman's contemporary Islamic practice and everyday piety derive from contemporary understandings gained from quick change and cultural innovation and influence, rather than centuries of urban, lived traditions.

The urban history of Amman that follows provides the groundwork for understanding the spectrum of consensus and Islamic practices found throughout the rest of the book. Some practices assert clearer and more lucid historical trajectories than others. This variation in religious life is due, at least in part, to the swift demographic, political, and economic changes experienced in social and urban life. In particular, this is the story of the emergence of a middle-class—an Islamic middle-class—Amman.

## The Unrecognizable Amman

In 1910, Father Raphael Savignac, a Dominican priest, made his first visit to Amman. He found it a barely habitable village inhabited by Circassian refugees from the Russo-Ottoman Wars. Five hundred members of this largely Muslim ethnic group from the Caucasus had come to Amman at the end of the nineteenth century. Of these, a mere 150 stayed and survived, using donkeys and wooden carts to farm this mainly rocky and barren, desert land and swords to defend themselves against raids by their Bedouin neighbors.

In 1925, Father Savignac and his colleagues returned to Amman, taking the picture in figure 1 and noting a new and appealing rhythm and visual aesthetic to the emerging town. He wrote that it was no longer recognizable as the Amman of a mere fifteen years prior:

> The Circassian village has been transformed into a small city, which has six thousand inhabitants, so we are told. They have widened the streets, built numerous homes and have multiplied the number of shops, for today it is mainly to Amman that the desert Arabs come for their purchases. There is nothing as picturesque as these *suqs* where cars, camels, donkeys and riders intersect with the war-pistol armed Bedouin, the Circassian with his cutlass at the belt, negroes and other dark-skinned types that come from the depth of Hejaz, numerous soldiers and elegantly dressed officers, and so on. (Savignac 1925, 110)[1]

Within the next century, local Jordanian literature would feature story after story of a swiftly changing, "unrecognizable Amman" (Al-Razzaz 2002; Schwedler 2010), creating a rhetorical device for residents and visitors alike. The short story "The Character of Amman," penned by a Jordanian, features a grandfather who returns to Amman from an unnamed, distant country after a number of years. While being accompanied on a tour around the city of his childhood by his resident grandson, the grandfather observes all

**FIGURE 1**    Roman Amphitheater, 1925. Courtesy of the École Biblique, Jerusalem.

the visible changes—the modern airport, the traffic circles and high-speed bridges and passageways, the abundance of Western four- and five-star hotels. Previously poor areas—Abdoun and Shmeisani—have become home to Amman's wealthiest residents, highest commercially valued properties, and most expensive malls and cafés. The old man continually whispers to himself, "They say it is Amman . . . but it is not" (Kaddoura 2007, 7). In literature, the Amman of memory is often not the Amman one encounters.

The unrecognizable Amman carries significance even into the Western and Orientalist imagination. The trope of not recognizing Amman as one would a neighboring Arab city, such as Damascus, Jerusalem, or Cairo, plays a major role in contemporary descriptions for non-Jordanians, including students and tourists. The traveler-oriented *Lonely Planet* guidebook describes it as "a modern Arab city rather than a great, ancient metropolis of the Orient: it has never rivaled Damascus or Cairo as a grand Islamic city of antiquity" (Ham and Greenway 2003, 98). The *Rough Guide to Jordan* takes the narrative one step further, describing parts of Amman as "indistinguishable from upscale neighbourhoods of American or European cities, with broad leafy avenues lined with mansions, and fast multi-lane freeways swishing past strip malls and black-glass office buildings" (Teller 2002, 77).

Even people already versed in the Arab Middle East struggle to recognize the city of Amman. Western scholars, students, and travelers I knew often

**FIGURE 2**  Roman Amphitheater, 2012. Courtesy of Austin Jessie Davidson.

referred to it as "Middle East Lite" and "a good place for people who hate Cairo," in reference to its crowds and pollution. Even modern scholars have been known to dismiss Jordan as "artificial" and "neither nation nor state" (Rogan 1999, 1). Contemporary Amman is frequently characterized in both native and foreign accounts in terms of what it lacks, and for which neighboring capitals are so well known: an extensive urban history.

A lengthy urban history could enable a city to make bold claims, such as being the oldest continuously inhabited city in the world, as in the case of Damascus. It might boast a dynastic history with a contemporary crowded urban environment of 25 million people, as in the case of Cairo. It might even claim to be the holiest and most violently contested city in the world, as in Jerusalem. Similar assertions continue in the south in the cities of Mecca and Medina, east in Baghdad, north in Beirut, and even west across North Africa in Fez and Marrakesh. These famed cities also often lay claim to being Islamic urban centers. Mecca and Medina saw the revelation of Islam. Cairo houses Al-Azhar, one of the oldest Islamic universities in the world. Damascus claims the seat of eras of Islamic dynasties. The list goes on. Amman's ability to make such assertions, however, is more highly disputed.

## Amman: An Urban, Islamic City?

As Janet Abu-Lughod (1987) articulates, Western Orientalists often turned to the theme of the "Islamic City," describing Islam as an urban religion that organizes everyday life by creating a religiously derived need for a congregational Friday mosque for obligatory prayers, a market (*suq*), and a community bath, or *hammam*. Their descriptions of urban, Islamic centers often include legal and Shari'a-based priorities for residential organization, such as the "rights of neighbors," and articulate a preference for gender segregation. Western writers often reference the case of Cairo or Fez or other North African cities to typify their descriptions. Abu-Lughod quotes Georges Marçais, who wrote in 1957:

> I have said that the center was occupied by the Great Mosque, the old political center, the religious and intellectual center of the city. . . . Near the mosque, the religious center, we find the furnishers of sacred items, the *suq* of the candlesellers, the merchants of incense and other perfumes. . . . The essential organ is a great market. (230–31)

A major difficulty with applying—or even comparing—this model to the case of Amman is that many of the Orientalist writers espoused these ideas before Amman was a community of any note. Georges Marçais' brother William, for example, wrote "L'Islamisme et la vie urbaine" ("Islamism and Urban Life") in 1928, when Amman looked much like the picture that opens this chapter. As a city of only a few thousand farmers and merchants, Amman lacked the "anchor" of deep Islamic intellectual and urban history as witnessed in Fez and its ninth-century Qarawiyyin Mosque, or Cairo's tenth-century Al-Azhar University. As the notion of the Islamic city captured the imaginations of Western Orientalists at the beginning of the twentieth century, Amman was still in its urban infancy.

Twentieth-century writings—by both Orientalists and academics—often mark residential patterns as another lens for understanding urban growth and change in these cities. Many recite the narrative that the great Middle Eastern, Islamic cities are characterized by old quarters or "an old city," which was later redefined with the influx of advanced capitalism, contemporary sources of wealth, and accompanying leisure and consumptive lifestyles, often heavily influenced by colonialism (see Abu-Lughod 1971; Eickelman 1974; Salamandra 2004; Zubaida 1989). The old heterogeneous-classed cities often emptied as populations moved into "new cities" and Western-styled suburbs (Abu-Lughod 1987, 170). The influx of new wealth and urban development changed physical forms for social organization, and the emergence of middle-class homogeneity became a primary defining characteristic of these suburban and residential new cities. In turn, old cities have survived as primarily lower-class areas associated with the influx of migrants from rural areas (Salamandra 2004, 29). In the urban shifting of many of these  great Islamic cities, class came to trump other forms of social organization.

This assumption of urban organization and residential patterning into "old" and "new" quarters does not hold true in the case of Amman, however. Although today's downtown area was settled first in the late nineteenth and early twentieth centuries, the city never developed in a way that drew a wall or gate separating an "old city" from a "new city." Growth occurred primarily in an east–west fashion along a seasonal stream of water, with settlement moving up the hillsides (Potter et al. 2009). Today, this means the largest socioeconomic separations lie between East and West Amman (Adely 2007a), which have become less distinct and more integrated with the life and lifestyles of "aspiring cosmopolitans" (Schwedler 2010).

This also means that neighborhoods in Amman are most often discussed in terms of the name of the hill or *jabal* on which they stand, or in terms of which of the eight numbered traffic circles or *da'irat* (sing. *duwaar*) is most expedient for movement in, out, or through. Many other Middle Eastern cities commonly named their neighborhoods according to the residents' ethnicity or family names (Abu-Lughod 1987). As a city that developed quickly, Amman became "a sort of lung that has provided much needed breathing space for populations in the region" (Al-Asad 2004). Rather than organizing around ancient Great Mosques, lively *suqs*, and an old/new city duality, Amman's urban processes have led to a much more socially and religiously diffuse and integrated middle class, urban Muslim-majority city, invented and reinvented with each "breath" of its recent history.

As a point in contrast, Damascus' modern history of development and modernization reveals different reflections and points of elaboration. According to Christa Salamandra (2004, 7–15, 25–47), the city's population was not quite 300,000 in 1945 but had jumped to 1.3 million by the early 1980s. During the first half of the twentieth century, despite war, famine, and colonialism, elite Damascene families were able to maintain their longstanding position and status. However, as the century continued, they lost out to new competitors and were systematically displaced from key positions, which were often filled by the newly powerful 'Alawis, among the largest group of rural migrants to the urban center. Despite also experiencing a capital influx that helped nationalize Arab sentiment and center economic and political power, class differentiations expanded and divisions along sectarian lines became pronounced, as did religious, urban/rural, and other forms of social distinction.

These events resulted in socio-spatial distinctions (Salamandra 2004, 25–47). Many families moved out of the longstanding urban center of Old Damascus, "the vestiges of backwardness," in search of a "modern" style of living of concrete apartments in detached or French-style houses with balconies (26). These formerly elite families have since cultivated a nostalgia for "a supposedly more homogenous urban identity in Old Damascus" (25), which has fueled new forms of consumer culture designed to construct and represent past and contemporary identities.

This twentieth-century process of developing a nationalist and unifying economic and political framework that simultaneously and contradictorily increases economic differentiation has also been explored in Cairo (Abu-Lughod 1971). In fact, Zubaida (1989, 83–98) extends this thesis to the Middle East in a larger way, arguing that old quarters were vertically and horizontally stratified in their socioeconomic organization. As Salamandra indicates, "In the Arab world, old walled cities surrounded by modern neighborhoods are a visual legacy of colonialism and post-colonial modernization projects" (2004, 31). Although this argument works in the cases of Damascus and Cairo (among others), it is impossible to extend it to Amman because the longstanding, walled Old City of Damascus or Old Quarters of Cairo, or those found throughout North Africa were simply not present there. Today's Amman was carved out of agricultural lands, not out from behind an Old City.

As part of the processes of inventing and reinventing Amman, the city and its neighboring areas have become an elevated site of notable, ancient religious events involving some of the most famous persons of the Abrahamic faiths. These sites are often used in popular discussions to elongate the city's history and to anchor Amman in more than the twentieth century. The interpretations and uses of these claims play a significant role in contemporary understandings of Islam and in practices of everyday piety of Muslims in Amman.

##  Ancient Islam, Rural Jordan

Geographically situated at the crossroads of Israel, the West Bank, Syria, Saudi Arabia, and Iraq, present-day Jordan has been historically understood to be a place through which people traveled on their way to more valuable and important lands, rather than a destination in and of itself. It was known to have strategic economic importance, however, as it linked the major trade routes of the Middle East between Egypt and Palestine, and Iraq and Iran. To be sure, the relatively few inhabitants enjoyed a certain measure of prosperity as they fed, watered, and hosted travelers and their animals—particularly under the Umayyad and Abbasid periods (661–1258 CE)—along these trade routes. However, a majority of the wealth and goods continued on into other, predominant lands (Salibi 2006, 7, 19). Jordan was a bridge, and an important one.

Early Arabic terms capture Jordan's position and value. For seventh-century Arab Muslim travelers coming north from Arabia en route to Syria, present day Jordan was known as "masharif al-Sham," or "the approaches of Syria." Inversely, for those traveling south from Syria to present day Saudi Arabia, the terminology was changed to "masharif al-Hijaz," or "the approaches of the Hijaz" (Salibi 2006, 6). This otherwise nameless tract of land became known as "Jordan" or "Al-Urdun" during the Crusades in the eleventh and twelfth centuries in reference to the River Jordan, which currently serves as the country's westernmost border.

Because of its strategic location and historically popular pathways, the areas surrounding Amman are rich with Jewish, Christian, and Islamic history. Stories about ancient prophets traversing the area are abundant. Abraham and his family are believed to have walked through Jordan on their travels between the lands of Arabia and Jerusalem. Mt. Nebo, twenty miles south of Amman, is the site from which Moses viewed the Promised Land. The tomb of Aaron, Moses' brother, is atop a mountain overlooking Petra. The tomb of Jethro—Moses' father-in-law—lies a few hours north of Amman. Zeid ibn al-Haritha, Mohammed's adopted son and the only Companion mentioned by name in the Qur'an, is buried in Jordan. The tomb of Abu 'Ubaydah 'Amer Ibn al-Jarrah, one of the Blessed Ten Companions or *Sahaba* of the Prophet Mohammed, is located within several hours drive of Amman.

Local geography is also anchored in Islamic history. The Dead Sea, Bahr al-Mayyit, is locally understood to be the ancient site of Sodom and Gomorrah. According to the biblical account, two angels traveled to Sodom and approached Abraham's nephew, the prophet Lot, who offered them food and lodging. In the course of the evening, men from Sodom came to Lot's house, asking for the guests to come out "so that we can have sex with them" (Genesis 19:5). Lot refused to give up the guests, and instead offered the men his two virgin daughters. Unsatisfied, the men of Sodom threatened Lot and attempted to break down his door. The angels protected Lot and his family by blinding the men, and urged Lot to take his family out of Sodom and away from its imminent destruction. The angels warned Lot and his family not to look back. Lot's wife did not heed their command, and as a result was turned into one of the pillars of salt (Genesis 19:26) in abundance in the Dead Sea area.

In the Qur'an, the story continues that Allah's punishment was to "turn the cities upside down, and rain down on them brimstones hard as baked clay, spread layer on layer, marked from your Lord" (Qur'an 11:82–83). The "layer on layer" serves as a rhetorical hook that has guided popular and local scientific understandings of the Dead Sea as the site of Sodom and Gomorrah in texts from as early as the first century (Daily 2010, 152). The stratigraphy of the Dead Sea includes organic phosphorus chalk derived from bones and exoskeletons that were compressed and refined over time, which many scientists cite as evidence of ancient human and animal remains. Dead Sea products marketed for healing powers both locally and internationally often include a dark mud composed of similar organic materials.

According to my informants, the religious texts, combined with the historical and linguistic precedent and the contemporary commercial reinforcements, all serve as evidence of the historical truth of an Islamic presence—the *real* Islamic presence—in and near Amman. Invoking ancient Judeo-Christian and Islamic history and placing such events on local maps has become the means by which Ammanis can and do elongate their history. Not only has Amman been an important urban location during the last one hundred years, the logic goes, it has been an important Islamic location back into the earliest days of mankind. Rather than tracing a singular, linear, Islamic history in and near Amman, residents punctuate and highlight these events to serve as representative of an entire history. They become an abstraction of historical Islamic and religious events and given a nostalgic timelessness in the push for Islamic authenticity. This serves to reinforce the idea of a singular, normative real Islam whose earliest days passed in and near Amman. As one informant summarized, "We have the same Islam as they had with the Prophet Mohammed, *Salalahu 'aleyhi wa salam* (Prayers and Peace Be Upon Him), and we have it in same places as the Prophets Ibrahim and Haroon, *'Aleyhi wa salam* (Peace Be Upon Him). Amman and Jordan are really important and holy places. You can just feel it."

## Amman Becomes the Capital

It was primarily because of the importance of regional trade and to preserve these sites of Islamic import that King 'Abdullah claimed his political ascendency in the new Hashemite-ruled British protectorate of Transjordan in the 1920s. Despite these advantages, the choice of Amman for the new capital was a surprising one. Other cities just to the north were more likely candidates for the establishing and centering of political power. Ajlun was a *sanjak*, or Ottoman administrative district for the province, and Salt—a largely Christian city—was the area's "only real town of note" until World War I (Robins 2004, 11). Irbid was a small, Muslim-majority town whose higher levels of wealth and facilities had been brought in by Palestinians in the West, Syrians in the North, and internationally by British missionaries (Salibi 2006, 45).

Despite the seeming appeal of preexisting administrative structures, established commercial enterprises, and institutionalized foreign involvement, demographic diversity made Amman the best choice. The area in and around the city was home to diverse populations. Some Arab Bedouin had migrated from Arabia after the advent of Islam. Many were of the Bani-Sakhr clan, who still comprise a large and powerful tribal faction in Jordan. Arab Bedouin were considered seditious, and the Ottomans had sought to subdue and pacify them by settling Muslim-majority ethnic Circassian refugees near them (Rogan 1994, 45–48; Rogan 1999, 18, 72–76; Salibi 2006, 27). Additionally, there was a small Druze community, made up of refugees from Syria seeking the protections of the British rather than the French (Salibi 2006, 118). As T. E. Lawrence described the diverse populations found around Amman in 1922:

> East of [Jerusalem] lay the Jordan depth, inhabited by charred serfs; and across it group upon group of self-respecting village Christians. . . . Among them and east of them were tens of thousands of semi-nomad Arabs, holding the creed of the desert, living on the fear and bounty of their Christian neighbours. Down this debatable land the Ottoman Government had planted a line of Circassian immigrants from the Russian Caucasus. They held their ground only by the sword and the favour of the Turks, to whom they were, of necessity, devoted. (1997, 340)

Diversity, it seems, was not a peaceful coexistence. By the period between the World Wars, the Circassian farmers were weary of Bedouin raids and Christians looked forward to a stronger, more stable environment. Both held favorable opinions of the Hashemites, "an Arab dynasty representing the best in the political traditions of Islam" (Salibi 2006, 85), who claim and draw legitimacy from their genealogical descent from the Prophet Mohammed (Adely 2012; Anderson 2005; Schwedler 2006).

As Salibi (2006) points out, Arab Christians also respected the *sharif* institution and tradition from which the Hashemites originated. The Ikhshidids, a Muslim, Turkish institution based in Egypt and in charge of Syria and the Hijaz in the mid-tenth century, appointed a *sharif*, or descendant of the Prophet Mohammed, as the first Emir of Mecca. This appointment had long-term effects, as it institutionalized the guardianship of the Holy Places as the trust of a future descendant. Hussein of the Hijaz, the father of King 'Abdullah, was the last *sharif* appointed by the Iskhidids (Salibi 2006, 20–21); this gave his son a favored position within the region, one on which he was able to capitalize. The institution of the *sharif* as a political and religious leader in Mecca and Medina established historical precedent for a direct descendent of the Prophet Mohammed to rule in the area well before the current nation-state of Jordan was envisioned.

The respect for the *sharif* by the Christians was reciprocated by King 'Abdullah, who saw them as "tolerant and fair-minded, without the least hint of religious fanaticism" (Salibi 2006, 85). In fact, the links between the Hashemite rulers and the large Christian families in Jordan were solidified when the Sukkar and the Abu Jaber families hosted the king in their homes and on their grounds during construction of the royal palace in the 1920s (Salibi 2006, 100).[2] Father Savignac wrote at the time,

> The people were duty bound to the choice Emir 'Abdullah made to this town as the headquarters for the Government of Transjordan. 'Abdullah still lives there under the tent by them awaiting the completion of the handsome palace, the construction of which has carried on already for several months. (1925, 10)

The desire for security and political leadership by both Circassians and Christians provided a welcome haven in Amman for 'Abdullah, from which he successfully struck out to gain political power over and subdue the semi-nomadic Bedouin (Rogan 1999; Salibi 2006).[3]

During the interwar and British Mandate period (1921–1946), 'Abdullah brought political power and authority of the British with him while adding form and shape to the new monarchy. The Mandate era elaborated new conceptualizations of land ownership and private property based on British forms and implementation. Establishing the rule of law in land ownership was well received by Amman's Circassian and Christian cultivators, and it fueled Abdullah's imposition of law and order as well as his political ascendancy until Jordan's independence in 1946 (Rogan 1994, 80–107).

After independence, two mass movements of people accelerated Amman's rapid development into a globally recognized capital city. The first was the settling of the Bedouin. In order to attract a population to reside in the sparsely populated and barren land at the inauguration of this new government and new nation, many of the post-1946 political campaigns focused on providing government services such as land reform and rule of law that protected cultivated farmland (Rogan 1994), projects that enhanced water resources (Amawi 1994), and efforts to provide education (Hefner and Zaman 2007). Some of these endeavors were funded by the British and U.S. governments and constituted significant changes. The United States initiated economic aid to Jordan in 1951 and military aid in 1957 (Sharp 2005, 2010). With the British government administering Palestine and Transjordan, the host of new services rendered to the new Jordanian populace further supported the settled merchant and agricultural classes and paved the way for the Hashemite Monarchy to "subdue" the Bedouin tribesmen through a father-son relationship of respect and exchange (Anderson 2005, 19, 33; Shryock 1997). The effective settling of the Bedouin created ethnic "Jordanians" who stood in contrast to their neighbors, whether ethnic populations such as the Circassians or the newly arrived Palestinians.

The second mass movement of people came with the waves of Palestinian refugees in 1948 and 1967. The emergence of "Palestinianness," in contrast to the Bedouin "Jordanianness," solidified ethnicity as a means for people in Amman to relate to the state and to each other.[4] Though the settled Bedouin were relatively socioeconomically homogenous—"a tribal, stable, rural and marginal population" (Robins 2004, 2)—an estimated 750,000 Palestinians came into Jordan, bringing with them better education, more merchant connections, higher levels of socioeconomic divisions, and psychological trauma from the process of dispossession (Robins 2004, 2–3). One reason for these differences is that Bedouin were largely organized around tribal affiliations that cut across class. Palestinians, on the other hand, came from a mode of sociability that emphasized class greatly and was conscious of urban/rural divides. In Salibi's (2006) words, "Arab townsfolk and the peasants lived, socially, in two different worlds" (130). This economically and socially differentiated population, coupled with another influx of up to 300,000 Palestinians in 1967, prompted much internal dispute regarding the cultural and religious identity of Amman and the prospects for its future. Economic opportunities that developed in the late 1950s with the U.S. investment mentioned above cemented a differentiation between merchant Palestinians occupying the private sector and the government dominated by ethnic Jordanians (Amawi 1994; Robins 2004, 3). The rise of the middle-class occupations—professional civil service and the private service sector—constituted a major impetus for the rise of the middle class in Jordan in general (Clark 2004; Nasr 2009), and characterizes much of Amman today. In fact, and as described throughout the book, "middle classness" has emerged as the primary form of social differentiation. OR UNITY?

Jordan's borders have been continuously in geographic flux from 1946 through the Civil War of the 1970s[5] and up to the 1993 peace treaty with Israel. It has also been in a condition of social flux throughout its nearly seventy years of existence. As people have established their livelihoods in Jordan—either as settled Bedouin and the resulting identification as "Jordanian-Jordanians" or "Palestinians"—the cultural and social landscape has changed. The differentiation of ethnicity derived from family origins in either the "West Bank" or "East Bank" of the Jordan River is easily observable in casual conversation. When discussing ethnicity, "West Bank" Palestinians frequently refer to themselves as "Jordanian" (*Urduni*), which references their country of citizenship but maintain "Palestinian" (*Filistini*) as an ethnic label. "East Bank" ethnic Jordanians often conflate citizenship and ethnicity by referring to themselves as "Jordanian-Jordanian" (*Urduni-Urduni*).

Mass movements of people alter the cultures of a place. Given the large degree of geographic and demographic change in Jordan's twentieth-century history, it is not surprising that people have also experienced and prompted a large degree of sociocultural change. The pre-1946 life of Bedouin outside Amman consisted of sparse populations living in relative social, cultural, and economic homogeneity (Robins 2004, 2). Though the Palestinians experienced a more urban-based, socially differentiated life and lifestyle in Palestine than did the Bedouin outside Amman, pre-1948 life in Amman was characterized by transformations of political systems and stabilities, strong economic trade (between groups and with traders coming through the area), and settled Christian and Circassian farmers and cultivators anchoring the city. At the more recent end of this extended period of change and these different modes for relating to each other and the state, there emerged a seemingly appealing means to cut Palestinians' and Jordanians' class and ethnic differentiations through a shared religious ethic—Islam—as a means to reorganize a modern society.

## The Islamic Revival and Contemporary Amman

Sunni Islam was upheld as a characteristic part of life in Amman from the time of its inception as a capital and economic center. The Jordanian

Constitution of 1952 stipulates that the King and his successors each be the child of two Muslims parents and that he be an adherent of the religion. As described above, the ruling family descended from *sharif* lines, which claim both a genealogical descent from the Prophet Mohammed and from the guardianship of the Holy Places. The ruling King of Jordan is born into an Islamic family genealogy and becomes the protector of a Holy Land and an ancient cultural and religious heritage. The ruler has, therefore, both an institutionalized birthright and a holy profession.

The populace, too, expects a visible Islamic practice from each other. The signs they seek have historical roots in the Islamic Revival or Resurgence that swept much of the Islamic world in the latter half of the twentieth century. The earliest pushes for an enhanced public role and space for religion began in Amman as early as the 1960s. At that time, public challenges to secular political regimes and nationalist systems were abundant throughout the Muslim world (Brown 2000, 124), most oriented toward an Islamist alternative. Many analysts point to political upheaval, especially in the Arab Middle East and regional opposition to Israel, as the turning point for the movement. Although the Arab states lost the Six-Day War with Israel in 1967, which "undoubtedly had a decisive effect on subsequent events in the region, Islamist politics would probably have emerged even if this very surprising and avoidable war had not occurred" (Brown 2000, 123). Of course the Muslim world is much wider than the Arab world and encompasses more than the Arab-Israeli conflict. Nonetheless, disappointment with the promises of political regimes in the 1960s and 1970s fueled the idea of using Islamically derived ethics and norms and legal and political extrapolations as a feasible alternative mode for organizing society (Brown 2000, 124–25). Demographic shifts and the growth of education also contributed to the spread and popularity of Islamically derived solutions to everyday problems (Brown 2000; Hefner and Zaman 2007; Starrett 1998). Combined with the dramatic events of the Iranian Revolution of 1979, much of the Muslim world was reimagining the role that Islam could play in daily life, including that of Islamic doctrine and understandings of Islamic law, or Shari'a, and reexamining Islamic modes for mediating sociality (Mahmood 2005, 3).

The Islamic Revival in Jordan as a localized mass movement can also be tied to political events: King Hussein's public support for the Shah in Iran, the country's continued relations with Egypt after Sadat's peace treaty with Israel, and its own peace treaty and normalized relations with Israel in 1994. The resulting cooperative relationship between the Muslim Brotherhood and the Hashemite Rulers has occupied volumes on the subject of the impacts of the Islamic Revival on political organization in Jordan (see, e.g., Droeber

2005; Gandhi and Lust-Okar 2009; Lust-Okar 2009; Moaddel 2002; Norton 1995; Norton 2001; Robinson 1997; Schwedler 2010).

Jordan, among other countries, witnessed a growth of public adherence to Islamic customs in ways that were shared throughout the region and went beyond political and legal organization: increased frequency of donning the *hijab* and Islamic dress, a rise in attendance at Friday prayers, more people fasting for Ramadan, and more men growing beards. Women, too, particularly students, were drivers of this alteration of public life. In the 1980s, the mosque at Yarmouk University had a large women's section that was often full, and women gathered there to study Islam in groups (Al-Khazendar 1997). Such reconfigurations of modes of sociability and the insertion of Islamically based forms of mediation, such as Shari'a, also adjusted signals and signs of religious distinction. They altered previously held symbolic notions of, for example, socioeconomic class. As a case in point, as Islamic dress grew in popularity and usage, particularly among women, it was no longer associated with the poorest social classes.

By the 1980s, active middle-class Muslims were a sizable demographic in Amman. They often both drove and rode the wave of Islamism in ways that pushed for a critique of Western habits and lifestyles and offered up alternative Islamized social norms and expressions (Clark 2004). They did so, in particular, by creating new Islamized consumption. One strong force behind this change was the development of mass communication (Armbrust 2000a, 2000b; Eickelman and Piscatori 1996). Prior to the mid-1990s, Jordanian television was dominated by two state-run channels, which were highly censored and guided by strict broadcasting schedules; one of the channels only aired for part of the day (Adely 2007b, 1679n24). Local stations also played notable programming such as the Arabic-language version of *Sesame Street*, *Iftah Al-Sim Sim* (literally "Open Sesame") and scenes of the King praying in heightened forms of religious expression. With a sizable receiver other stations and their programs were available, such as Egyptian films on Friday nights and Israeli programming. As one Palestinian informant discussed with me, her knowledge of the Hebrew language came from watching Israeli TV during her late-1980s and early-1990s childhood.

Since the mid-1990s, however, satellite TV has revolutionized Jordanians' access to global and Islamic voices, growing the average number of TV stations in one's home from two Jordanian and two regional stations to hundreds from around the world. Satellite programming is currently widely variable in its content. Jordanians now have access that ranges from American TV series such as *Friends* to Syrian and Turkish Ramadan soap operas, from religious programming that features ultra-conservative preachers in Saudi Arabia to converts to Christianity espousing the "evils" of Islam from some undisclosed location, and even pornography. Nearly every home in Amman has a satellite dish, where the cost of installation is minimal or "do-it-yourself." No monthly subscription is required, as in the United States. Satellite dishes stand prominently on rooftops or cling precariously to the sides of buildings across the landscape of the city. The service has revolutionized the kinds and amount of information available at any given time in a Jordanian home.

Through the settling and establishment of Amman as the capital of Jordan, through mass migrations and political, social, and religious movements, and through technological advancements such as mass communication, a set of cultural symbols and reference points has emerged that is shared across tribe and ethnicity and found in an emergent middle class. The social field for contemporary life in Amman has changed once again, as Islam is now widely understood through a distinctly middle-class lens, particularly by those who might be considered part of an aspiring middle class.

## Aspiring Cosmopolitans and Being Middle Class in Amman

Throughout this book, when I refer to "Amman," I typically mean West Amman, the smaller, wealthier, and more globalized and internationally connected part of the city. With some exceptions, my informants came from West Amman. East Amman is the historic city center and downtown area, and generally houses a lower-middle-class working and professional demographic. West Amman has emerged as more financially and socially influential. Characterized by four- and five-star hotels, expensive restaurants and bars, large malls, and a new Dubai-inspired high-rise project, 'Abdali, West Amman is considered one of the most metropolitan and globally connected cities in the Arab Middle East. However, my informants from East Amman were also connected to international influences, typically through family members abroad, or had adopted many elements of a more aesthetically modern lifestyle in their movements into West Amman. As one of my informants from East Amman explained:

> Sarah, you know why we're friends and why I can talk to you? Because you understand my world. You know what Starbucks is and you know where Mecca Mall is. I can talk to you about my life—who I am, what I really believe. You understand the way I dress and why I want to work. You know, my in-laws [who live in East Amman] don't even know what Starbucks is. They've never even heard of it. Can you imagine?!

My East Ammani informants were often more closely associated—culturally and socially—with West Ammanis than with others from East Amman. These conversations reveal that "middle classness" is a predominant force in people's lives, influencing their cultural referents, social relations, and religious life.

As Jillian Schwedler (2010) has described, the neoliberal economic reforms implemented by the Hashemite regime at the end of the twentieth and the beginning of the twenty-first century created new spaces for the "aspiring cosmopolitans" of Amman. Despite divisions between West and East Amman, increasing numbers of eastern residents are crossing to the west. New patterns of work and leisure have combined with easier access to private commercial spaces and employment in the service sector. In these spaces, both East and West Ammanis prioritize cosmopolitan constructs of economic, political, and cultural forms of sociality that closely resemble those of the elites. They emphasize inclusiveness rather than "internecine conflict, resurgent nationalism, and all sorts of bloody 'othering'" (Schwedler 2010, 555), particularly through the practices of elite and exclusive consumerism learned through service-sector employment and leisure-time patterns in commercial spaces such as malls and coffee shops. Working-class Jordanians are now able to emulate the consumption habits and patterns of the elites as "aspiring cosmopolitans." West Amman typifies both real and idealized middle-class lives and lifestyles.

Starbucks in Amman, as described above, has become an index for a host of symbolic and social affiliations. The coffee shop is a point of entrée into shared time, shared space, and a shared frame for meaningful relationships. These points overlap. People spend time in a number of different Starbucks, from the wealthiest residential neighborhood of Abdoun to the commercial center and outdoor shopping mall area of Sweifiya to Mecca Mall, one of Amman's largest indoor shopping centers. In those places and times, and as demonstrated in the quote above, the ability to divulge one's sense of self to another and develop a close friendship is engendered. That these neighborhood Starbucks are ubiquitous in West Amman is notable, as it places one's friendship, literally, on the map. Mapping one's sociality according to the neighborhood Starbucks in which you have shared coffee represents an immense restructuring of time and space for purposes of meaningful interpersonal connections. Social and cultural capital are now being built in terms that refer to commercialized venues, elevated consumption, and leisure time with friends over and above the more traditionally valued family arrangements. Middle classness can trump tribe and clan affiliation, and elevating consumption with peers over and above family relationships is a significant shift for social organization in Amman.

Residents of Amman, when meeting for the first time, often inquire about the other person's family name as a means to better determine whether the person is Palestinian, Jordanian, or another ethnicity such as Iraqi or Egyptian; which part of modern-day Jordan or modern-day Palestine the person is from; whether the person is Christian or Muslim; and whether the two have family members or contacts in common. I recall a conversation in which I was telling an upper-class Christian male friend in Amman about a close female friend of mine from a lower-middle-class background, who is Muslim and lived in East Amman. I revealed her last name to him, to which he replied, "Ooh, I know her family. They're from the village next to mine near Karak.[6] We're like family." Despite the fact that these two Christian and Muslim families have resided in different parts of Amman for generations, these conversations reveal that tribal affiliations, much like ethnicity and religion, have a certain durability influencing cultural knowledge and forms for social interaction. Such connections, however durable they may be, can be trumped by reference to class. East Ammanis from lower-middle-class backgrounds are now brought into the cultural milieu of Amman's middle class, adding shared consumption and economic practices to the fore of common identity markers.

Much of Amman is college-educated (Adely 2012) and, as such, education represents a form of socialization into middle-class positions. This is consistent with the larger trends that place Jordan as the most literate country in the region (Baroudi 2002). Yet, educational access for girls is still relatively recent:

> In the 1995–6 school year, the proportion of the population in eligible age groups enrolled in secondary education was 67% for boys and 73% for girls (with a total of 70%). National enrollment rates were just below 90% for those who are age 16. They began to drop off to 72% at age 17 and 62% at age 18. (Adely 2004, n1)

As Fida Adely points out, the formal public school system for girls is a relatively new social space with new opportunities and tensions (2012). With same-sex government-funded educational environments until university, publicly educated students do not experience a mixed-sex classroom until they reach marriageable age. In my work as an Instructor of English at the University of Jordan, we discussed the topic of same-sex classrooms, which was met with widespread support from all the students who had experienced the sex-segregated public school system in Jordan. Higher education was many of my informants' first experience in mixed-sex environments, and most students demonstrated their belief that middle-class educational experiences could also be heavily gendered, even segregated.

Beyond education, a person's place of employment was frequently an extension of the mixed-sex experience of university and a place that solidified middle-class sociality. By the time of their first post–bachelor's degree job, most of my informants did not feel a particular sense of crisis or difficulty in working in a mixed-sex environment, having resolved most of the tensions during university. In fact, most women viewed their working environments as one of the few socially sanctioned spaces in which they could meet other women of similar social class, expand their social networks, and meet potential marriage partners without engaging in behavior that would otherwise threaten their reputations. Outside of arranged marriages and the university setting, many women looked to their working environments as one of the few places in which they could attain these other life goals.

In addition to these points of integration under the umbrella of social class, a predominant feature of the people involved in my study is that they were in the process of establishing and negotiating identities as middle-class Muslims. This was particularly true when they were confronted with new economic practices—often for the first time in their personal lives—in which they had to establish what role Islam and Shari'a would or would not play as they balanced competing interests and negotiated personal identity with public normativity. In this way, they were all engaged in questioning the place of religious belief and practice in their daily lives. Religion played an important role, even if they couched certain choices or understandings not in explicitly religious terms, but in ethical terms that resonated with principles derived from Shari'a.

The following chapters elucidate the points for negotiating the telltale signs of the Islamic Resurgence: "Reciting the Qur'an, keeping the fast, wearing the veil, avoiding alcohol, giving alms; not necessarily anything strictly political" (Hefner 2005, 21). To that, I would add engaging in economic practices. Ammanis are unable to take life as Muslims for granted (Berger 2009), and have not been able to do so since the beginning of the twentieth century.

## The Development of Modern Amman in Images

A pictorial depiction of Amman during its swift twentieth-century development helps to shed light on how quickly life and lifestyles changed. Visually, life in Amman at the beginning of the century was striking. The land was rocky and hilly, relatively open and uncultivated with little green growth. The pictures here show some of the initial colony of 500 Circassians (Rogan

1999, 74). For those who stayed and survived, this land eventually proved fertile[7] and they managed to make a living with tools like the wooden carts and cutlasses shown in figures 3 and 4.

In the 1920s, Amman underwent a change from a collection of Circassian villagers to a small town with a political centering facilitated by King 'Abdullah. During this period, Amman saw the construction of large, durable homes, an influx of modern technologies such as electricity, and the development of a robust service sector that included support for religious life through measures such as the construction of the King Hussein mosque and its public fountain.[8] These are a few of the enduring symbols of Amman. The large white buildings constructed at that time are of limestone, still the primary building material used today and throughout much of the West Bank and Jerusalem. In fact, when traveling to Jerusalem for the first time, I was struck by how similar the cities looked. In the 1920s, the barren lands at the highest peaks of the hillsides remained largely uncultivated.

**FIGURE 3**    Circassian farmers, 1914. Courtesy of the École Biblique, Jerusalem.

**FIGURE 4**   Circassian resident, 1914. Courtesy of the École Biblique, Jerusalem.

**Figure 5**  Amman *Suq,* 1928. Courtesy of the École Biblique, Jerusalem.

**Figure 6**  Downtown Amman, 1929. Courtesy of the École Biblique, Jerusalem.

**FIGURE 7**   Downtown Amman, 2008. Photo by the author.

In 1928, another Dominican priest, Father Michel Abel, visited Amman. He wrote:

> The center of the Ammonite kingdom is indeed beginning to become a true capital, even quite a modern city. Stalls, shops, offices, and garages line the length of valleys that intersect at the foot of the acropolis, and a motley crowd livens up the new bazaars. In front of this rapid blooming of growth, the ancient colonnades and various monuments are found in the lower city, as reported by the 19th century travelers and guides. (Abel 1928, 591)[9]

Father Abel would have witnessed a *suq* that looked like the one in figure 5. Many of the changes of the 1920s—the durable construction of homes, the provision of modern amenities such as electricity, the development of support for religious life, and the strong service sector—came to rest solidly as characteristic of Amman, the new capital, by 1930.

In 1928, Father Michel Abel would have witnessed an Amman that looked like the one in figure 6, with the King Hussein mosque's minaret visible from great distances. This same area is now downtown Amman, Wist al-Balad (or colloquially, al-Balad); see figure 7.

As a result of the rapid development in the 1920s, migrations to this new capital and urban center surged. The earliest waves of new residents included Syrians, Palestinians, Lebanese, and Iraqis, as well as Kurds and Armenians, expanding the population from 10,500 in 1930 to 45,000 a decade later (Kadhim and Rajjal 1988; Potter et al. 2009, 84). Between 1930 and 1945, the population of Amman grew from 45,000 to a staggering 250,000. A 555% population growth rate within 15 years is difficult to accommodate in immediate and instantaneous construction efforts. As a result, by the time of the 1952 census, as many as 29 percent of the population were still living in tents and a further 8 percent in natural caves (Abu-Dayyeh 2004). This trend is mainly attributable to the influx of Palestinian refugees and the living conditions created by the five refugee camps in Amman. Between the 1967 Six-Day War and 1970, Amman's population is estimated to have risen from 330,000 to about 500,000.

The physical development of contemporary Amman meant accommodating a swiftly growing and diverse populace, both in terms of housing and other public spaces and services. It is important to note that the durable housing has been provided for an otherwise liminal population, the Palestinian refugees. This and eligibility for Jordanian citizenship demonstrates an emerging vision for a wholly constructed city, both in terms of permanent structures and sociocultural forms. The development of electricity provided a buoyancy to other developmental efforts. The grounding of public life around structures and services that support personal interactions—green public spaces and centers for religious life—further supports a vision of a modern city that is integrated and supportive of a diverse public sphere.  Finally, although agriculture may have been a means to center and solidify early migrants (Rogan 1994, 1999), the priorities for land use are eventually given to residential housing, which inevitably results in urban sprawl.

The development of an aesthetically, architecturally, and technically modern Amman does not necessarily translate into homogenous understandings of Islamic practice in everyday life. Rather, "meaning is something conferred" (Barth 1993, 170); it is not inherent in Islam or even in Shari'a. Therefore, meaning—as both "authentic" and "Islamic"—is constituted by the individual act of interpretation and practices in economizing processes. The consumption of religion and modernity constitutes a consumption of "intellectual commodities," often understood as an Islamic middle-class endeavor. As discussed in chapter 3, consensus in understanding how to live one's life in this economically modern context and as a pious Muslim is still being debated and decided, even as such processes reside under buildings that may share a common limestone exterior.

# CHAPTER 3

# Making It Meaningful

*Ramadan*

*Abu Huraira (Allah be pleased with him) reported Allah's Messenger (may peace be upon him) as saying: "Every (good) deed of the son of Adam would be multiplied, a good deed receiving tenfold to seven hundredfold reward . . . with the exception of fasting, for it is done for Me and I will give a reward for it. . . . There are two occasions of joy for one who fasts, joy when he breaks it, and joy when he meets his Lord."*

—From the sayings of the Prophet Mohammed in the hadith,
as cited in Sahih Muslim Book 6, Hadith 2567
(Muslim ibn al-Hajjaj 2000, 674)

*For most people, Ramadan has just become all about the food. They think that because they fast all day they need to eat, eat, eat. They forget that the fast is about more than just eating.*

—University student, 2008

During the first week of Ramadan, 2007, I took a two-hour taxi ride from the northern Jordanian border with Israel back to Amman. It was mid-September, and the weather was still hot. I was sitting in the back seat of the non–air conditioned taxi wearing long sleeves and jeans (standard daily clothing for me), seated uncomfortably on the passenger side facing directly into the sun. The windows were rolled up with the exception of a small crack next to the driver, and the music was turned off so I had nothing to distract me from the heat. I rolled down the window next to me in the hope of getting a cooling breeze, but the air outside proved to be just as warm, and its blowing into the taxi made it feel as though I was next to a furnace. I started to slide out of the sun but because only the driver and I were in the taxi, I wanted to avoid moving into his direct line of sight (via the rearview mirror) to avoid any hint of impropriety, so I shifted back into my original position. Then I remembered that I had a bottle of water from the Arab market in Nazareth in my bag. I opened up the still-cool bottle and started drinking.

The taxi driver heard the rustling of the bag and the opening of the water, glanced back and, as his shock turned to anger, nearly drove us off the road. "What are you doing [Shu biti'amilee]?!" he shouted. "I'm just drinking water [Bishirib mai' bess]" I answered. Seeing his anger grow, I continued, "I'm not Muslim and I'm a girl [a tactful way of saying that I was menstruating, when Muslim women are not required to fast, but which they must make up later on]. I'm not fasting [Ana mish Muslima, wa bint. Mish musawama]." He replied:

> *Haram! Haram!!*[1] How can you do that?! Don't you know it's Ramadan?! This is our holiest month and the month when we fast and pray and think about Allah and worship. We don't even listen to music these days [gestures to the radio]. It doesn't matter that it's hot, and that you're not a Muslim, and that you're a girl. Everyone knows that.[2] You're drinking water during Ramadan and that's disrespectful to us and to our religion. And, you know what else? It's illegal. You can't drink water in public. You're going to get us both put into prison.

I immediately put the water bottle away and apologized profusely to the driver, which thankfully brought an end to an extremely awkward and uncomfortable moment. Afterward, however, I couldn't stop thinking about this incident and what it said about the norms of public behavior with respect to Ramadan. On the one hand, of course, Ramadan is a matter of personal piety and religious practice—something private between each believer and Allah. On the other hand, Ramadan is also very much a matter between believers and others in society. As such, there is a fundamental—and government-legislated—shift in what is considered appropriate in terms of public displays of religiosity and authentic Islamic piety during this holy month, quite apart from the other months of the year. Consequently, certain norms of public behavior and of personal religious practice become amplified during

Ramadan, especially during the daily give-and-take of communing with one's coworkers, friends, and family.

The religious precepts of Ramadan—praying, fasting, and repenting, as well as expressions of popular religiosity and Islamic egalitarianism—have been the subject of numerous anthropological studies over the years. More recently, anthropologists have turned their attention to the socially significant and extra-religious meanings of Ramadan. Christa Salamandra (2004), for instance, has shown how the cultural practices associated with Ramadan serve to engender and perpetuate social hierarchies rather than egalitarianism. We know that Ramadan soap operas serve as reflections of and perpetuators for cultural knowledge of the nation-state in Egypt (Abu-Lughod 2005). Also in Egypt, the commercialized aspects of Ramadan serve as a signal of the penetration of capitalist modes for markets and for a mass consumerism that accompanies the religious and secular rituals associated with the month (Armbrust 2000a, 2000b, 2002).

Although such work has been important for revealing the localized, political economy of Ramadan practices, contemporary Amman presents a particularly fascinating case for study in that, as a city of 2.5 million people, it requires one to take into account a plurality of religious pieties on display at any moment in time. Far from a unitary response in religious piety—everyone praying and fasting for the same reasons—practices and pieties here are conducted and justified by all kinds of discursive and socially sustained modes. This chapter focuses on these discursive justifications and rationalities—especially references to Shari'a, or Islamic law, and norms and ethics that "command right and forbid wrong" (Cook 2000)—used to make meaningful this shift in social, cultural, and religious practices during the month.

Islamic practices and beliefs are particularly subject to normative expectations during Ramadan: everyone should fast, pray, heighten their "good" behaviors, and draw closer to Allah. The pressure to live according to these normative expectations is intense and pervasive, leading to, in essence, a "bottom line" of what are considered to be the most essential elements of appropriate Islamic belief and practice. The rationalities used to understand and justify these shared practices are derived from an array of religious and Shari'a-based sources, as well as from extra-religious understandings. For example, in order to manage the deleterious effects of fasting during Ramadan, some people sleep away the hunger and headaches, while others use the fast for various health reasons such as losing weight or "detoxing" from alcohol drinking. In other words, not everyone justifies adherence to these practices in the same ways—each individual makes Ramadan meaningful on his or her own terms.

The process of making the normative practices of Ramadan meaningful to each individual believer is essential to understanding the larger argument of this book about the cultivation of a neoliberal Islamic piety in Amman. As I will show, there is a "spiritual economy" at play during Ramadan, one in which economic practices become integrated into the everyday experience of Islamic piety, and vice versa (Rudnyckyj 2010; Scott 2009). While Ramadan is not the only time when this spiritual economy is evident, the heightening of normative expectations makes it an especially good time to see both the Islamizing of economic practices and the economizing of Islamic practices.

## Ramadan History

Ramadan, the ninth month of the Islamic calendar, is a commemoration of a set of historical events that occurred at the advent of Islam. It is also a religious command to fast during the month. How Ramadan became a holy month is well documented. It is believed that Mohammed went into a period of personal spiritual reclusiveness on Mount Hira, just outside Mecca, in the year 610 CE. During that period, the angel Gabriel came to him and began revealing the Qur'an with the word "Read!"[3] Though the exact date of the revelation is unknown, it is believed to have occurred during one of the odd-numbered nights during the last ten days of the month: the 21st, 23rd, 25th, 27th, or 29th. The most common interpretation is the 27th, which is often referred to as "Laylat al-Qadr" or "Night of Power." It was also during this month that the Battle of Badr redefined the new Muslim community.

The Battle of Badr occurred in 623 CE (2 *Hijra,* according to the Islamic calendar), on the seventeenth day of Ramadan. It is one of the few battles discussed in the Qur'an, and is often cited as the decisive moment in the power struggle between the followers of Mohammed and the presiding and powerful tribe in Mecca, the Quraish. This first large-scale engagement between the two forces and the subsequent victory of the Muslims is often attributed to divine intervention. After receiving the call from God to "Fight them until persecution is no more, and religion is all for God"[4] and the command to pray in the direction of Mecca rather than Jerusalem,[5] the first Muslims were charged to engage in warfare with the Quraish. As a Quraishi caravan came toward Mecca from Syria, its vulnerability and fear of a raid by the Muslims prompted its leader, Abu Sufyan, to send for support and troops from among the Quraish in Mecca. By the time they reached Badr, the Quraish outnumbered the Muslims three or four to one. On the seventeenth day of Ramadan, Mohammed and his companion, Abu Bakr, prayed. Mohammed turned to him and said, "Be of good cheer Abu Bakr; the help of God hath come to thee. Here is Gabriel and in his hand is the rein of a horse which he is leading, and he is armed for war."[6] According to the Qur'an, when the Quraish and the Muslims charged at one another, the Muslims were guided by "a thousand angels"[7] and God "cast terror into the hearts of the disbelievers," adding that "it is for you [the Muslims] to strike off their heads and to smite their every fingers."[8] The Quraish turned in retreat to Mecca. The battle lasted only a few hours.

While many Muslims take the account literally, the role it plays in solidifying Ramadan as a holy month is significant. The advent of Islam and the revelation of the Qur'an brought the voice of God to the Muslims during the month of Ramadan. The involvement of supernatural agents for the victory at Badr during Ramadan only served to solidify that God was actively and divinely intervening in Muslims' lives, and Allah continues to do so in exceptional ways during the month.

If the revelation of the Qur'an and the Battle of Badr are well known, the origins of fasting during the month are not. The word "Ramadan" comes from the Arabic root *ramida* or *arramad*, meaning "scorching heat," but its exact connection to fasting is unclear. It may be a reference to the belief that the fast "scorches" away sin (al-Isfahani 1991, 203). According to the *ahadith*, there is an injunction to fast on 'Ashura, the tenth day of the month of Muharram,[9] which establishes fasting as a means to make particular days sacred through ritualized eating and drinking. The Ramadan fast may also be tied to summer solstice or an extension of the Jewish holiday of Yom Kippur, which likewise includes the practice of fasting.[10] Regardless of the speculation surrounding the origin of the practice, as the fourth pillar of Islam, fasting from sunup to sundown is perhaps the most well-known aspect of Ramadan to non-Muslims today.

Fasting in contemporary Amman can be interpreted in various degrees of strictness but it begins with the basic assumption that during the period of fasting one should not ingest food or drink. Some even avoid taking medication, while others go so far as to abstain from swallowing their own spit or even applying gloss or lipstick. Furthermore, a fast can be broken with practices that have nothing to do with what passes one's mouth. For example, one's fast may be broken with one's hands by touching a member of the opposite sex who is not a relative, or with one's eyes by gazing lustfully at a member of the opposite sex. Typically, fasting becomes a practice enforced by immediate family members once an individual reaches puberty and—as described at the beginning of this chapter—enforced by the government in public, visible spaces. Some individuals, such as travelers and menstruating women, are exempt completely from fasting but must make up the days later. Others, such as pregnant or breastfeeding women and the very elderly and infirm, are exempt completely from fasting and are required to compensate or restitute through specified acts of charity.

The larger intent behind observing Ramadan is to achieve heightened piety so, in addition to fasting, Ammanis often pay careful attention to ensure they pray the required five times per day and try to pray more often, often in the *tarawih* prayer.[11] Personal comportment changes during Ramadan, as many strive to avoid gossip, slander, and backbiting. Men avoid looking at women lustfully and women typically avoid wearing provocative clothes, cosmetics, and perfumes that could attract a man. There is a focus on charity, with one's mandated charitable giving, *zakat*, due at the end of the month. Additional charitable donations and gestures such as giving money to beggars on the street (*sadaqa*), are valued. It was commonly asserted among my informants that if a person dies during Ramadan, ascension to *jenna*, or paradise, is expected.

In a normative sense, Ramadan is considered a time for inner reflection, self-control, cultivating one's religious practice, and giving to the poor. One's mind and body should be focused on Allah. The month ends with 'Eid Al-Fitr, or the "Little Feast," which often includes days off from work and time spent with family and friends.

## Enforcing the Fast

Regardless of one's personal religious practice or status, all people in Amman are required to uphold Jordanian law, which means that they are forbidden from public consumption of any kind during the daytime hours. Smoking cigarettes, drinking, and eating on the street or in a public space are all strictly prohibited and enforced by local law. This strictly imposed rule of law has had detrimental consequences for those who choose to violate it. In one story I heard during Ramadan 2007, a thirty-year-old man was rumored to have been arrested after he lit a cigarette on the street. It was said that he died that night in prison.[12] Whether true or not, such stories serve to enhance the rule of law on this point, reinforcing the expectation that dire consequences are in store for those who violate the fast.

To further legislate an environment conducive to heightened Islamic piety in public, all alcohol sales are forbidden in Jordan during the month of Ramadan. I once interviewed a member of the Abu Jaber family (distributors of Amstel Beer in Jordan) about this and was told, "Of course we can't sell alcohol during Ramadan. It hurts sales, yeah. But our sales the month before are always really good." The latter comment is an allusion to the fact that before the month begins, there is a rush to "stock up" on alcohol, especially by Christians but also some Muslims. The Christian Orthodox Club is forbidden to *sell* alcohol during Ramadan. However, they are not forbidden to *serve* it. As such they have developed a system by which people bring in their own alcohol—hard liquor, beer, or wine—and it is served to them throughout the month. The Orthodox Club sold no alcohol, in adherence to the law, but Christians and others who wanted to feel as though they were having a night out as they would outside of Ramadan were able to have alcohol served and consume it without violating the law.

Four-star and five-star hotel restaurants, along with a few other establishments that typically cater to foreigners and tourists, have special licenses to operate food and alcohol services and are closely regulated through special permit. For people unable or unwilling to refrain from smoking, these hotels provide a safe and legal venue in which to light up. The Intercontinental Hotel in Amman is one such space. On my way to meet another American for lunch at a restaurant in the hotel, I witnessed the lounge full of Jordanian men smoking cigarettes.

Requirements for adhering to the law extend to all businesses that sell food or drink. By default, businesses in the food industry are not allowed to open during daytime hours unless they have a special permit to operate. Special permits are most frequently granted to businesses that have a large foreign—and presumably non-Muslim—clientele. If a business violates the terms of its Ramadan agreements and the government finds out, the business will most likely be shuttered for the remainder of the month. During Ramadan 2007 I heard a rumor that the Gloria Jeans coffee shop next to the University of Jordan had been shut down for the month and its managers arrested after serving coffee to foreign students without the special permit.[13]

A similar incident occurred during Ramadan 2008 involving Books@ Cafe, a bookstore/café that is popular with twenty- and thirty-somethings in Amman. Located in prime real estate in the reinvigorated neighborhood of Jabal Amman, "Books" (as it is commonly termed by its regulars) hosts a diverse crowd. Known for being a harassment-free space for women, gays, and foreign workers, Books is also one of the few places in Amman that serves both *argeelah* ("hookah") and alcohol, as well as offering decent food, free Wi-Fi, and outdoor and balcony seating with expansive views. The story unfolded in a series of postings on www.7iber.com by the storeowner. As reported, the Ministry of Tourism and the Hotel and Restaurant Association had issued Books a special permit—for the third year in a row—to remain open, selling both food and alcohol during the day. As a three-star tourist establishment, it was one of the few exceptions to the more usual four-star and five-star spots with similar permits. The night before Ramadan began, the police entered Books and, according to the owner, "asked us to close down. 'This is the holy month of Ramadan!' they barked. Since we are officially licensed and they could provide no official papers, we refused to close" (Jazerah 2008).

The story did not end there. Shortly after Ramadan started, a Security Committee (Al-Lajna Al-Amnia) was formed to monitor and enforce food and drink sales and consumption in Amman during the month. The Committee included representatives of three offices: the Hotel and Restaurant Association, the Ministry of Tourism, and the Governorate or regional administrative offices. On September 17, 2008, the Security Committee came to Books. This is the story recounted by the angry owner:

They then [the Security Committee] walked into the kitchen while many of us including my brother were standing and witnessing. One person proceeds to tell our chef that there are cockroaches, insects, mice in the kitchen. Every one was baffled and were telling him to show us what he was talking about! Of course there was nothing, but with every accusation, he ordered one of his committee members to write it down and then adds, "Let them get what they deserve for serving alcohol in this holy month." Our chef kept asking the guy to show him where he saw cockroaches, mice, however the inspector was not there to listen; he was just there to write us up and penalize us.

Despite the fact that only representatives from the Ministry and the Governate [sic] were there—no one from the Hotel and Restaurant Association. The guy then tells us we should not be serving alcohol on the terrace; we immediately pulled all liquor sales indoors.

Sunday night, we get shocked with the visit from the police with an order to close. There was no reason within the order. Of course, they only come at night so that there is no one to call or anything to do. When we showed them our papers, they kept calling us a night club. We are licensed as a restaurant. To them, if alcohol is served, then it is a night club. This is the logic we encountered, regardless of the fully accredited and legal license.

To our shock, the order started with the same Ministry of Tourism representative who received us like we were dirt at the ministry. He had sent a document with 18 accusations at us including the basic cockroaches, insects etc. Including another accusation "jalsat 7ameema wa tabadol al qubal." Roughly translated into "intimate gatherings and exchange of kissing." He also mentions that someone told him to go and form his prayer ablutions with beer! The document stated that this was all happening on the terrace, in public and in front of us and everyone! The guy was lying through his teeth!

For now Books@Cafe is closed. (Jazerah 2008)

The rumor among my friends and colleagues was that the people in residential units around Books had complained about food and drink present in their line of sight during daytime hours, as consuming customers were outside on Books' balconies. The government, it was rumored, felt compelled to "respect" the rights of Muslims to fast without temptation and public viewing of eating and drinking. Even though Books operated under the legal entitlements of their Ramadan permit, the popular understanding was consistent with the owner's statement that the cited health code violation was a sham. Furthermore, it was believed that this was the only way to close Books; to revoke the permit would have been legally difficult. In total, the Security Committee closed sixty restaurants and bars during Ramadan that year (Jazerah 2008). Many—if not all—had also received the proper permits in advance from the government.

As this story suggests, where, when, and what one eats and drinks during Ramadan is a highly public and contested, even legal, issue. The morality at play here is one in which justifications argued on the basis of "individual choice" or "market demands" are considered inadequate, even illegitimate; to argue that there is enough of a clientele to stay open during the day in Ramadan and to give individuals the choice to consume or not is beside the point. Furthermore, the claims made by the owner of Books—that the closure violated the terms of the Ramadan permits the store had been granted for several years—might have been technically correct but the fact was that there is fluidity and porousness to what is considered right and wrong. The legislating and governing bodies can and do change their minds, asserting their assessments and reassessments of the right and wrong in people's actions, even over and above consistency in rule of law.

This contestation of practices during Ramadan goes beyond the obviously public spaces of hotels, restaurants, and bookstores. A car or vehicle, such as the taxicab in the story at the start of this chapter, is an ambiguous space that is neither completely public nor entirely private. During Ramadan 2008, while an American friend was visiting me in Amman, the two of us picked up a few cupcakes at the local mall to snack on one afternoon. After we were told that we could not sit in the café and eat them I asked the cashier, "What do pregnant women do when they need to eat?" He answered, "They sit in their cars." We, too, sat in my car to eat the cupcakes. Likewise, the Starbucks drive-through was open, but one had to be careful not to drink when at a stoplight and under the watchful eye of the people in the neighboring car for fear of receiving disparaging looks and comments. Individual choice in an enclosed space, even for people who are not required to fast, is superseded by a dominant public ethic that invokes line of sight as the threshold criteria for public chastisement.

These are some of the ways that a more restrictive and austere public life is enforced during Ramadan. It is a legislated and popular shift in normativity, and it is a collaborative—even assertive—morality that dictates the adherence to certain religious practice in public spaces. Everyone feels the impact, even the pregnant or menstruating women and Christians who are not required to fast. The same is true for people who choose not to fast for another reason, such as non-practicing Muslims and atheists or agnostics from Muslim families. Foreigners are also required to uphold these laws, although much greater lenience and space is given to them than to Jordanians.

Within this framework of legislated governmental support, the publicly recognized and authorized ethics for practicing piety in public also shift during Ramadan. Even if behaviors in public or semi-public spaces are not, strictly speaking, illegal, the tenor for these highly normative ethics is already in place; the governmental regulations further produce and legitimate a morality and public ethic about proper comportment. The tacit collaboration of state and society in enforcing Ramadan practices is the norm, and it permeates all public and semi-public spheres that one may encounter. Civil society theorists have discussed the important impacts of state-society collaborative dynamics on public norms and ethics (Hefner 2000, 55–57; Norton 1995; Norton 2001). In the instance of Amman, the state-society dynamic is overwhelmingly collaborative, and the collaboration is ultimately aimed at illiberal and religious ends (Tobin 2013).

The list of prohibited public practices during Ramadan extends well beyond alcohol sales, eating, drinking, and smoking, and crosses over into the more murky realm of heightened social norms that alter public behavior. Men and women refrain from touching each other in public, chewing gum, applying anything to the lips such as balm or lipstick, dressing in a way that reveals or suggests their shoulders, elbows or legs, wearing cosmetics and perfumes, even carrying unopened food and drink. I was frequently advised to wrap my water bottle in a black plastic bag, so as not to draw attention to a substance with which one could break a fast. "Line of sight" is again invoked: it is a general rule that if someone might struggle to maintain his or her own fast by seeing someone else engage in (or even remind them of) a behavior, it is a violation of public ethics, and perhaps also illegal, to engage in it within the public eye. This sort of ethics is usually discussed in terms of "respect" or *ihtiram*. That is, people of all religious faiths and kinds of personal practices are implored to keep their consumption out of sight "out of respect" for those fasting and "out of respect" for Islam.

## With a Hand, a Tongue, and a Heart: Minority Experiences of Ramadan

This normativity—legitimized by both the government and the public—is illustrative of a central tenet of Islamic ethics, the concept of "commanding right and forbidding wrong"[14] (Cook 2000). 'Umar ibn al-Khattab has identified the commanding of right and the forbidding of wrong as a primary tenet of the religion, which some also regard as the "sixth pillar" of Islam (Gammer 2004, 131n49). The concept is based upon the Prophet Mohammed's statement, "Whoever sees a wrong, and is able to put it right with his hand, let him do so; if he can't, then with his tongue; if he can't, then in his heart, and that is the bare minimum of faith" (Cook 2000, 32n2; the references to this in the Sunna and the accompanying *isnaad*, or chains of transmission, are extensive). This injunction to put right the wrongs with a hand, a tongue, and then a heart—solidified as a core Islamic concept in the second century of the Islamic calendar—plays out in interesting ways here. The multilayered support for these norms and ethics include the "hand" of the government, the "tongue" of the public, and the "heart" of respect. That is, a person needs not only to abide by the letter of the law and refrain from public consumption or suffer repercussions by the "hand" of the government, but also to avoid situations such as drinking coffee in a car that would prompt a chastisement with a tongue. Furthermore, one must adopt these behaviors "with respect," an attitude of apparent heartfelt deference and support for these norms. It is not simply a matter of what one does or says, it is *how* one does or says it. Orthopraxy here is expanded to include both method and outcome.

While the extensive inculcation of these ethics and norms during Ramadan affects everyone, the fact is that not everyone experiences them in the same way. That is, the meaning of Ramadan and its traditions varies from individual to individual and from group to group. In Amman, it is estimated that 3 to 5 percent of the population is Christian. Some Christian neighborhoods, such as an area just outside of Amman named Fuhais, are known for public displays of Christianity, which are distinctive and include practices such as the public placement of decorated trees during the Christmas holiday season. Generally speaking, however, Christian pieties and religious practices are less visible than their Muslim counterparts. Practitioners do not display publicly their religious observance beyond a piece of jewelry with a crucifix, or rosary beads around the rearview mirror of their cars. Although some Orthodox Christians fast during Lent or other Church seasons by adhering to a vegan diet, they do not fast during Ramadan. Nevertheless, they must adhere to the legislation forbidding public consumption. They often express frustration with the governmental and Muslim-majority ethics and public restrictions placed upon them. A middle-aged, Jordanian Christian woman described a trip to the French supermarket and department store, Carrefour, during Ramadan:

> I went to Carrefour to buy our food. . . . And everyone kept staring at me. I didn't understand why, until I realized I was chewing gum. I was walking around Carrefour and not fasting, and everyone knew it. But, I'm a Christian. I don't fast for Ramadan. So, you know what I did? I started chewing really loudly and cracking the gum. It's not my holiday. Why do I have to follow their religious rules? I hate it. I hate Ramadan so much.

This woman's act of chewing gum, which some would consider sufficient to break a fast, evoked stares from the people around her; the "tongue" of the public. Her response, to chew loudly and crack the gum, carried with it a certain measure of "disrespect" and antagonism. In so doing she was pushing the boundaries of acceptable public comportment of respect for a non-faster during Ramadan. In other words, even though she was not observing Ramadan, she still felt the constraints of the legislated and enforced set of laws and public ethics.

Likewise, a young Christian female described the month of Ramadan in her work as a pharmaceutical sales representative:

> Everyone I work with is Christian, so we eat lunch together and spend the time in the office drinking coffee and tea together. But we just got this new boss. He's Muslim. So now we have to eat in the bathroom to respect him and his religion. Eating in the bathroom is disgusting. I don't understand why we all have to change what we're doing for one person. Why can't he respect us? Why do we have to respect him?

The presence of one Muslim within a community of Christians, particularly where he occupies a position of power and authority, is enough to alter the public tenor and set of ethics within a Christian-majority office. Furthermore, as public ethics of not eating or drinking were altered, so too were sentiments of "respect." That is, the informant is really questioning who has a more morally justifiable right to claim their notions of public ethics—the single Muslim boss during Ramadan or the demographically larger community of Christian employees. Or, to state the matter differently and in a way that further emphasizes the assertive moralities in play: a principle of religious majoritarianism prevails even when the demographic majority is not present. Ramadan here is not typified by a model of individualized liberalism. The individual's "right" to chew gum at the supermarket or to eat lunch at her desk are not supported during Ramadan. In this case, as in other cases I witnessed and heard about in Amman, the presence of a single Muslim was enough to evoke the "need for respect" and, by extension, invoke the hand, the tongue, and the heart to alter and "correct" social behaviors.

Of course, how "respect" is determined in situations such as these is critical. Not surprisingly, the terms by which it is defined and invoked reference distinctly Islamic ethics. In a conversation with one of my Muslim friends, she gave a fairly typical assessment of non-fasters:

> The Christians in Jordan are always respectful. They are. The women dress more conservatively during Ramadan, and maybe they have alcohol, but they always have it at home and never in loud parties. We don't have to see it. But the Muslims that don't fast, they're always the ones that are not respectful. They should fast, but they don't. And it's like they rub it in our faces. They are the ones that have the loud parties with lots of alcohol. They have no respect.

In this instance, "respect" is defined in terms of line of sight: by women's dress and removal of alcohol. These are also two primary ways that the Islamic Resurgence has manifested itself in orthopraxy in recent decades.

The sentiment above serves to affirm not only that Christians are altering their public comportment to adhere to this legislated and normative sense of Ramadan ethics, but also that Muslims who are not fasting are perceived to lack the appropriate respect that Christians have. As Muslims, they can and will be subjected to the injunction of commanding right and forbidding wrong. Normativity here is strong and clear: Muslims *should* be fasting and, by extension, *should* be promoting these public ethics of a normative Islam. They are judged by my friend as acting outside the norm and, therefore, disrespectful. The injunction to command right and forbid wrong on the part of non-practicing Muslims is a particularly important source of agitation in processes of developing and solidifying normativity, and further speaks to the encompassing and illiberal nature of this morality. Indeed, according to my Ammani friends and informants, non-practicing Muslims are the most offensive and threatening group because their liminal position—as both legal Muslims and non-fasters—carries the potential to undermine the governmental and public collaborative morality in play.

Amman has a vibrant, if small and relatively ignored, gay community. There is a dance club, an online magazine catering to homosexuals, various neighborhoods known for "cruising," and bars where gays can meet without fear of persecution. By large consensus in Amman, homosexuals are typically considered outside the majority Muslim community and frequently discussed in terms of "deviance." As a result, Ramadan for some in the community is often not about raising one's level of religiosity but about tempering one's "bad" behavior.[15] In an interview, one homosexual Muslim in Amman described what Ramadan means to him:

> Well, first it's a time to detox [laughs]. I don't drink during Ramadan. But, we have, like, our own Mardi Gras. You should have seen the party the night before Ramadan started! Yeah. I pray five times a day. Well . . . [pauses], I try to pray five times a day [laughs]. And I fast when I'm not traveling. And when I'm not going to the gym [laughs]. I spend time with my family. I see them every night for *iftar* and it's really great. But really, Ramadan for me is about trying to be a better person. And I definitely detox.

As the informant indicates, there is a lighthearted measure of incorporating the push towards heightened religiosity, but the larger rationale is about refraining from alcohol and orienting toward the family in a movement to inculcate a stronger sense of "being a better person." These practices are not necessarily placed within a religious framework, and working out one's piety in religious terms is, at least in this case, tertiary.

This is also an instance where calculative agency serves to economize Islamic practice. The informant fasts when he's not traveling, as is permitted according to the scholarly tradition. However, he also fasts when he's not "going to the gym." Deciding when to fast is done in terms of planned physical exertion, a calculation that exists outside of the scholarly work that the *'ulama* have established. This is also true for Ramadan as a time of "detox": my informant engages his agency by calculating alternatives between public normativity, family rituals, and personal health.

Ultimately, of course, piety comprises a spectrum of practices and beliefs. Outside of the month of Ramadan the diversity is widest. During Ramadan, however, in the face of assertive moralities in orthopraxy—particularly fasting—additional rationalities and legitimations emerge that both uphold and reproduce the normative Islam while still finding personal meaning in the rituals. The effect is the economizing of Islamic practice. Not all Muslims in Amman engage in Ramadan practices to enhance their devotion to Allah. In fact, their presence serves as a critique of constructions of Islamic piety that are defined in opposition to simplified notions of liberal societies. That is, it is not all about heightened religiosity for this portion of the population. Nor do they necessarily prefer this illiberal construction of morality that so clearly defines the month and their parameters for practice. Nonetheless, these friends and informants reported a measure of acquiescence and then exertion to make Ramadan meaningful and fulfilling for themselves, but oftentimes for non-religious ends.

## Consuming Ramadan, Making Meaning

There are commonalities in how the month of Ramadan is passed for those in Amman regardless of their devotion to Allah. One of these has to do with the fact that Ramadan has become an intense period of time for religious consumption—not just in the pursuit of material ends as individuals are keen to sate their thirst and hunger, but of socially sustained, religious ones. Not only is the month a time when families gather for longer periods and with greater frequencies, but also one when families consume large quantities of food together and deal, in community, with this shift in ethics and norms. Heightened and altered consumption here is of religious and material goods, and is done in community and socially organized settings.

Ramadan is characterized by long evenings passed with family and friends during which the fast is first broken by consuming dates and water, followed by soup, salads, and a large meal that often consists of rice and meats with dairy products such as yogurt poured on top. Special desserts are the norm, such as *getayif* (or *qatayif/'atayif*), which resembles palm-size pancakes folded over and stuffed with either walnuts and cinnamon or cheese. Special, sweet drinks are preferred, such as *tamarhind* (tamarind) and Qamr ad-din, a dried sheet of apricot "concentrate" that is mixed with boiling water and sugar. For the women who typically prepare the meals and large, nightly feasts, a taste of the food is important to adjust flavors and spices; this can be difficult while one is fasting. I witnessed a fasting wife prepare an elaborate dinner for her family one afternoon. To taste each dish, she spooned some of the dinner from the pot into her mouth, chewed for a moment, and then spit it into the sink in order not to break her fast by swallowing.

This extensive meal is a daily affair during the month, and many people complain of the high prices of food, hoarding, and lack of goods available in the supermarket. A common complaint is typified by an informant who said, "Prices are so expensive right now! And the shelves were empty! There's nothing there—even at Carrefour!" Alternatively, many people go out to dinner at local restaurants and pay even more for a more elaborate meal or buffet. These are familiar rituals during Ramadan throughout the region (Armbrust 2000a, 2000b; Salamandra 2004).

After dinner many people are at home to watch the daily installment of a Ramadan soap opera such as the Syrian historical drama *Bab Al-Hara* ("Gate of the Neighborhood") or *Noor* (literally "Light," as adapted from the Turkish title "Gümüş" or "Silver"), then attend the local mosques to pray *tarawih*. After the conclusion of the soap opera and *tarawih* prayer, many people visit the homes of friends and family or go out to cafés to drink coffee, smoke the water pipe (*argeelah*), see local artists and shows, and play cards.

One popular event is *sohour* Ramadan, which translates roughly to "staying up late into the late night/early morning of Ramadan." It is also the name of the pre-dawn meal that people consume before a day of fasting begins. *Sohour* Ramadan events are in outdoor tents, often associated with four-star and five-star hotels around the city. Sometimes they occur in people's homes. Usually they are heavily supplied with the seasonal foods mentioned above and with a later, sometimes catered meal in the middle of the night. *Sohour* Ramadan is also a time to see and be seen. I attended a *sohour* Ramadan at the home of a retired high-level government official. In attendance were the Director of Jordan's Fulbright program and his wife, the Ambassador from Sweden and his wife, and the editor of the country's most prominent English-language business magazine, *Jordan Business*.

Such events are becoming more common throughout the region, as elites who are otherwise non-observant Muslims use the Ramadan consumptive moments to reinforce social differentiation. Going to restaurants for *iftar*, for example, enables the elites to go out for a social occasion *and* display religiosity at the same time (Salamandra 2004, 95). Hosting a *sohour* Ramadan event provides an opportunity to display status markers of modernity—fine food and drink, elite and prestigious guests, enjoyable entertainment, and high levels of conspicuous consumption—within a framework that acquiesces to the hand, tongue, and heart of commanding right and forbidding wrong during Ramadan. In this way, *sohour* Ramadan is not a means to pursue one's personal piety and devotion to Allah, but an orthopraxic means to entrench the public norms, ethics, and symbols for Ramadan, to Islamize economic practices in conspicuous consumption, and to create a meaningful Ramadan experience. In this way, *sohour* Ramadan is a socially sustained means to consume both religious and material goods.

Such Ramadan rituals also constitute an economizing of Islamic practice by conspicuous consumption of religion. Many homes and streets are decorated with colored strings of lights lining doorways, balconies, and windows, which not only enhances the festive quality of the month, but—more importantly—"announces" people's religiosity and adherence to public norms and ethics and constitutes a symbolic gesture that reinforces the commanding of right and the forbidding of wrong. It does all this while adding to the "atmosphere" of the season in a way that evokes affective responses and a sense of meaning. The lights are often in the shapes of symbols associated with Ramadan: lanterns, cannons, and crescent moons, as well as sayings such as "*Ramadan Kareem*" or "Blessed Ramadan."

## The Marketization of Ramadan, the Marketization of Islam

The Ramadan rituals and traditions just described reflect a certain degree of change over time, largely consistent with the swift development of Amman. Informants frequently referenced the increased commercialization and elaboration of the holiday celebrations in comparison with years past, particularly through advertisements and public consumption in restaurants. In a regional English-language magazine, *Sayidaty*, an 89-year-old named Hind describes Ramadan 50 years before—in the 1960s—when she was in her late 30s:

> There was no sophistication at all. We only had to prepare one meal. Life is much more complicated now. People tend to seek personal pleasures and satisfaction rather than showing gratitude to the Creator of all things. ("Ramadan," 101)

Hind characterized the Ramadan holidays in her younger years as simpler and people in contemporary times as more complicated and sophisticated, following personal pursuits rather than religiosity and piety in the Ramadan fast. Her observations are consistent with the argument that despite—or perhaps because of—the legislated and enforced restrictions on consumption during Ramadan, there is wider diversity of religiosity, which displays both an economized Islamic practice and an Islamization of economic practices. As Hind attests, Islamized consumption during Ramadan has risen as a primary mode for experiencing the month. In particular, the rise in the commercialization of Ramadan is another realm in which there is a heightened sense of the "festiveness" of the holiday and reason for sociality, particularly through multiple shared meals and experiences of consumption throughout the night, rather than exclusive growth of personal piety. As the state legislates and enforces restrictions on consumption during Ramadan, the times in which consumption occurs become rife with symbolic depth, such that the act becomes a primary means to enact calculative agencies in Islamic and economic practices.

Heightened levels of consumption and commercialization during Ramadan are frequent targets for criticism (Abu-Lughod 2005; Armbrust 2002; Armbrust 2006; Salamandra 2004), in Jordan as well as in neighboring countries. One particular subject of complaint is "an association of corporate-sponsored materialism with morality" (Armbrust 2006, 208) during Ramadan by the promotion of heightened levels and types of consumption during a time otherwise designated for the pursuit of heightened piety. Many corporations have introduced seasonal foods and targeted commercials. As a case in point, during Ramadan Starbucks now sells date-flavored Frappuccinos and merchandise that highlights symbols of the season. Burger King and McDonald's display advertisements with partially eaten food products shaped into symbols of Islam, such as the crescent moon and praying "French Fry fingers."

Figure 8 is a Nokia ad that avoids using overt symbolic representations of Islam to commodify Ramadan. Rather, it uses a form of sociality amplified during Ramadan—reconnecting with family and friends—as a means to try to sell more Ramadan applications. The domed architectural form is an abstract and generic mosque shape: the idea is that one's experience of Ramadan will be enhanced by Nokia's mobile phone applications in an economizing of Islamic practice.

In figure 9 the Amman skyline has been reproduced as a UPC symbol with the crescent moon above, implying that during Ramadan the entire city is available for sale. Even the crescent moon is represented as part of the UPC code, implying that Islam itself is available for purchase.

Food and its public consumption have become a significant part of how orthopraxy in Ramadan is made meaningful for many in the Islamization of economic practices. Some restaurants offer only a buffet dinner without the regular menu offerings, and some only open after *iftar*. Still some open for *sohour*, or the last meal of the night, which is often accompanied by the playing of card games, from around 2:00 a.m. until the *athaan* signals *fajr* (sunrise) and the beginning of another daytime of fasting. In any case, a cover charge of between 5 and 10 JD ($7.50–$14.00) to sit and consume publicly at or

**FIGURE 8**   Nokia Ramadan advertisement, 2008. Photo by the author.

after the nightly *iftar* is common, even if one is only looking to spend 5 JD for *argeelah* and tea. Public consumption of food, tobacco, and drink here stands for a whole host of other important types of consumption that make up "the Ramadan experience" and an elaboration on Islamic piety.

   As a particularly salient case in point, most four- and five-star hotels offer *iftar* and *sohour* Ramadan in "Ramadan Tents," which provide a large, covered

**FIGURE 9**    UPC Amman skyline with crescent moon, 2008. Photo by Osama Hajjaj.

area for people to enjoy a table-served three-, four-, or five-course dinner, followed by dessert and *argeelah* and a concert or comedy show, often
complemented by other events such as games for children, fortune tellers, and
henna hand painting.[16]

A local Jordanian wrote about Ramadan tents, and in his narrative described the feeling of being in the tent, saying that

> maybe deep in my soul and my sub-consciousness, I feel a bit freer than usual. Maybe the tent is a symbol of open space and freedom of movement that our modern way of life in the city is stripped of . . . Living in peace, quiet, and close to nature makes you feel closer to God and religion, and since I miss these things in my real life out there, being here under this tent restores part of the harsh imbalance.

He then goes on to describe the tent:

> Under the fluffy colorful ceiling of the big tent, you can treat yourself and friends to various types of sweets, entertainment and distraction until the very early hours of the morning, while playing game after game of cards. A musical band with a leading singer can play classical pieces of Arab music. . . . Waiters are dressed in special 19th- or 18th-century attire with the red cylinder-shaped hat better known as "*tarboush*." They offer you, in addition to the very popular *argeelah*, a rich assortment of little snacks. (Quna 2008, 73)

These two sentiments are in sharp contrast: the tent provides a space in which one can grow closer to Allah and Islam, feel freer, and restore something that the modern life does not provide, which seems contradictory to the actual description of the tent as full of entertainment and distraction with cards, music, and waiters dressed in Ottoman-era costumes. The feelings it evokes contrast with the mundane, even profane, details of the mechanisms by which this kind of consumption occurs. Still, this demonstrates that consumption is both materially and religiously—even spiritually—meaningful for consumers during Ramadan, particularly when conducted in social groups. Furthermore, people are willing to pay large sums to corporations and other commercial ventures for a re-creation of some era "gone by" (and one that, in actuality, never existed in Amman) in order to "feel the Ramadan spirit." Ramadan tents provide an elaborated Islamized experience of consumption. To some people, it looks and feels like a ruse as the drive for profits is "masked" by heightened religious commodification and consumption.[17] However, the promises of material, social, and religious "value" are so high—and seemingly fulfilled—in Islamized consumption that the critiques of commercialized Ramadan remain mere "cultural complaint." Such protests lack the authority of constructions of piety such as in Islamic history or Shariʿa. They lack an authentically Islamic authority (Asad 1986, 1993; El-Zein 1977) while providing a modern aesthetic. Consumptive experiences provide for multiple and highly personal kinds of values and provide for "the Ramadan experience."

These processes of co-production occur, as Comaroff and Comaroff have argued, because "just as culture is being commodified, so the commodity is being rendered explicitly cultural—and, consequently, is increasingly apprehended as the generic source of sociality" (2009, 28). "The Ramadan experience" in tents and in other sites of amplified, public consumption both reinforce the holy month's commodification at the same time that these often aesthetically charged expressions of Ramadan become personally meaningful and sustained in practices of sociality. The value of "the Ramadan experience" is retained and even heightened in replication.

As a result, and because Ramadan consumption is a powerfully social and religiously charged affair, and as *iftar* has taken on a more institutionalized, commodified, commercialized and "packaged" form, more people are willing to spend more money for a complete meal and accoutrements each night in the search for an Islamized and meaningful consumptive experience. As an example, I met up with an American friend for dinner one evening. We tried to find a restaurant that was serving dinner before *maghrib*, without success. We stopped at the international chain Pizza Company, only to find the restaurant packed to fullest capacity with people eagerly awaiting *maghrib*, as the smells wafted by of the hot buffet of soups, salads, pizzas, pastas, and desserts, all ready to be eaten. It was minutes before *maghrib*, and we were offered a table "after one hour" and notified that the buffet dinner cost 25 JD each ($35.00). We were also told that we could not order a la carte or off the menu. Rather than spending $70.00 for the buffet at a pizza place, we opted to go across the street to a popular middle-range Lebanese fast-food chain, Zataar wa Zeit, but found the restaurant empty, save for an elderly and disabled woman with her middle-aged daughter. There was no buffet and only a minimum of staff was on hand. When we asked if they were serving food, the waiter said yes, then added, "But according to the law we can only serve you at the [time of] *al-athaan*." We both ordered basic falafel sandwiches and snacks (for about 5 JD, or $7.00, each). We—as well as the two other women in the restaurant—were served before the *athaan* and the staff ate at the time for *iftar*.

Ramadan consumption and commercialization has also increased within the home, as exemplified by television soap operas (Abu-Lughod 2005; Armbrust 2000a, 2000b, 2002, 2006; Salamandra 2004). During my time in Jordan, the Ramadan soap operas or serials (in Arabic, *misalsalat*; literally "links" or "chains") occupied significant time and space in both people's homes and while passing the Ramadan evenings. According to the September 2007 edition of *Jo*, "It's an institution. It's an addiction. For an entire month, it's practically the only thing there is to do. The Ramadan TV serial is a unique feature of Arab life" (63). In Amman, the most popular soap opera in 2007 was *Bab al-Hara*, a Syrian-produced historical drama that dominated the airwaves. In 2008, however, *Bab al-Hara* began to be outpaced by a Turkish soap opera, translated and dubbed as *Noor* (Kimmelman 2010, 63). By 2009, it appeared that *Bab al-Hara* would enter its fourth season in 2010 with only mediocre reviews. *Noor*, on the other hand, had become a huge success, with a line of other, more highly crafted Turkish soap operas ready to fill in when *Noor*'s ratings started to slip. The Ramadan consumer is becoming more sophisticated in the pursuit of modern and authentic Islamic experiences: she is seeking higher production values, more attractive and appealing characters, and more contemporary and relevant plotlines.

Ramadan *misalsalat* have been understood as more than a mode for increasing consumption; in Egypt, they are thought of as a nation-making, citizen-defining craft (Abu-Lughod 2005; Armbrust 2006), and in Syria, as a tool for elite constructions of place-making and "authentic Damasceneness" (Salamandra 2004). Jordan's case is somewhat different: there, Ramadan soap operas remain a popular media form but because they are produced, directed, and distributed by non-Jordanian outlets, they do not serve as a mode of informing national identity.[18] Historically, Ramadan soap operas came into Jordan from Egypt, long considered the "hub" for Arab cinema and media, then from Syria, and most recently, from Turkey. Their imported status prevented Jordanians from cultivating a national identity through these media spectacles, but the shows promoted heightened consumption and middle-class life and lifestyles, both in the content and in the context in which they were watched. The commercialization in homes during Ramadan—from what is eaten to what is watched, heard, and repeated—serves as a serious avenue by which religious consumption is enacted and Islamic practices are economized as economic practices are Islamized, and as market practices and knowledge distribution make meaningful "the Ramadan experience."

## Laylat al-Qadr: The Night of Power and Weddings

Other Ramadan-specific invented traditions include those associated with Laylat al-Qadr. It is believed—generally but not in total consensus—by Muslims familiar with the textual debates on the topic that the revelation of the Qur'an by the Angel Gabriel to Mohammed started on an odd-numbered night during one of the last ten nights of the month of Ramadan. Because of the significance of this night, it is a night of extraordinary power and a time when the heavens and the earth are considered closest in their proximity. The Qur'an (97:1–5) says:

1. Lo! We revealed it (the Qur'an) on Laylat Al-Qadr.
2. Ah, what will convey unto thee what Laylat Al-Qadr is!
3. Laylat Al-Qadr has more blessings than a thousand months (83 years and 4 months).
4. The angels and the Spirit descend therein, by the permission of their Lord, with all decrees (orders).
5. (The night is) Peace until the rising of the dawn.

The Prophet Mohammed did not indicate on which night these verses were revealed. Historical records were not kept, but tradition—and the "signs" and "feelings" of Islamic scholars—have led most to believe that Laylat Al-Qadr is the night of the 27th. Interpretations and exegesis of the Qur'an 97:3 indicate that this is the most powerful night of Ramadan. Everything that happens is said to carry the same power as if it were done 83.3 times: one prayer equals 83.3 prayers, one hour in the mosque equals 83.3 hours, and completing a reading of the Qur'an is the same as having done it 83.3 times.

Because of the promises of extra blessings, many Muslims economize and maximize their religious practice that night. People stay up all night praying and reading and meditating on the Qur'an, in the belief that the prayers of the sincere will be answered. Many people, particularly men, sleep in the mosque that night, alternately napping and praying. Although this a is common practice throughout the month, given the extra blessings promised in the Qur'an for Laylat Al-Qadr, many make a particular point to do so on the odd-numbered nights during the last ten days of Ramadan, in hopes of shoring up blessings for eternity. Ideally, this is an evening for those most serious pursuit of religiosity and heightening of one's personal devotion to Allah. It is also a time for heightened consumption of religion, with the idea that this strategic consumption may serve as a springboard for heightened spirituality and blessings. As one informant said, in a kind of cost-benefit approach to the consumption of Islam, "You don't know if it's true or not [the increased blessings], but it doesn't hurt to try and find out."

Scheduling wedding receptions and parties for Laylat Al-Qadr is not uncommon. If people desire to get married during Ramadan, the choice can be made to have the wedding on the 27th, in the assumption that the Night of Power is a particularly fortuitous and auspicious one for the bride and groom, as the newlywed's marriage will surely be supernaturally blessed. During Ramadan in 2008, I attended two weddings that were scheduled in a fashion tied to Laylat Al-Qadr.

On the 26th day, I attended a wedding reception in a neighborhood near my house. My friend, Aminah, had technically been married a few days prior: the legal and Islamic commitment to marriage—the *nikkah*—is made before more public wedding celebrations and the consummation of the wedding contract are performed. The *nikkah* was a small and short event in a local *zawiyya*, a type of community center that hosts classes and religious events, and in this case a regular Sufi *dhikr*. All of the women sat upstairs in an opaque, glass-encased women's room, while men congregated in a larger, more open-aired space below. Aminah, unveiled and dressed in traditional garb, was seated on a white plastic outdoor chair between her mother and mother-in-law.[19] The Sheikh's wife sat nearby. The rest of the women who came to observe, myself included, sat veiled and on the floor. The Sheikh read the marriage contract, which was broadcast via a sound system into the women's room, and to which the father of the bride agreed as a proxy for her. Afterward, the bride and other women cried, the Sheikh's wife passed around sweets (which were not eaten at the time, due to the celebration of Ramadan), and many women tried to steal a glance at the new husband and male attendees through cracks in the opaque glass pane that separated the sexes. The entire event took about fifteen minutes. Aminah and her family then headed back to her house to begin preparations for the wedding party on the night of the 26th.

Aminah's wedding party was originally scheduled for the night of the 27th of Ramadan, in accordance with aims of attaining the promised blessings for the bride and groom. However, the date was changed to the 26th. As Aminah told me:

> I wanted it to be the 27th. [She blushed, looking shy and embarrassed] We would be blessed—not just because it's our wedding night, but also because, you know, if you feed people *iftar* during Ramadan, you gain blessings from that too. But so many people said they didn't want to come to the wedding if it was Laylat Al-Qadr. They wanted to spend the night in the mosque and reading the Qur'an and worshipping Allah. So we moved it [the wedding] to the night before. It will still give us the blessings of getting married [during Ramadan] and feeding people [*iftar* during Ramadan].

Strategizing one's religious practice and life choices to maximize blessings during Laylat Al-Qadr is considered and weighed, particularly as it involves including others, who are calculating their own practices. Laylat Al-Qadr is perceived to be the only night of the year that carries this level of spiritual importance—even given the uncertainty of the exact date during the last week of Ramadan—and some seek to take full advantage of it.

At Aminah's wedding party, the men and women were again segregated, with men inside the Sheikh's house and the women outside in the covered driveway. Nearly twenty-five women and children sat on the ground around the edges of the driveway with tablecloths covering the concrete and filling in the middle. The food was provided as the day's *iftar*: it consisted of plates of lamb and rice. In addition, there were salads, 7-Up and water to drink, and chocolate cake for dessert. There was neither music nor dancing.

The next night, on Laylat Al-Qadr, I attended another wedding. This event was small and lively, with about forty people in attendance. Pictures of the unveiled bride and her family and friends were taken beforehand, and the evening commenced with everyone in the family living and sitting rooms, a mix of men and women around tables on which sat small bowls of dates. The guests engaged in small talk until the *athaan* sounded, at which point everyone started eating dates and drinking water to break their fast. Many of the men got up at that time to go pray together in another living room, while many women began eating a hearty lentil soup. After the men returned from praying, some of the women, particularly the older ones, got up to take their turns to pray in the living room. Everyone remaining at the tables proceeded through the buffet line for a large dinner of traditional Arab mezes such as hummus and falafel, followed by entrées like maqlubah[20] and salads. After dinner, there was music fed through the family's stereo for the women to dance to in the living room in which everyone had earlier prayed. I asked the bride why she scheduled her wedding for Laylat al-Qadr. She answered:

BRIDE: We didn't schedule it for Laylat al-Qadr. No one knows when that is.
ST: Then why did you pick the date you chose?
BRIDE: It was just the date we could get our family together and get the caterers. It was Ramadan, so we have the blessings [of feeding others], and it's meaningful.
ST: But it was the 27th of Ramadan, and that's when most people think it is Laylat al-Qadr.
BRIDE: Oh. I never thought of it that way.

These two stories confirm that during the month of Ramadan, there is a heightened striving for religious practice and personal piety, particularly by consuming Islam. There are many moments that serve to create an economization of Islam, as discussed in chapter 1, which, in turn, amplifies the religious tenor of the practice and the Islamization of the economic practices in moments of co-production. When one considers these moments of co-production, one response may be to consume more—more religious knowledge, more practices that re-embed religious knowledge, more material practices that re-entrench religiosity in one's identity construction.

In Aminah's case, the intended scheduling of the wedding on the Night of Power was overt and conscious. The blessings believed to be promised were sought out and it was only after receiving resistance from others, who were competing to take the blessings of the night for themselves, that they had to reschedule. A commercial, consumptive event and economic practice—a wedding—was explicitly being used as a springboard for heightened religiosity and maximized spiritual rewards. In the second example, the overt and conscious process never occurred; the wedding was a consumptive endeavor that was not explicitly religious in the choice of day. It was a coincidence. However, once the bride was conscious of the coalescing of dates and events it appeared that the knowledge and awareness could have made a difference for personal practice and piety. In the first case, the wedding planning seems to have necessarily derived from the Islamic and pious implications for personal practice. In the second, there were no overt implications for personal piety, perhaps because a conscious alignment of the dates and events had not occurred.

## Competitive Pieties

For Ammanis, Ramadan is characterized by expressions and contestations of moral dominance. While the explicit aims of the month are egalitarianism and shared experiences that reduce socioeconomic hierarchies, at every level it involves negotiating tensions that arise from competing notions of moral correctness. Historically, the month began with a battle in which the rightly guided Muslims were able to overcome the militarily dominant Quraish. Contemporary understandings of this battle have established the "real Islam" as the dominant discourse and idiom for Ramadan. In the context of today's Amman, the Jordanian government legally enforces the dominance of localized Islamic moral correctness. Pressures for pietistic orthopraxy eclipse orthodoxy, creating serious tensions for some Ammanis. They experience additional tensions as the commanding of right and the forbidding of wrong strongly situates not only what Ammanis do, but also how they do it. Economized practice creates further contests as one's interest in maximizing the opportunities for enhanced blessings in Ramadan require formulating how one spends time and energy.

This results in what I call "competitive pieties," which place claims of dominant moral rightness against others in contests of authenticity. Some authors have discussed competitive pieties as external manifestations in dress and comportment that are meant to serve as indicators of greater religious commitment.[21] The competitive spirit in Amman not only features some-times-exaggerated practices and claims of fasting and exemplary moral be-havior, but also takes a personalized form as individuals overcome internal struggles in order to economize and maximize their rewards. Competitive pieties here are simultaneously about a kind of resignation to and adop-tion of the dominant discourses and expected practices, while principles of economization prompt them to engage earnestly and make the experience meaningful. Striving to achieve dominant moral standards and practices is part of neoliberal piety during Ramadan.

Ramadan, however, is only temporary. The limits of competitive pieties are revealed at the end of the month when the push to fast and pray ends, laws change, and consumption reverts back to the typical form. Though certain elements of society may be keen to see the ethics of Ramadan con-tinue beyond the month, the temporality of moral accommodations passes, the majoritarian ethics and moralities shift, and Ammanis—in their diverse forms—go back to drinking alcohol, skipping prayers, or any measure of other practices until the next Ramadan.

Issues of temporality and rationalities in personal and public piety, particu-larly with consumption as a mode for expressing and negotiating religious life, continue. In chapter 4, women engage the question of whether to wear the *hijab*, as well as the accompanying ethics and consensus regarding the practices that surround such questions.

# CHAPTER 4

# Love, Sex, and the Market
## *The* Hijab

> *I have a big crush on this guy. He's handsome, so smart. But he's very* mutidayin *(religious). And I'm not. I don't wear the* hijab. *And he called me "walking* fitna." *It means, like, disorder or unrest, but he means I'm seductive or alluring and that I'm keeping him from his proper religion. Then he said that I have "a remarkable personality and a lit soul." I guess it's sort of flattering, but it's not very nice. I mean, it's because I can be myself with him that he likes me, and it's because I'm being myself with him that he feels like he's compromising his religion. Then, he said that some women just "are* fitna" *and that I'm one of them—that I'm "walking* fitna."*
>
> —*Female student*

The *hijab* defines relationships between men and women. As a result, there is a strong sense of normativity at play with the *hijab* in Amman, as there are certain *hijab*-associated behaviors that a woman should adopt, oftentimes on behalf of the men they encounter. The *hijab* should stand for a commitment to everything that would prevent *fitna*: modesty in dress, socially distant and impersonal interactions with men, a general support for men and their religious practice rather than a distraction from it, and the creation of significant obstacles that prevent a man from knowing that a woman has a "remarkable personality and a lit soul." Normativity here also indicates that men have a vested interest in the *hijab*, as it affects not only their relationships with women, but also their ability to maximize their religious practice. Even though it is women who wear it, a gender-inclusive importance renders the donning of the *hijab* a salient category for morality and ethics among the wider public.

As discussed in chapters 1 and 2, in Amman the Islamic Resurgence brought forth a set of well-defined practices for a normative orthopraxy in public Islam, including "reciting the Qur'an, keeping the fast, wearing the veil, avoiding alcohol, giving alms" (Hefner 2005, 21). In the case of Ramadan in chapter 3, however, the localized interpretations of such symbols and practices such as keeping the fast—in both legal and extralegal terms—are met with a wide variety of responses in piety and practices. Although one may be legally required to keep the fast in public, how one maintains it in private and in socially sustained forms while constructing the action as personally meaningful is highly diverse and contested. These are also economizing practices, as seen by the realm of Islamized consumption. Robust and comprehensive implementations of "commanding right and forbidding wrong" can and do result in the co-production of economized Islamic practice and Islamized economic practice. They also result in illiberal constructions of society, at least for a time (Tobin 2013).

The *hijab*, or Muslim women's headscarf, is a case where issues of temporality and non-Shari'a-derived rationalities for Islamization and economization come to the fore. They do so without the same legal requirements or legitimations as Ramadan. While not legally required in Jordan, the *hijab* still carries a strong degree of consensus and normativity. Because of this, the *hijab* is a particularly salient case for homing in on the questions of public practices and their grounding in Shari'a and non-Shari'a-derived logics for economization. As we will see, these logics and rationales are invoked more frequently and with wider diversity than was the case during Ramadan, where the state and legal regulation regulated public practice. The debates over what constitutes the right *hijab* in an authentic, modern, and real Islam are subject to various, also Shari'a-justified, counterarguments and alternative interpretations, which can be bolstered by Shari'a sources of knowledge beyond Shari'a. As such, the *hijab* represents a realm in which diverse pieties and practices are asserted and contested, while certain notions of normativity, moralities, and public ethics are socially and culturally—rather than legally— enacted, contested, and sustained.

My study focuses on two types of women involved in processes of Islamizing economic practices and economizing Islam around the *hijab*: those for whom it is already an adopted part of life and others who do not wear the scarf, have personally questioned, contested and negotiated the idea, and most frequently have opted to "not yet" adopt. These two set of experiences tell the story of how the normative, orthopraxic expectations for donning the *hijab* are balanced against other personally weighed interests, concerns, and authoritative sources for economic and Islamized practices. The chapter highlights how such practices are understood, negotiated, and enacted in moments of Islamized and economized co-production. It also explains how such practices are justified and made meaningful, authentic, and modern through reference to various sources and kinds of knowledge. As such, these processes further reify the normativity of the *hijab* and work in the constitution and reconstitution of actors in economized and Islamized practices, which carry very public repercussions and implications.

## Understanding the *Hijab*

The idea that more women in the Middle East are wearing the *hijab* each year is a generally accepted truism of the post-Islamic Revival context. The scarf carries with it a kind of "semantic versatility" in its symbolic representations (Shirazi 2001). It is an outward and visual sign of the multidimensional and complex realities of life and relationships found throughout the Muslim world. Beyond claims of internal religiosity and orthodoxy (Mahmood 2005), a discourse about personal choice emerged, as have expressions of modernity and cosmopolitanism in Islamic dress and fashion (Khosravi and Bayat 2008; Stratton 2006; White 1999). Additional motives often cited for wearing the scarf include protection against harassment by men, even if the outcome is actually an increase in catcalls and groping,[1] and individual ethics and preferences for a certain aesthetic of modesty and privacy (El Guindi 1999a, 1999b; Fernea and Fernea 1997). Recent analyses indicate that donning the *hijab* is mediated by all kinds of extrareligious and local references to ethics grounded in social class, status, even politics and traditions (Ask 1998; Khosravi and Bayat 2008; Smith-Hefner 2007, 389).

What makes the recent emergence of the *hijab* movement notable in Jordan is that many of the roughly 60 percent of women donning the *hijab* are young, middle-class, well-educated members of Amman's social landscape (Adely 2012).[2] Negotiating the normativity of the scarf symbolizes involvement in the city in a modern and authentically Islamic way, as women enact a measure of freedom of mobility, freedom to work, and freedom to engage contemporary economic practices. Still, at the core they have a "complex mix of motives" (Smith-Hefner 2007, 412). Whether these are pietistic, economic, personal, political, or some combination, engaging in the debates about veiling and the normativity for wearing it has become a means for women to acknowledge and engage demands for personal pieties while si-multaneously attending to the more pragmatic demands of everyday life (Afshar 1998; Hefner 2000; Smith-Hefner 2007, 412).[3] Regardless of re-ported motives, in Amman negotiating the *hijab* has become a reference point against which women evaluate their self-interests in economic practices and pursue them in a modern and authentically Islamic manner.

This chapter also examines the normative ethics of the *hijab* in Amman and the depths to which they have penetrated the lives of both women and men in light of competing interests and understandings. The sources of knowledge that inform, create, and frame logics of behaviors, especially Shari'a, also build some consensus in the ethics and moralities of public, normative understandings of the *hijab*. Without the state playing a legislative function as it does in Ramadan, people achieve consensus-building through these other strategic and calculative processes. As we will see, processes of Islamizing economic practices and economizing Islamic practices take place in some of the most intimate spaces of life, including employment at the Islamic bank.[4] Despite the presence of Shari'a-derived morals and ethics in such intimate spaces, as well as the their use in knowledge debates and nego-tiations within those spaces, their utilization and employment is not neces-sarily tied to religious piety per se. That is, religious norms for orthopraxy in these spaces is in generally high consensus. Yet they can be and are wielded for non-religious, actor-centric purposes. This demonstrates another mo-ment of co-production in the Islamization of economic practices and the economization of Islamic practices. Wearing the *hijab* is not always or neces-sarily motivated by reasons of personal piety. It and its accompanying ethics are often used as a tool to attain more distinctly actor-centered and actor-oriented ends, broadly defined.

## Why the *Hijab*?

Deepening religious piety is frequently assumed to be the primary motiva-tion behind donning the *hijab*. At least, the normative assumption is that it *should* be. This motivation and the eternal spiritual implications of wearing the scarf are told and retold as part of popular lore that demonstrates clearly the economization of and normative ethic for wearing it. Take this example, often recited as common rumor, but retold on a popular general-knowledge cultural website for Sunni Muslims[5]:

> Do you know when you'll die, sister? The death rate for youth is in-creasing! I will give you an example of a girl. A true story that really

happened. This happened in Egypt, Alexandria last year in Ramadan. The man was telling me that his wife wears *hijab*. Living in front of them was a young girl who was not wearing *hijab*. The girl had good things inside her heart, like all of our sisters in Islam. However, she didn't understand the meaning of the *hijab* and the meaning it has in Islam. So this man's wife (and this is obligatory for all the women who wear *hijab*) had good relations with this girl. She didn't ignore her just because she didn't wear the *hijab*, no, she was friends with her. So one day the young girl came to ask the wife if she'd come shopping with her to buy some jeans. So the intelligent wife who knows that she has to call the girl towards Allah agreed to go shopping with her, but under one condition: that the girl would also accompany her to an Islamic *halaqa* [gatherings for giving lessons about Islam] that was about to start. The girl agreed.

So they went to the *halaqa*, which was about repentance to Allah. The girl was so inspired by what was being said, and started to cry until she kept repeating one sentence over and over again, "I've repented Allah, please someone cover me." The people told her okay let us take you home and you can put the *hijab* on. But she refused, wanting to be covered right at that moment with the *hijab*, she couldn't go out without it. So they got her a scarf and a dress, and she left the building with it on. And as soon as she left to cross the road, a car hit her and she died. I swear this is a true story. She died after she had repented. She is lucky that she repented before she died. So never give the excuse [for not wearing the *hijab*] that you are still young, because you never know when you will die.

As this story so vividly demonstrates—as do others retold in popular circles that dramatize the eternal implications of the *hijab*—there is an urgency and immediacy in appeals to don the scarf for the deepening of one's piety, "because you never know when you will die." Though compelling, this style of "*hijab* evangelism" utilizes a calculative logic to promote a certain kind of Islamic practice: repent and wear the *hijab* now, because the end of your life is uncertain and could be quite near, and wearing the *hijab* has eternal consequences. Despite combining these calculative logics with emotive tactics, such highly compelling messages in social media are not, in and of themselves, enough to convince women to put on the *hijab* en masse. Visible and socially sustained practices of the *hijab* require additional forms and types of calculative engagements, particularly those that are actor-generated. It often takes additional rationalities and logics before actors will enact such normative moralities.

As a case in point, Amr Khaled—the Egyptian accountant-cum-televan-gelist and "Sheikh of Cool"—has spoken out in favor of the *hijab*. In fact, a number of journalistic sources have named him the single most impor-tant factor influencing young women in this practice (Stratton 2006). His talks often reinforce the normative ethic that women should wear the *hijab* and appeal to calculations of enhanced spiritual blessings and ethics, many of which compound with some notion of a gendered contribution to the "public good." Not only is the *hijab* beneficial for eternal rewards, he says: it is also a facilitator of good things on earth. Such appeals invoke non-explicitly "Islamic" but culturally applicable moral constructions of the "good girl," such as "proper beauty," "bashfulness," and "shyness." In his *Lifemakers* video dated October 21, 2007,[6] Amr Khaled says:

> Islam . . . made the beauty of women of a higher value in men's eyes by providing protection [in the form of *hijab*] to that beauty from uncon-trolled lusts and desires, and instead ordering men to respect greater the inner beauty of her soul. Thus, the real value of women is associated with the degree of her bashfulness and her abidance by it.
>
> A veiled woman will be rewarded for wearing the veil continuously, as her veil invites those who see her to obey Allah. Seeing her obeying Him. On Judgment Day, veiled women may find their rewards as large as mountains. Can you imagine this?! They will be struck thinking they did nothing in life worth all these rewards! But they get rewards whenever anyone sees them wearing the veil! Some girls give up the veil and some women cannot stand adopting it. These women must be unaware of the importance of wearing the veil and how Allah—the Rewarder—will reward them for adopting it.

Consistent with the chapter's opening quote, this ethical construction places women's "greater" beauty in the soul and constructs the *hijab* as a kind of covering—a protection—against that overwhelming and overpowering reac-tion that surely men will have to the "lesser" beauty of her body. Beyond moral imperatives and appeals to a certain kind of interaction with men, a scarf also serves as an icon to Allah, leading both the woman herself and oth-ers around her to enhanced piety. These pursuits of moral, right living by protecting oneself and men from their lusts, cultivating a "real value" as a woman defined by her soul, and seeking eternal rewards that multiply as oth-ers come to see them on earth all combine in calculations and economized practice that reinforce the public ethics and normativity of the *hijab*.

With such compelling normativity for donning the *hijab*, women who do not wear the scarf are in a position where they must justify and legitimate

their actions. The normative assumption is that a woman who does not wear
the *hijab*, but should, "didn't understand the meaning of the hijab and the
meaning it has in Islam," and "must be unaware of the importance of wearing the scarf and how God—the Rewarder—will reward them for adopting
it." This logic makes visible the notion that unveiled women are ignorant.
Islamic knowledge, it assumes, is singular and compels action.

However, deepening one's piety is not the sole reason for donning the
*hijab*, nor does wearing it necessarily represent a move from ignorance to
knowledge. Rather, the case of Amman demonstrates that the scarf is an avenue for enhanced agency and a medium for pursuing a publicly sanctioned,
modern and authentic Islamic self in contemporary society.[7] It is both an orthopraxy in coherence with strong public consensus and a means to achieve
other, typically actor-centered ends.

There are overlapping and reinforcing motivations for the pervasive wearing of *hijab*. First, the heightened and altered forms of consumption associated with it create meaningful experiences for consumers when the religious
motivation or point for spiritual fulfillment is not viable or primary in importance. Second, the moralities and ethics for the donning of the *hijab*
are another element of "commanding right and forbidding wrong." In this
case, however, the government has not legislated the practice as was the case
during Ramadan, so the injunction relies upon socially sustained implementation: men harassing women, and women chastising women who do not
wear the scarf; men and women praising women who start wearing it; and
the gossip that surrounds those who wear the scarf, but not "correctly."
Such mechanisms of social enforcement are powerful and deeply penetrate
women's everyday lives. The symbol of the *hijab* has brought forth an important space in contemporary life in Amman in which the role of religion
and religious ethics are debated and enacted in processes of economization
and Islamization. It infuses even non-religious purposes and spaces with religious rhetoric and logic, even at the times when personal piety is not the
actor's first concern.

The two primary ethics of the *hijab* are religiously derived and locally
understood. The first is a generally agreed-upon notion that once a woman
assumes the veil, she should continue to wear it in the presence of men to
whom she is not related for the duration of her life, exhibiting dress and
comportment and that are "consistent and responsible" (Smith-Hefner 2007,
400). The second, a more highly contested ethic, is that a woman may technically follow the Shari'a-derived ethics of exposing only one's face, hands, and
sometimes feet, but demonstrate a certain measure of contested, fashionable
flair with flashy jewelry, bright colors, luxurious materials, and tight jeans in

a sustained assertion of modernity and cosmopolitanism. These cases demonstrate that questioning consensus and logics for legitimation and pursuing other needs and interests do not automatically result in heightened religiosity. Rather, they reveal that the penetrations of certain notions of Islam found in the *hijab*, including normative ethics and moralities, into new spaces in one's life. Women's resulting adaptations and responsiveness are part and parcel of authentically Islamic life in modern Amman.

## The *Hijab* Is Forever

In Amman, wearing the *hijab* comes with certain ethics of use that are continuously discussed and negotiated as women establish and place themselves in relation to localized, normative notions of "the real Islam" and other competing interests that are less explicitly Islamic. First and of primary importance is a guiding ethic that, once a woman puts on the *hijab* for the first time, it should stay on in what, thereafter, become negotiated and contested spaces for the remainder of her life. The *hijab* is forever. The overarching idea is that the donning of the scarf should be routinized and dependable as a means of showing an authentically Islamic practice (Kaya 2010, 528–29) that is "consistent and responsible" (Smith-Hefner 2007, 400). In the strictest interpretations and understandings which, in this case, are also normative, the *hijab* should only be taken off in front of men who are spouses or *mahram*—men whom the wearer may not marry, such as brothers, fathers, sons, in-laws, uncles, and boys before the age of sexual awareness.

Within the urban areas of Amman, little acceptance or legitimacy is granted for a more contextualized donning of the *hijab*. For example, if a postpubescent female decides to wear the scarf, she is strongly discouraged, even disallowed, from wearing it one day and not the next. This is in contrast with other contexts, such as some parts of Indonesia and even the rural areas of Jordan, where the veil is part of girls' socialization into women. A "training veil," if you will, is worn in a less circumscribed manner (Adely 2004, 2007a, 2007b, 2012; Smith-Hefner 2007, 402–03). In urban Amman, it would be simply unthinkable to show up one day with a headscarf, and the next day without one, and then the following day with one to classes at the university, professional offices, even around the neighborhood or with extended family and friends. Of all the *hijab*-required spaces, the public areas where men and women interact in a physically shared space or in vocal exchanges are the most strictly monitored.

During my time in Amman I often studied at a Caribou Coffee café in a local mall. As a non-Arab, non-Muslim American, I did not wear a *hijab* and this was no surprise. The high school- and college-aged male employees were always respectful and friendly to me, looking me in the eye and asking out of curiosity about my school and work, but they were never flirtatious or inappropriate. I was also a student in a local Islamic studies school where I was required to wear a *hijab* to class. One day, a friend offered to meet me at the Caribou Coffee and then drive me to school. I took the opportunity to put on the scarf and matching *abaya* before arriving at the café. This altered the staff's treatment of me. Immediately, they refrained from looking me in the eye, asking questions, or making friendly conversation. They took my order and refused to offer me my change out of their hands, preferring to place the money on the counter to avoid accidental hand touching. The change in behavior due to my *hijab* was remarkable.

During the following visit to the café, I was again without the *hijab* and clearly reflecting my position as a non-Arab, non-Muslim American. The young staff members again looked me in the eye, greeted me politely. Then, before taking my order, they began asking questions. "Weren't you here in the white *hijab*?" one asked. "And the *abaya*!" another responded. After explaining that I had been on my way to a class at an Islamic school, a third employee stated, "Because, you know, we don't do that here. Women don't wear the scarf one day and not the next. It's disrespectful to our religion. *Muhajabat* [women who wear the scarf] need to take it seriously."

The notion of "respect" here echoes the "commanding right and forbidding wrong" discussion in chapter 3. Again, although the "hand" of the Jordanian government is not pressing in on normativities of the *hijab*, the "tongue" of the public certainly is, as is the "heart" demanding respect. Consistency is a way to show "respect," which further integrates normative notions of the *hijab* and creates a cultural context in which putting on the scarf is further defined in terms of values such as "significant," "important," and spiritually and socially "weighty."

The notion that "the *hijab* is forever" constitutes a major discursive space in which women are able to postpone wearing it or jettison the discussion in general. One can start at age fifteen, thirty, or fifty, and unless one is "ready" to wear it for life, space is typically given to continue the processes of discernment and decision-making as part of the "respect" of the religion and the further entrenchment of the normative practice in play. "Postponing" the decision does not undermine the ethic of veiling. In fact, it reinforces it as this discursive space operates in acceptance of the terms of this normative ethic. As one of my university students, who began wearing the *hijab* during the middle of the semester, said:

I wasn't sure that I wanted to [start wearing the *hijab*] for a long time. Not because I didn't think it was right, but because I just didn't know if I was ready. I just didn't want to put it on and take it off again. . . . It's a big commitment. You have to really think about it.

The normativity and morality of wearing the *hijab* as the "correct" or "right" thing to do is perpetuated by this decision, and further adds to the significance given to the decision: it is a "big commitment."

Accepting the logic and normativity of the scarf and invoking the socially acceptable deferment because one is "not ready" also serves to demonstrate that actors can accept and reproduce the logic and normative ideas of the *hijab* without actually having to engage in the practice. One can use the morality of the *hijab* to pursue one's self-interest and demands and not don the scarf. In economized terms, it is a "path of least resistance" model of piety and self-interest that demands few investments for personally favorable outcomes. One is not structurally challenging the normative modes for piety, but using them to achieve what one may want, which can include not wearing the scarf.

The college students I met were not the only ones who put off the discussion by claiming they were not "ready yet." Many middle-aged women who chose not to wear the *hijab* used the same reasoning. "Maybe," one middle-age woman speculated to me, "[I will put on the *hijab*] when I'm a grandmother, and I can wear the scarf as an elegant old woman." In order to avoid the pressure and notion that all Muslim women should wear the scarf, postponement has become a socially acceptable means of disengaging the debate and disarming pressures the women may feel.

After one puts on the *hijab*, there is continuous negotiation and contestation of the degree to which one's body and head must be covered in spaces where men who are not of one's *mahram* are present. A party where only women gather and do so outside the purview of men is a primary excepted space in which removing the *hijab* is considered acceptable. This is also true in a space wherein men are present, but that has been transformed as a distinctly gendered women's area. That is, men may be present as workers or servers, but not as party attendees. By extension, their status as men becomes marginalized. Rather than always a clear-cut demarcation, this rule is applied in gradients when men occupy spaces at the social and physical margins.

The engagement party of an upper-middle-class Palestinian friend of mine was conducted in the courtyard in front of the house and over to and through the driveway in an "L" shape form. The male DJ set up in the balcony that extended from the second-floor and over the back half of the driveway, which had been set up for dancing. Round tables marked the dining area, which occupied the front half of the driveway and rounded the side of the house. At the end of the dining tables in the front yard, the buffet for both men and women was set up. For the entirety of the party, women congregated outside in the driveway and front yard, and men were inside the house. The only interaction between the sexes occurred at the buffet area in the front yard. Despite the fact that a significant number of neighboring apartment buildings looked out upon the driveway and courtyard and that the DJ was male, many women removed their headscarves while dancing in the driveway below. Others placed the scarves loosely on their heads while sitting and eating in the front of the driveway, at this more "intermediary" space at the tables next to the buffet, and then secured them tightly when in the buffet line. This graduated application of the ethics of the headscarf indicated that neither the DJ nor the peering neighbors were considered to assert a gazing eye commanding "respect." While women were in the line of sight of men, the men were not in direct line of sight of the women. As a result, it seemed, the women could disregard them.

When I asked another party attendee about this graduated application of the ethics and women removing their headscarves on the dance floor in the view of men, she responded with the normative ethic that, according to Shari'a, the women "clearly shouldn't be doing it." She added, "But people here have some money." This is a moment in which the compelling aesthetics of modernity and cosmopolitanism integrate with Shari'a-derived norms. The actors engender an Islamic middle-class generative moment as they continue to wear the *hijab*, but do so in stylized ways that demonstrate an altered and graduated adherence to normative ethics, but adherence nonetheless.

This scenario represents one way that the ethics associated with the *hijab* can be negotiated and utilized for more actor-centered ends; for many women, wearing the scarf tightly around her head was not conducive to showing off her coiffed hairdo. The normative idea that women "shouldn't" remove their headscarves is circumvented by practices that enable women to exert other preferences and options of personal interest, particularly those found in aesthetics of middle-class modernity. Furthermore, they are able to do so until they are in a position where the normative ethic of the *hijab* is unavoidable: when standing face to face in the buffet line with men. The ethic of keeping the headscarf on in the presence of men remains the primary guide. However, the women were able to ignore the fact that men were present, as both the DJ on the balcony and the neighbors in higher-storied apartment buildings were above their line of sight. Unless they looked up, they could avoid and ignore the men who were peering down on them. That this was an engagement party attended by some people with money demonstrates that a temporal suspension or alteration of the strictest application of the normative ethics of wearing the *hijab* is possible on some social terms among the Islamic middle class.

## Rejecting Normativity: Removing the *Hijab*

Despite such strict ethics and discursive pressures, some women do opt to remove the *hijab* completely at some point in their lives. This is relatively rare, however. I knew of only two people who elected to do so. This practice is a particular challenge because, if a woman removes the *hijab* after first wearing it, the assumption is that her morals have declined. A good friend of mine, Ayisha, wore the *hijab* from middle school through her early twenties. I met her after she had taken off the headscarf. Ayisha's father was a relatively well-known Islamic scholar whose work is used in current Islamic studies. However, he was part of an Islamic intellectual, speculative theological movement that some in Jordan consider outside of more "mainstream" Sunni sects, the mu'tazili.[8] Ayisha once described the mu'tazili in a tongue-in-cheek fashion as the "freemasons of Islam, in the sense that they are rejected by most Muslim cults on allegations of rationalism." Because of her father's work, Ayisha grew up surrounded by Islamic scholarship and was quite comfortable discussing and debating Islamic law, sources of knowledge, and interpretations in a highly intellectualized fashion. One afternoon, we were discussing my work in a local Islamic studies course, and Ayisha recounted her history of self-described religiosity. As she explained:

> This reminds me of the days when I used to go to *dars deen* (religion class). They used to teach us everything. We'd memorize Qur'an and *hadith* and *du'aa'*, and learn *tajweed* (stylized reading of the Qur'an), and we'd ask for *fatwa* there to see if something is *haram* or not. Of course, I used to go there to do something with the free time I had and to meet new people. But, I never believed in the things they'd say unless it makes sense to me. *Dars deen* started when I was in the second grade and ended when I became a teenager.

In this passage we see some of the first hints of Ayisha's personal disagreements with more mainstream interpretations, as she "never believed in the things they'd say" unless they made sense to her. Ayisha's upbringing utilized multiple sources of knowledge as a means of assessing what was "believable" and what was not. Furthermore, as is the theme throughout this chapter, in contemporary society the pursuits of piety also involve pursuits of self-interest. In this case, Ayisha is reflecting on her religion classes as a way to spend her free time and meet people. Studying religion here is also about being in community.

Whenever Ayisha and I were around her neighborhood, she would wear a large straw hat until she was either back inside her house or we had driven beyond her neighbors' sight. Ayisha explained to me that the hat was to prevent them from gossiping about her choice to remove the *hijab* and "to keep mama happy"; it was difficult for the neighbors to clearly discern that she had removed the *hijab* when an oversized hat covered her head. After entering a private car or taxi and driving a few blocks, she would remove the hat and any headbands, neck scarves, or other accoutrements on or around her head. The straw hat represented a transitional time in the gaze of the neighborhood, until Ayisha was able to remove it without fear that people who knew her previously as a *muhajaba* would see her and gossip about her.

This need and desire to wear a hat and avoid gossip stemmed from the serious discussion brought about by removing the *hijab*. By doing so, Ayisha became known as a woman in "moral decline." She had former professors refuse to acknowledge her when she saw them at the University of Jordan, and some of her childhood friends did not or could not recognize her without the *hijab*. When we went out, I often heard her say to people, "It's me— Ayisha!" Then, after a pause in which she would not be recognized, Ayisha would add, "Without the *hijab!*" ("*Gheir al-hijab!*").

As a result of such encounters and the association of moral decline with removing the *hijab*, Ayisha developed a poor reputation. Gossip frequently circulated that she was experimenting with lesbians and having frequent, illicit sexual encounters with men and women, drinking alcohol, and taking drugs. Such moral decline, it was often speculated, would be remedied if only she would wear the *hijab* again. People who were still friendly with her assumed that her act was merely a phase similar to the rebelliousness of an adolescent, rather than a full choice by an adult woman with a Master's degree from a major European university. Although they did not attribute Ayisha's removal of the *hijab* to ignorance, as Amr Khaled would, the construction of her behavior as "adolescent-like" carries a similar condescending tenor. In fact, they pressured her frequently to "get over it" and "just wear the *hijab* again" with the reasonable expectation that this would reverse Ayisha's "moral decline."

Ayisha never spoke with me directly about her choice to remove the *hijab*. We talked and joked during my fieldwork period about the ways that people responded to her, but it seemed too difficult a subject to ask her about directly. She never brought it up. At the same time, Ayisha said, during the conversation recounted above:

> All those years of Islamic education, hopefully [they're] not gone in vain. I mean I don't remember everything, but there are things that I never forgot. I especially liked *tajweed*, because it was, in a way, thought-provoking.

In this, Ayisha spoke fondly of her Islamic education and held onto what she learned there. In the end, she found that the *tajweed*, or the musical recitation of the Qur'an, was one of the elements of an Islamic education that stuck with her and prompted her to think. Had some of her friends heard this, it might have given them hope that a *hijab*-less Ayisha was not beyond moral redemption.

In fact, these normative understandings of wearing the *hijab* "consistently and responsibly" (Smith-Hefner 2007, 400) carry over even when women leave Amman for a life abroad. This is the case for another woman I know. Reem is a mother of three. She married immediately after high school and is now—after a decade of marriage—divorced. She filed complaints and police reports that her husband was abusive, which she feels fell on deaf ears. She and her children are now living in the United States with her parents, who provide childcare while Reem finishes her bachelor's degree. Some time after the divorce, Reem stopped wearing the *hijab*, and did so in a very public manner: she started posting pictures of herself on Facebook with new hair-cuts and styles, form-fitting clothing, and even revealed arms and shoulders. This drew widespread, public condemnation by her Facebook friends and prompted discussion among my own. I asked her about her decision to take off the *hijab*:

> A lot of times when I went for job interviews in the U.S., they were fine on the phone but in person it was their tone, their attitude of me in the *hijab*. I wasn't looked at properly or at least [it seemed] to me because they looked at me as if to ask, 'Why you looking for a job? Why would you want to work here?' as if me in *hijab* would represent their place [of employment]. I pondered on that for a long time. Like would a *hijabi* work in a retail environment? And a lot of times a lot of people felt uncomfortable with *hijabis*. They told me this after the fact. Like after I removed my *hijab*, people told me how uncomfortable they felt with me wearing it. How they felt awkward because I was showing my faith to them, as if I was better. I said I wasn't trying to show I was

better than them, and I'm sorry if that they got that impression. But I was just doing something that I felt was closer to God.

It bothered me for a long time, then finally I took it off. I've had jobs on and off and, yeah, I think it could be because I wasn't wearing the *hijab* because a lot of these places where I work, these people I know have this attitude towards women in *hijab* as they complain about the customers. So I have to do what I can for my kids' sake.

A lot of people [in Amman] think I took it off because of the abuse I faced with my ex. I said if that was the case, then I would have taken off the *hijab* right after I moved to the U.S. I didn't take off the *hijab* until a year and a half later. So still going through these struggles of wanting to change to become a better person, but not lose my whole identity in the process.

Someone gave me this long, long email about how I should keep it on, and all the verses and *hadiths* that support it, encourage it, and force it. I told them that I've seen all the verses and know all the verses—just, I feel personally in my heart, it's not for me. And I don't think these people will get that as to why would anyone want to not wear it.

Though I do have to mention, that when I wore my *hijab* I didn't get hit on all the time by perverted guys or guys in general. They always respected me and treated me as if I was their sister. Now [pause] it's so hard to get that sometimes.

The case of Reem is an interesting one because it reveals the ongoing tension and dynamism of sources and interpretations of Islamic norms. That is, the new context of the United States provides a different set of practical and daily needs for life within a community, in this case finding gainful employment while studying and mothering three children, which requires extensive calculation and planning. At the same time, the preexisting normativity is still in play: Reem feels that she *should want* to continue wearing the *hijab*, and is in fact encouraged to do so by friends in Amman who send her all kinds of justifications for the normative practice based in *hadith* and Shari'a. Furthermore, others speculate that she removed the *hijab* as the result of her very difficult divorce, implying a moral decline. For both Ayisha and Reem, the processes of taking off the *hijab*, rejecting the normative ethic, and exposing themselves to scrutiny and chastisement were painful and very public.

These accounts demonstrate that the economic calculations of Islamic practices with the *hijab* are the very means by which those Islamized actors are constructed. That is, as Reem is "going through these struggles of wanting to change to become a better person, but not lose my whole identity in

the process," she is negotiating the difficult calculative tensions that exist between new contexts and needs—such as those of gainful employment abroad
for a recent divorcée with three children—and the strong role that Islamic
normativity, consensus, and the moralities of the *hijab* play in women's lives.
As a result, she decides that "it's not for me" even as she is working "to
become a better person." The choice to remove the *hijab* drew not only the
concerned condemnation of friends who implored her to put it back on, in
accordance with consensus of interpretations from Shari'a and the *hadith*,
but also unwanted attention from men. Still, these difficulties are not overwhelming her calculations and her decision-making processes. Nor are they
prompting her to put the *hijab* back on.

Of course, not everyone who relocates to the West is subject to the same
contextual shifts and is so moved to stop wearing the *hijab*. Another Ammani
friend wrote to me about her visit to a local car dealership in the United
States:

> At the Honda dealership, the receptionist asks me, "I know, you're
> Muslim, right?" I thought to myself . . . "*Al-hamdulilah* [Praise Allah]
> . . . yes!" I nodded. She asks me about *hijab* and what it represents . . .
> but the whole thing made me think that it is such a blessing to be
> noticeably Muslim. Like if someone gave you a lottery ticket and they
> called your number, wouldn't you be like, "Yes, yes, that's me! I win!"

This is a clear case in which the public visibility of the *hijab*, which is even
more pronounced in the Muslim-minority context of the United States than
the Muslim-majority context of Amman, is likened to a lottery. For this
informant, one can "win" in Islam as one can "win" in the lottery.

These stories remind us that not everyone will respond to new or altered
circumstances, sources of knowledge, and internal states in a singular, predetermined way. Islamic normativity of the *hijab* is powerful, and negotiating
it is a continual process that points to the fluidity and the porousness and
contestation of different economized practices of piety in everyday life. Islamic practice here is not unitary, nor are behaviors that are often read as
"rejections" of normativity.

## Rejecting Normativity: Downveiling

One need not remove the *hijab* entirely in order to fall prey to gossip and
speculation about one's loose morals. Many women employ a "downveiling"
strategy as a means to follow the most essential, normative forms of veiling

in orthopraxy, but add more shape to the designs or substitute long, loose clothing for the most strict *abaya* (Herrera 2001). It is also a way to express aesthetics of modernity and Ammani middle-class cosmopolitanism. However, to do so can be socially risky, in that it may bring forth the ire of those who would prefer to see *abaya*-stylized Islamic dress and the accompanying ethics "done properly" and according to localized interpretations.

Marwa is a college-educated, professional Palestinian woman who had lived in East Amman and identified with middle-class economic practices in employment and consumption, while her family perched precariously between middle class and lower-middle class. As an expression of her modern aesthetic, she wanted to downveil in less covered and more revealing forms of Islamic dress. Marwa wanted to trade in her black *abaya* and white *hijab* for long skirts, long-sleeved shirts, and colorful scarves. At the same time, she refused any potential suitors, pursued her education, and made it a career goal to teach Arabic abroad. Marwa indicated to me that she wanted a love match for a husband and intended to "wait to get married. Wait until I find the right one to marry." Marwa exerted her agency and did so through a highly personalized narrative of choice and self-determination, which included dictating what she wore, whom she married, what she studied, and where she lived. Because this complex of highly personalized desires was structured in an actor-centered way that was seemingly dismissive of the family's authority and in ways that brought a rejection of normative forms and styles of dress into the equation, the family began to suspect that that her intentions were morally suspect and less than pious.

In fact, upon the declaration of her decision to downveil, many family members ostracized her for her "moral decline." At least one of her brothers cut her out of family interactions entirely and continues to ostracize her. At the time she made her life-altering announcement, the whole family was living in the same house, and one of her brothers, Mahmoud, went upstairs into her closet and confiscated all of her clothing except the *abayas*. He refused to return Marwa's skirts, shirts, and colorful headscarves for over a week. This was his way of "encouraging" her to continue dressing conservatively.

The family rejected Marwa's attempts to alter her dress to a different kind of stylized Islamic practice and accused her of moral decline. As a result of having her propriety questioned, she found it possible to engage in other, associated behaviors without additional derision. In a calculated way, this "freed" Marwa from a bundle of behaviors that hinged upon the Islamicness of her dress. Marwa was now able to refuse marriage proposals, teach Arabic abroad, and express her own moral and ethical agency. Whether or not she kept the *hijab* at that point likely would not have mattered: she had already rejected the moral complex of the lifestyle that "should" orient her, pursuing international travel without a male escort, rejecting the idea of entertaining male suitors for arranged marriages, and choosing longer skirts and shirts.

Because of these discursive and familial arrangements, Marwa stopped wearing the *hijab*, dove into her education, taught Arabic in several different countries, and returned to a lukewarm reception by her family years later. I asked her brother, Mahmoud, how he felt years later about Marwa's life choices. He answered, "At first I didn't understand. I was really mad at her for like two years. But now, I'm married myself. I understand her decision to postpone marriage. It's a big deal with a lot of responsibility. I respect her decision to delay this." His reflections on her other decisions were left unsaid.

However, when I asked another member of the family about his response, she replied with sarcasm, "Ooh, Mahmoud is such a progressive husband. Ask him when the last time was that he let his wife leave the house by herself!" Then she added seriously, "And the issues are really not all about her getting married or not, and he knows that." The "issues" are the larger normativities related to the *hijab* and her rejection of them by downveiling. One could surmise that, given Mahmoud's first, strong response of confiscating her clothes, he now respects one aspect of her decisions to some degree and is now less angry. Meanwhile, her other decisions do not appear to incite the same kinds of anger (although this might simply have been the image of himself that he wanted to present to me). Either way, these family relationships are still in tension, as one sibling has completely cut her out and continues to do so. Furthermore, when I visited Marwa's family when she was present, she wore the *hijab* in the neighborhood, loosely and seemingly unwillingly. It appears that Marwa—like Ayisha—has made calculated and localized compromises for the sake of the family, neighbors, and the neighborhood.

## The *Hijab* Is About a Certain Type of Modesty

Another ethic of the *hijab*, which is hinted at in Marwa's story, is less generally agreed-upon but much more widely discussed than the first. It is about the kinds of dress and comportment that should accompany a headscarf. For many women there is a tension between being modest and being "feminine" and sexually attractive. In general, there is some controversy regarding women who wear *hijab* and tight, or form-fitting, clothing that reveals her physical shape or the outline of her figure. Despite some controversy, such dress and fashion is common (Kaya 2010). A male informant told me that this style is unacceptable according to Islam and is "disgusting," whereas one of my female informants said, "Why don't I wear the *abaya*? It's not me, not my style. I prefer to be fashionable." Regardless of where one falls in the debates, they take up considerable amounts of time in conversation.

As a case in point, I was once riding down the escalator in a local mall with several girlfriends who were wearing headscarves and *abayas*. Coming up the escalator was a woman wearing a brightly colored headscarf, jeans, and what appeared to be only a black tank top covering her body from the waist up, leaving her shoulders and arms completely exposed. It was highly unusual—even shocking—to see a woman in a scarf and such scant, form-fitting covering and with so much flesh exposed. My friends and I all stopped talking and stared at the woman, until, up close, we realized that she was, in fact, wearing a long-sleeved shirt underneath the tank top. However, the shirt was flesh-colored and completely invisible from a distance. Based on the ensuing conversations with my friends, the damage had been done: the woman could make you think that she was so exposed, and therefore her dress violated more normative, but contested, ethics of modesty and was forbidden, or *haram*.

Such fashion—both Islamic and eye-catching—is found throughout the Muslim world. As Smith-Hefner (2007) and White (2002) discuss, the wider consumer audience for veils and *hijab* fashion has prompted a wide array of Islamic dress, further diversifying modes for religious and self-expression, challenging and negotiating economic and Islamic practice while reproducing the normative ethics of the *hijab*. Women's dress often combines new materials—chiffons and silks (which are generally conceived of as *haram* or forbidden for men to wear[9])—with stylized prints and patterns, vibrant colors, and decorative trim to lend an aesthetic appeal and personal distinction to the *hijab*. Furthermore, the styles of wrappings vary. Smith-Hefner (2007) discusses a "movie-star" style in Indonesia called *disko* (disco), *kafe* (café), *gaul* (social) or *fongki* (funky) veils. These styles prompt the ire of conservatives and male militants, who publicly berate their wearers for "besmirching the name of the *jilbab*." These trendy new veils are sexually alluring and, therefore, a serious threat to an Islamic social order (413).

Drawing attention to impurity in dress is considered widely to be part of the injunction to command right and forbid wrong. Islamic scholarly debates—as early as those of Maliki Yahya ibn Umar in the tenth century—discuss problems such as nudity, the presence of women in the public baths, and "their coquettish habit of wearing squeaky sandals" (Cook 2000, 368). Official debates by jurists occurred on the acceptable amount of flesh that could be exposed—no "larger than a *dirham*[10] in their dress" (314)—and on the leeway given to "merely personal" duties such as "beards, hair, and dress" (553). Certainly unofficial groups have engaged in berating "any woman whose dress flaunted her sexuality" such as those conducted by Ibn Ibrahim in Saudi Arabia in the 1940s and described by 'Abdullah al-Qarawi in the 1960s (191). There is also some historical, legal, and social justification for women chastising other women about their dress: in the mid-twentieth century Lutf Allah Safi Gulpayagani told a woman that she should command right and forbid wrong by reprimanding improperly dressed women with whom she interacted socially (*Majma' al-Misa'il*, 1:434n1, 324, cited in Cook 2000, 548–49).

Historically speaking, the *hijab* has not always been considered an Islamically unqualified good. "To be veiled" can also mean a kind of hiding or separation from Allah, and it carries some negative connotation in the Qur'an (Mernissi 1987, 93–94, 97). In fact, the practice of today's *hijab* does not appear to be rooted in the earliest understandings of the word, concept, or theological import (Mernissi 1987, 97). Unfortunately, little is known about the developments of today's *hijab*. It appears that the precise stages of the processes by which it became obligatory are documented by Islamic scholars in localized cultural and "established" forms, rather than in any kind of "developmental" form (Stowasser 1994, 93). In other words, classical legal documents, *ahadith*, and Qur'anic exegesis are formulations of the system as established by the extra-Islamic practices of the Sasanian and Byzantian states and secured in the religious establishments of the Abbasids who were responsible for formulating Islamic law and moralities (Ahmed 1992, 79–101; Stowasser 1994, 93).

Much of the debate about the *hijab* in Amman seems to hinge upon the localized understandings of *'awra*, which translates literally as "genitalia" (particularly female) or "nakedness." Medieval jurists left the word *"hijab"* generic and conceptual, instead focusing legal rulings on other previously specified terms for female clothing such as *jilbab, izar, khimar,* and *niqab* (Stowasser 1994, 92). By leaving *hijab* relatively vague and pairing it with *'awra,* medieval scholars were able to avoid getting bogged down in the specifics of obligatory clothing, preferring to be ambiguous in the culturally and geographically diverse context (Stowasser 1994, 93).

Still, some guideposts exist that trace the development of *'awra* as conceived of today. According to Stowasser (1994), Shafi'is and Hanbalis (two schools of Islamic jurisprudence, or *madhhab*), rendered the decision that the entire female body—including the face, hands, and feet—was *'awra* and should be covered. Two other schools, Maliki and Hanafi, defined *'awra* with an exclusion for the face and hands, justifying this position with a strong *hadith* that the Prophet Mohammed instructed "believing women" to show the face, hands and "one hand's breadth" of the forearms (Tabari *Tafsir* 18:93, cited in Stowasser 1994, 93). However, there are conflicting rulings within each *madhhab* over time, so it is not possible to determine a clear trajectory.

With this historical, cross-cultural, and legal context in mind, in Amman the point of contention revolves around the idea that this kind of dress is *technically* sound. That is, the women are exposing a minimum amount of skin and adhering to localized and conservative interpretations that a woman should show only her face and hands. At the same time, they challenge this adherence with form-fitting, sexy outfits such as tight jeans and long-sleeved, even flesh-colored, shirts, large earrings, heavily applied cosmetics and perfumes, and colorful *hijab* tied in new, fashionable styles. This combination, many people believe, violates the *spirit* of the ethic of the *hijab*. Though a flesh-colored shirt technically covers the entirety of one's 'awra, critics argue that because it invokes an imaginary version of the very flesh it covers, such clothing is too risqué and does not conform to the spirit of modesty enacted by the *hijab*.

In this way, the discussion gets at the question of the localized normative ethics for certain behaviors and social postures that are expected of women who wear the *hijab*. They are expected to embody the normatively loaded "modesty." This state varies between social groups and is contextualized and negotiated by circumstance, but the normative idea in Amman is that women should both cover their skin and hide their physically attractive bodily features from men. They should also cover their 'awra from other women. (When women are with women the 'awra typically referred to their buttocks, genitalia, and breasts.) For example, a friend of mine tried to sunbathe topless at the rooftop pool at the all-women's gym I attended. She was approached by a gym employee several minutes later and told that removing her bikini top was *haram* because she was not allowed to reveal her 'awra. Similar ethics prevailed at local Turkish-style baths for women, saunas, and jacuzzis.

Localized understandings also dictate that once in a headscarf, women should refrain from revealing any of their hair. This is despite the fact that the *hijab* style in the Gulf countries permits the revealing of short bangs across the forehead, as seen in many television programs from the Gulf, Internet-based interactions with Gulf residents, and visits to Amman by Gulf Arabs in the summertime.[11] Such women, while often admired by Ammanis for their wealth, are often disparaged as part of larger, community-wide conflicts of aesthetics with Gulf residents.

It is estimated that over a million Gulf residents spend the summer in Amman every year. In the summer of 2009, the city hosted 2.5 million summer residents from neighboring countries, most of them believed to be from the Gulf countries. The traffic congestion during these months is significant, typically caused by large SUVs displaying license plates from Saudi Arabia, Kuwait, and Dubai. The noticeably different male fashion of long, white *thobes* or *dishdashes*, more typically worn by Jordanian men to the mosques on Friday, are donned by male Gulf residents throughout the week. The "Gulfies" or *khalijis* are frequently the subject of disparaging comments by Ammanis. For example, the "fanny pack," popular in the United States in the 1980s, is sometimes seen around the waists of male Gulf residents, prompting giggles from Ammanis who might have owned one themselves twenty years ago. Gulf women are frequently the subject of jokes about multiple wives, "mounds of children," and ignorance of husbands' evening homosexual and illicit affairs.[12] These are, of course, all speculative matters. However, one friend summed up her perspective on the summer "Gulfies":

> They drive their huge gas-guzzling Hummers all over traffic, ignoring our laws and endangering people on the road. They don't care about getting tickets because they can just pay the fines without any trouble. So what if they're rich. They don't have to go around like they own the place. They should respect us!

"Respect" here is invoking yet another instance of "commanding right and forbidding wrong," although the grounding in localized ethics as mediated by class rather than Islamic law is particularly strong.

It is, perhaps, due to the general public dislike of the summer "Gulfies" that Ammanis also reject the women's fashion and Islamic styles. This demonstrates a case of a modern and authentic Islamic ethic deriving from rejection of and disassociation with a complex grouping of behaviors: Ammanis reject the Islam of the Gulf because they object to its practitioners' attitudes, driving habits, personal spending, and personal and family lifestyles. This demonstrates that, despite the access to alternative Islamic norms and styles and routine exposure to other acceptable fashions of the *hijab*, the idea that a woman should not reveal any of her hair is less contested and more frequently accepted in Amman.

At the same time, and in a way that creates much tension, women frequently express a desire to be "cute" or "sexy," and attempt to do so with a personal style. As one jeans-wearing informant mentioned, "I'm just not the kind of girl who wears skirts." With regard to footwear, one informant said:

> I had these really cute ballerina shoes that just cover the toes, but then there's like the rest of the foot [exposed] . . . I've never heard of anyone getting turned on by this much [indicates a 2–3 inch space with

fingers] skin of a foot. But when I think about it, it probably is *haram*. The *hadith* that I know is that you're not supposed to expose anything except your hands and face . . . But they say that *hadith* is weak . . . I guess you don't need your feet to show. But have you ever heard of a man getting turned on by this much of a foot? I guess I just really like the shoes.

Herein lies the tension between covering, certain notions of modesty, and the desire and expectation to be attractive, which is resolved with an actor's calculative agency, intellectual reasoning, and Qur'anic knowledge. The normative ethics that derive from the Qur'an and *hadith* do not necessarily translate into the most extreme or conservative forms of Islamic practice, even if the populace sees and understands the reasoning and even if some scholars advocate for it.[13] Rather, as this example demonstrates, women are calculating their own notions of correct and incorrect practice and actively promoting a certain *hadith* as "weak" when its commands conflict with their own interests and desires. This is a moment of co-production in which economic practices are Islamized and Islamic practice is economized. "But have you ever heard of a man getting turned on by this much of a foot?" is a springboard into alternative economic practices that have the potential to undermine the most austere and literal forms of normativity.

As the informant mentioned, there is a prevalent notion in Amman that only a woman's face and hands should be displayed. Ammani women frequently cite the following Qur'anic verse in conversation: "And tell the believing women to lower their gaze and be modest, and to display of their adornment only that which is apparent, and to draw their veils over their bosoms . . ." (24:31). The phrase "only that which is apparent" is generally interpreted in Amman to mean a women's face and hands. At the same time, however, shoe stores that feature strappy high heels and open-toed footwear are abundant: thirty-three stores there in three major malls carry women's shoes that reveal their feet, one of which is named, ironically, "Wahhabi Shoes." (The Wahhabi movement is known as one of the most austere fundamentalist Islamic movements.) Only three stores in the same malls are categorized as "Islamic Wear."

The delegitimation of the *hadith* against displaying one's feet as "weak" is another means by which women are able to negotiate that tension between sources of Islamic knowledge and self-interest, particularly in the name of fashion. Wearing sexy, strappy high heels or "cute ballerina shoes" is a form of actor-centered economic practice. One is able to invoke knowledge-based, viable alternatives for claims of Islamization in order to pursue the points for self-expression in economic practices that one might be keen to do.

Class differences also come into play here. Three of the largest and most expensive shopping centers—Mecca Mall, City Mall, and Barakat Mall—feature stores, products, restaurants, and services that are far outside the price ranges of lower-class and even many middle-class Ammanis. Caribou Coffee, where I often studied, is in Barakat Mall. A small "specialty" drink costs the equivalent of between $3.50 and $5.00, and 500 grams (1.1 lb.) of roasted coffee beans cost nearly $20. Caribou Coffee is located on the same floor as a French handbag store, Longchamp, downstairs from a combination English-language bookstore and sushi restaurant, and near a multiplex movie theater that shows first-run American and occasional Arabic movies, even offering VIP seats with food service and extra space. Unlike Cairo's, these malls do not attract high numbers of lower- and lower-middle-class shoppers who wander the mall, unable to afford the offerings (Peterson 2011). In Amman, this may be due to the costs associated with getting to the mall: a one-way taxi ride from East Amman to Mecca Mall costs approximately $7.00. This hardly makes for an affordable—or enjoyable—afternoon journey. The three stores designated as "Islamic wear" are themselves high-end shopping experiences. I purchased two *abayas* in two different stores. Each cost more than $65.00 and, as the salesman told me, were the most inexpensive they carried.

These points of class-mediated negotiation for personal dress, social pressures and expectations, and self-interests are spaces where Islamization of economic practices occurs and modern and authentic Islam is expressed, debated and contested, and renegotiated. My Ammani informants demonstrated a strong resistance to the extremely austere Islam requiring covering and maintaining "modesty" in front of both women and men at the expense of personal styles and interests. Yet, it is these personal styles and interests that lend themselves to experimentation with various normativities. That is, according to the localized interpretations of Islamic rulings and localized moralities, one need only be revealing nothing but the face, hands and feet to be considered "technically correct" and to fulfill the demands of normativity with the *hijab*. However, these normative interpretations and moralities do not extend with the same degree of consensus to tight jeans, a long-sleeved and tight shirt, and strappy high heels, thereby leaving the ethics of their use more open-ended and underdetermined.

Due to these uncertainties and lack of consensus in normativity, one can be both sexy with strappy heels and enact a modern and authentic Islam in agency-centered ways. Such adaptability and flexibility by consumers is in a complex interplay with a localized and negotiated kind of Islam. To be "technically correct," covering everything except the face and hands, is a highly calculative and economized way to be considered "just Islamic enough" to fulfill the normative requirements, and any number of stores carry clothing that a shopper might be interested in purchasing to complete the outfit.

## The *Hijab* and Islamic Bank Employment

During my time spent researching at the Islamic bank, women's dress—particularly the *hijab* and cosmetics—occupied a surprisingly large portion of conversation when women discussed their jobs. The bank required all female employees to wear both the *hijab* and cosmetics, though style and amount of coverage varied. It was a human resources requirement, and one's *hijab* and cosmetics were part of the employment evaluation: women's work performance was measured according to their *hijab* styles and the amount and style of cosmetics. Some women wore long skirts with neutral-colored *hijabs*, adding the minimum of cosmetics required by their employment contracts. Others wore tight-fitting pantsuits, bright scarves, flashy jewelry, and a heavy application of eyeliner and lipstick. The one clothing item forbidden at the bank was denim, even as skirt material. However, the Social Committee, a formal employee group who organized overnight and day trips throughout the region for bank workers, was advocating for "Casual Thursday" when denim skirts and jeans could be worn.

As mentioned above, Islamizing economic practices and economizing Islamic practices occurs in intimate spaces, including the workplace. The Islamic Bank can be understood as an intimate space for several reasons. First of all, when they are not at work women's freedom of movement may be severely restricted to areas around their homes (Hanssen-Bauer, Pedersen, and Tiltnes 1998), even if they have achieved a high level of education. In fact, for the girls in Fida Adely's 2004 study, school was the only space outside the home that the girls were permitted to go to on their own (358). Working at the Islamic bank is at times the only space outside the home that its young female employees are permitted to visit independently. After high school graduation, the university and the workplace become, for most women in Amman—including those who work at the Islamic bank—"one of the few opportunities to develop non-kin relationships and participate in a somewhat public arena" (Adely 2004, 359). The bank also provides one of the very few socially acceptable spaces in which women can talk with men without risking their reputations. "Coworkers" or "colleagues" are frequently considered socially acceptable relationships in which one can have more friendly or open conversations with men, of the sort that would not be considered "modest" or "proper" for *muhajabat* in many other public spaces.

During my time at the Islamic bank, one female employee, Eman, had "not yet" put on the *hijab* outside the bank and in her everyday life. She was a practicing Muslim, in that she prayed and fasted for Ramadan. She openly discussed her desire to uphold her vision for Muslim values and, most notably, was a proponent of Islamic banking, believing that it could "end poverty." Still, as most women indicate when they do not wear the scarf, Eman was "not ready yet." However, employment policies required that all women wear the *hijab*. To the Islamic bank, Eman wore a loose-fitting scarf that revealed the hair above her forehead in a style that more closely approximated the fashion of Iranians or Gulf residents. The colors she chose were often bright greens and blues and matched her equally bright outfits. However, because she revealed a portion of her hair above her forehead, Eman was the subject of gossip by the other women at the bank. As one fellow employee explained,

> I don't understand why she just doesn't wear it [the *hijab*] the right way and do it [cover her hair]. I know she doesn't wear it outside the bank. Sometimes I even see her putting it on when she's walking into the bank. Can you imagine?! If she's going to wear it here, she needs to do it right.

Following her statement, many of the women within earshot in the office started nodding their heads in agreement. Eman's style was, in wide consensus, considered disrespectful and donning the *hijab* on the street incorrect.[14] As this informant indicated, the fact that Eman did not wear the *hijab* outside the bank was not a legitimate excuse for not following the "right" way at the bank.

The main issue with Eman appeared to be that, as a Muslim and therefore subject to Islamic normativity and ethics about the *hijab*, she *should* wear it in a way that reflects this. She is a practicing Muslim, and others fulfilled the injunction to "command right and forbid wrong" with her. In contrast, I was never once asked to wear the scarf, nor was it even suggested that I should cover my hair, even though this was required for all female bank employees. I am not a Muslim, nor was I technically an "employee." (I did not receive a paycheck.) Therefore, it was assumed that I would not don the *hijab*.[15] Eman, on the other hand, was both a Muslim and a bank employee. As such, she was expected to fulfill the normative morals associated with both roles.

Eman's story demonstrates the limits to the claims that one is "not ready yet." There are times when the normativity in place—particularly when backed by official legislation, policy, or other "hands" commanding right and forbidding wrong—is so overwhelming that to reject it is no longer possible. In this case, it is conceivable that, if Eman wore the *hijab* outside the bank full-time and did so in a way that was both revealing of her hair *and* constructed as a classed choice, no one would have been bothered.

Beyond questions of *hijab* style and the revealing of hair, *hijab* color was also a major topic of conversation. Valentine's Day—locally celebrated as 'Eid Al-Hob—fell in the middle of my internship period, and the consensus was that the color red made a woman look very attractive and "hot." Even male employees at the bank weighed in on this discussion. Talal said, "It's true. When a woman wears a red *hijab* she looks hot. Even if it's just a picture of a woman in a regular *hijab* [white or black], but the background of the picture is red, it makes her look hot." Another man in the office looked up from his computer and added, "It's true, you know."

Because of this heightened attention, many women economized their Islamic practice and either sought to wear red regularly in an effort to catch a particular man's attention, or in the days surrounding the Valentine's holiday in an effort to maintain her reputation as "modest" and still stand out. Nada, attempting to capture the interest of a coworker at the bank, purchased a new red coat and matching red-patterned scarf. The combination was eye-catching for a woman who typically dressed stylishly but in more neutral colors. She explained, "I'm modest. You know, I don't dress like this [in red] or talk to men. But, I really like Khalid. I wish he liked me. This is my one chance to show him that I'm beautiful. Maybe he will notice me." In an environment in which mixing between the sexes is primarily professional, Nada utilized the festive atmosphere and temporal suspension of strict notions of modesty associated with Valentine's Day to vary from her typical neutral-tones in hopes of catching a crush's attention, without compromising her reputation as both pious and modest.

These expressions of sociality, *hijab* color, and motivations all point to ways by which the women were economizing their Islamic practices and Islamizing their economic practices. There is nothing inherently Islamic about St. Valentine's Day. In fact the holiday has been banned in Saudi Arabia. Yet women in the bank utilized the normative ethics of the *hijab* to extend their Islamized dress into a new color at a new time of the year. For actor-centered motivations such as attracting an officemate, these expressions of Islamized economic practices are strategic and calculated, and ultimately serve to reinforce the normative ethic of the *hijab*. These women are wearing the *hijab*, and are continuing to preserve this overarching ethic.

Regardless of the style or color, and despite the fact that wearing the *hijab* was a job requirement, women understood their dress in terms of "choice," a primary factor that kept most from quitting their demanding, relatively

low-paying jobs. Throughout the bank, women indicated that their positions were no different than those they would occupy at a conventional
bank. There was nothing uniquely "Islamic" about working the same job in
an Islamic bank, but women felt free to choose what they would normally
wear anyway.

My informants frequently made comparisons with other banks—both
conventional and Islamic—as a means to reiterate that wearing what one
wanted was important to female employees. As one noted, "It's really hard
for us [women who wear *hijab*] to get a job at the conventional banks. They
hire mostly Christians. It's like marketing for them—they have a better 'face'
for their bank. It's sexier." Whether or not this is actually an employment
practice at conventional banks, the idea was repeated frequently enough to
make it clear that the female employees at the Islamic bank believed it. I inquired about perceptions of working for the competing Jordan Islamic Bank,
and was given the near inverse of the reasoning applied to the conventional
bank: that the other Islamic institution was too restrictive in what it required
female employees to wear. As one employee noted, "I would never work
there. Did you know that they require all the women to wear an *abaya*, a
white *hijab*, and they are forbidden from wearing cosmetics? This is too
much for me. This is not the real Islam."

## Conclusions

Queen Rania of Jordan was interviewed by the Italian magazine *Correire della
Sera* about the *hijab*. Her response was that "we shouldn't judge women by
what is on their heads but by what is in their heads . . ." (Al-Abdullah 2007).
In this chapter, I have demonstrated that women are very much judged for
both what is on their heads and what is in their heads. That is because
women in Amman are subject to a multitude of means—both Shari'a-based
and non-Shari'a-based—by which the injunction to command right and
forbid wrong is enacted in the realm of the *hijab*. Though the *hijab* is not legally enforced by the government in the way that Ramadan is, the injunction
is socially carried in ways that range from stares and reprimands to threats
of disowning a child or not acknowledging a former student. There is consensus about elements such as the notion that Muslim women should cover
their hair and necks. However, women face much tension and dynamism as
they economize their actions and legitimate their calculative engagements,
particularly in authentic Islamic reference to the Qur'an, or a Shari'a ruling,
or *hadith*. Justifying one's "technical" behavior in the pursuit of an authentically Islamic identity that meets contemporary demands is often done in

reference to Shari'a, even if such behavior is believed to violate the "spirit" of the law. Women engage in some notion of these normative and ethical behaviors as a means of self-fulfillment, demonstrating that economized and Islamized practices can be and are mobilized for other, non-orthodox ends.

An authentic Islamic identity is not one that fits other, often Western, definitions of "authenticity," in which a desire or decision has been predetermined prior to a specific context and then enacted. Authenticity with the *hijab* does not, in fact, "demand that external signs be produced by internal dispositions" (Kaya 2010, 528). Although this consistency between internal states and outward manifestations seems to be the official line produced by the likes of Amr Khaled, the cases described here demonstrate that intentions on the part of the woman donning or removing the *hijab* are not what people see when the normativities and Islamic ethics have been threatened or violated.

In fact, consistency between internal and external states can limit the real power that other mediating forms of justification and knowledge carry; one can "lose" bargaining power in calculative agencies if the internal and external states must align. As a result of the flexibility engendered by separating internal and external states—orthodoxy and orthopraxy—and placing each of them in reference to doctrinal normativities, we find that people frequently live in a much more complex and negotiated arena that may use one to reference the other. However, complete consistency between internal states and external manifestations in line with some form of normativity in the *hijab* is not something people are actually living all the time, if at all.

In the absence of government-mandated practice as was seen during Ramadan, Shari'a-mediated and calculated justifications for economic action become much more elaborate and less singularized. This is because a "complex mix of motives" (Smith-Hefner 2007, 412) and the resulting actions—of both Islamic and economic natures—are fluid and porous, responsive to the changing circumstances and situations in which actors find themselves. While there is consensus about aspects of the normativity of the *hijab*, but less than was witnessed during Ramadan, the economization, Islamization, and valuation of contested and negotiated understandings of Islam in economic practices continues. The impacts of Islamizing economic practices and economizing Islamic practices are pronounced. The next chapter of this book elaborates these processes in a context of even less determinacy in Islamic economics.

# CHAPTER 5

# Making It Real

*Adequation*

Dr. Hamid was the head of the Retail Department at the International Islamic Arab Bank, one of the two Islamic banks in Amman. As one of the few Ph.D. holders in the bank and an older male in his early 60s, he was a major force at the bank, both internally and externally. Employees and other administrators frequently deferred to him and his advice, even above Human Resources and higher levels of bank management. Customers delinquent on their loans or requesting repayment extensions came into his office—embarrassed, ashamed, and using the formal address of "Dr. Hadritak"[1]—to have their individual cases reviewed, evaluated, and judged. Dr. Hamid made final and lasting decisions about bank and employee policies and when to use legal enforcement against delinquent clients. The bank employees often reported to me that much power resided in his hands.

While I was in a meeting with Dr. Hamid, he pointed out to me that the bank's general manager had recently published a letter to the editor in a local newspaper, which highlighted a new bank policy on title transfers for vehicles (discussed in detail in the next chapter). The letter concluded by welcoming other banks to compete with this new instrument for financing cars. Dr. Hamid then turned to me and said, "But you know what? The general manager is wrong. We don't need to compete. We don't need to use these new products and tricks. Do you know why?" Dr. Hamid leaned back in his leather office chair, raised his arms up before resting his hands behind his head and exclaimed, "Because we have Islam!" Surprised, I immediately pointed out that the rival Islamic bank in Jordan, the Jordan Islamic Bank, also "has Islam." Dr. Hamid responded, "But we don't have to compete! Don't you see? We can just be ourselves and be our Islamic bank and that will sell us. We don't have to compete. We don't have to think about the Jordan Islamic Bank." Then he moved in even closer to me and, almost whispering, added, "No one likes them anyway."

Dr. Hamid and his perspectives on the applications of Islam and Shari'a to Islamic banking came to represent what many bank employees, especially young professionals in their 20s and 30s, felt was a frustrating management style, characterized by "old" or "outdated" policies, employment regulations, and marketing notions. They particularly criticized his belief that it was unnecessary for the bank to compete by way of innovation and by updating their Islamic financial methods and products. Dr. Hamid asserted that the way Islam infused throughout the bank would be enough to promote and sell its financial tools and instruments, and that the bank's claim that what they were practicing was "the real Islam" was sufficient for attracting and keeping customers. In the employees' critiques of Dr. Hamid, they articulated a modern and cosmopolitan vision for a different way of conducting Islamic banking and of interpreting and applying Shari'a, one that is highly adaptable to new economic and social circumstances, responsive to shifting contexts, and relevant and applicable in everyday life for contemporary Muslims.

Dr. Hamid's reputation among the employees as "outdated," "old," and not particularly modern was reinforced when I revealed to some of them that he tried to convert me during one of our interviews. Dr. Hamid and I had been sitting for over three hours while he explained, in tremendous detail, the services and products of the Retail Department. I felt that I achieved good rapport and had an overall friendly encounter with Dr. Hamid. However, by the end I was exhausted, having conducted the lengthy interview in Arabic. As I started putting my notebook away, he leaned across his desk, folded his hands in front of him and asked, "Sarah, has anyone invited you to Islam before?"[2] I smiled and sighed, having received this "invitation" from a number of friends outside the bank. Based on the good rapport I had established with Dr. Hamid, I joked, "Is that a new nightclub? Are you inviting me to a new disco?" Although Dr. Hamid smiled, he did not laugh. He understood that I was making a joke, albeit not a very good one, as it was a bit irreverent for the serious topic of conversation. The following conversation ensued:

DH: Sarah, you're not a Muslim are you?
ST: No, Dr. Hamid, I'm not a Muslim. You know I'm a Christian.

DH: You know that we [Muslims] believe in Judgment Day, right?

ST: Yes, I know.

DH: On Judgment Day, Allah is going to ask me why I didn't invite you to Islam. So I have to do this. I have to ask you if you want to come to Islam. If I don't do this, on Judgment Day, Allah is going to ask me, 'Where is Sarah? Why didn't you invite her?' So I'm doing this because, if I don't, the sin is on my head. It's my responsibility. I can go to the *nar*, the fire, for eternal damnation if I don't do this. Do you understand me?

ST: Yes. Thank you.

DH: Ok, has anyone invited you to Islam before?

ST: Yes. Thank you.

DH: Do you want to return to Islam?[3]

ST: Thank you. Thank you very much. I understand. Thank you.[4]

I was not particularly upset or offended by the conversation, as it was a relatively common occurrence with a number of my Muslim friends and acquaintances in Amman. It appeared to me that Dr. Hamid was responsive to his understandings of his Shari'a-based responsibilities on the Day of Judgment, and was simply trying to clear his conscience. I was quite surprised, however, at the degree to which the employees of the Islamic bank were upset and offended. Most employees were surprised, even shocked, and spoke openly with me about it. I had not anticipated the strong reactions that I witnessed from them. In fact, rumors of this conversation spread throughout the bank, prompting many employees to approach me with questions of "Did he really?!" Many employees expressed emotions ranging from incredulity that anyone at the bank would have suggested I needed to convert, to strong frustration at his action. As one female employee, Sharifa, summarized:

> He shouldn't have done that! It was inappropriate and unprofessional. Don't be offended. I'm so sorry. Clearly, you know about Islam. You're at an *Islamic* bank! He doesn't understand. He treats everyone else like he knows best too. It's not just you. Don't take it personally.

Dr. Hamid's reputation as old and outdated, effectively "not-modern," was particularly revealed in these two different scenarios. In the first case, Dr. Hamid represented what is perceived to be an older model of Islamizing economic practices in banking and finance: change the name to "Islamic," alter some technical arrangements, and what you have is a singular, Islamized economized offering. In the second scenario, we see Dr. Hamid expressing an economized Islamic practice. He was trying to convert me as a way to prevent the sin of omission, that is, of not telling me about Islam, from falling on him. He was acting in the "here and now" as a means to prevent spiritual problems in the afterlife. The employees understood that the ways in which he approached the Islamization of banking and finance and the economization of Islamic practices were lacking in tact, in style, essentially in an accessible aesthetic. His attempts at wielding his economized Islamic practices fell flat, leaving many employees embarrassed and apologetic on his behalf.

In responses such as Sharifa's, the employees of the Islamic bank also contested Dr. Hamid's interpretation of Islamic doctrine and methods for contemporary applications. They rejected his relatively narrow understanding of his responsibilities on the Day of Judgment and his understanding of Shariʻa in his attempts to convert me. They also rejected his relatively narrow understanding of the commercial value of Islam; that "Islam sells itself" was not a popular idea. Furthermore, Sharifa's quote articulates a preference for a more "appropriate" and "professional" boss with a wider and more appealing—and aesthetically modern—management style, which overlaps with their perceptions of his religiously oriented narrowness. Based on this and other conversations I had with employees like Sharifa, I saw that many had a desire for a supervisor who wielded Islam in a different way. They wanted someone who was willing to use Shariʻa to listen to the employees, utilize their unique knowledge and experiences, and adopt a more innovative edge over the competition in a way that they found persuasive and compelling. In short, they wanted a supervisor who would more closely reflect their vision for "the real Islam."

In this chapter, I explore in depth the tensions between the desire on some people's part for a more Islamic—and highly economized—way of life, and the realities of a complex modern economy in their highly diverse manifestations. As such, this chapter further expands the discussions of economy and negotiations of Shariʻa in chapters 2, 3, and 4. It demonstrates that Islamic economics, banking, and finance are relatively recent emergent spaces in which questions of the role and place for a singular Islamic economic practice deriving from a narrow interpretation of Islam and Shariʻa are being challenged. The notion of a singular interpretation of Islam- and Shariʻa-derived ideas in economic practices is deeply questioned by the very producers of the banking industry, such as the employees I discuss above. The diversity of professional and personal pieties by the producers of an Islamic economics debunks the notion of a singular Islamic piety in economic practice, further diminishing consensus beyond that found during Ramadan in chapter 3 and with the *hijab* in chapter 4. Furthermore, the processes of

Islamizing economic practices and economizing Islamic practices are conducted in moments of co-production, and a framework of "adequation"
enables us to gain insight into many of these moments in the fields of Islamic
economics, banking, and finance.

## Realities, Tensions, and Adequations

These interactions with Dr. Hamid and employees such as Sharifa highlight a
major tension within this Islamic bank. On the one hand, employees such as
Dr. Hamid, who are producers—Islamizers—of banking and finance, envision Islam as a total way of life and therefore see Islamic banking as a robust
and comprehensive way to engage in economic practices that are based in
Shari'a, irrefutable, and singular in their construction and enactment. As the
logic goes, just as there is one "real" Islam, there is one "real" Islamic bank.
On the other hand are the practical and everyday realizations of the critical
employees and the consumers of Islamic economics and Islamic banking
that contest these assertions. They understand the Dr. Hamids of the bank as
putting forth but one possible approach to integrating Islam into economic
practices. These critical employees assert that a Shari'a-based approach to
Islamic economic practices must be open (even to non-Muslims), relevant,
efficient, well-managed, appealing, modern, and authentic if it is going to
succeed. As a result, and much more than the cases of Ramadan and the *hijab*
demonstrate, consensus in Islamic economics, banking and finance are highly
contested, divergent, and fragmented.

Both Dr. Hamid and the critical employees are attempting to realize their
vision for understanding and enacting "the real Islam" in their approaches
to economics and banking and finance. These attempts are made visible
through the lens of "adequation," which is defined as "bringing one's concepts in accord with reality, words with things, mind with matter" (Maurer
2005, xiii–xv). Adequation asks the question, "How adequately does this
reality represent the ideal truth?" "The real Islam" becomes manifest in economic actions through adequation, which enables the realization of abstraction, value, substance, and standardization as simultaneously real, or concrete,
and Islamic.[5] Debates about an authentic and real Islam and their manifestations are, therefore, debates about adequation.

Through adequation, we see widely diverse attempts at reconciliation between the everyday realities of Islamizing economic practices and economizing Islamic practices vis-à-vis Shari'a. Producers and consumers aim to
"make adequate" their economizations by injecting Islamic references, values, or ideas into economic processes and their associated institutions and

by altering their doctrinal stances or beliefs to align with public demands for Islamic practice. As a result, these various practices become rationalized, valued, maximized, legitimated, and sometimes monetized in their reference to Shari'a. These moments of co-production (Islamizing economic practices and economizing Islamic piety) aim to reconcile Islamized abstractions and realities "on the ground." Processes of adequation are particularly salient in the production of Islamic banking and finance, and in the wider production and integration of economized practices and Islam.

As Bill Maurer discusses (2005), the questions of adequation ask, "To what degree does this reality adequately represent ideas?" While he raises this question specifically to the case of money by asking questions about the source and location of value, the concept has roots in social thought and philosophy. One can trace this line of inquiry from Nietzsche to Heidegger, and from Kant to Aquinas. Maurer emphasizes that these great thinkers believed that the knowledge of truth came from the adequation of thought. These philosophers and their intellectual predecessors used adequation to articulate the ways in which "truth" stood for the adequation of knowledge. Debates about "truth" are debates about adequation.

The concept is also found in linguistics and linguistic anthropology (e.g., Cole 2010; Stern 1931), in which debates about pre-performative and per-formative conceptions and usages of language are marked. Gustaf Stern, for example, used adequation as a way to understand the processes by which words shift in meaning when the attention to the referents change (Maurer 2005; Stern 1931, 318). Debbie Cole looks at the case of Indonesian poetry to understand reflections of diversity in adequation, which she defines as the "social pursuit of linguistic sameness" (Cole 2010, 1). Debates about language and reality are, therefore, also debates about adequation.

In Islamic studies we also see adequation invoked in several divergent ways to understand Islam in the contemporary world. In one case, Seyyed Hossein Nasr believes that conditions of the modern era include the amplification of the self and the authoritative knowledge that derives from the self, which complicates understandings of Islam as a knowledge and tradition that ex-isted before and outside of the self (1979, 1980, 1983). Islam is, in this view, complicated by conditions of the modern self.

Abdelmajid Charfi (2010), in another case, believes that Islam is embodied and that, as such, one must understand the historical conditions that shape and condition its adequation in the contemporary era of globalization. Islam is, in this view, created by temporal selves of historical and modern times. While the first position posits that Islam and the contemporary world exist in tensions with knowledge and authority, the second argues that Islam and its expressions will be shaped by the very processes that constitute it today.

There is, however, a third view that best explains adequation for my purposes. In *Understanding Islam* (1998), Frithjof Schuon sets out "not so much to give a description of Islam as to explain why Moslems believe in it" (xvii), asserting that Islam is understood as the religion of truth, or "the religion of the Absolute" (6). Schuon, who first published this work in 1963, presciently understood the dilemma of Islam in twenty-first-century urban Jordan: while a singular Islam is asserted as "the real Islam," the content of such truth statements is diverse and highly divergent. As Schuon saw it, "the Absolute is less difficult to grasp than the tremendous abysses of its manifestation" (71). The manifestations of the moral and social aspects of Shari'a, he says, are "adequations of the will to the human norm; its aim is to actualize, and not to limit our positive horizontal nature" (80). In other words, conforming one's actions to socially constructed normative doctrines is one way in which our "horizontal nature" in social relations is actualized. Engaging the real Islam, in Schuon's framework, is to acknowledge that Allah is the Absolute "objective immanence" (185). Then one works out this "metaphysical doctrine" in pursuit of aligning intelligence with truth (158) and in modes of sociality.

In processes of adequation in Amman, actors align, negotiate, and alter their practices in relation to public norms. In doing so they generate and reveal the real Islam as they see it, often in sustained social or "horizontal" relationships, particularly in the fields of Islamic economics, banking, and finance. As we will see, adequation exists in these fields in the everyday processes that seek to align them with abstract representations articulated vis-à-vis Shari'a. These tensions play out with powerful advanced capitalist, often neoliberal, realities already in place. Producers of these fields, such as Dr. Hamid and the critical employees, aim to "make adequate" their vision for Islamic realities by injecting Islamic references, values, or ideas into these economic processes and their associated institutions, marking them somehow distinctly and singularly "Islamic." Adequation reveals the Islamizing processes at play in banking and finance efforts.

At the same time, adequation reveals additional economizing processes of Islamic piety. In adequation we see Islamic practices become rationalized, maximized, even monetized by reference to Shari'a. These moments of co-production aim to reconcile realities with Islamized abstractions and are repeatedly interrogated with questions such as, "How adequately does this reality represent my understanding of Islam and of Shari'a?" and "How adequately does this reality represent my understanding of proper economic practices?" The actions of Dr. Hamid and the critical employees speak to very different methods and understandings of the answers.

Following Charfi's (2010) argument that understanding the adequation of Islam requires grounding in the historical conditions that have shaped it, it is also important to acknowledge that there is a historical, Islamic undercurrent for these idealized aims of Islamic adequation in contemporary Jordan. Many Islamists understand the period of time in which Islam was revealed to the Prophet Mohammed and his earliest converts to be one in which "there was little divergence between ideals and reality. It is regarded as a period of ideological inspiration or guidance" (Clark 2004, 13). Contemporary Islamists often seek to re-Islamize or re-implement the "perfect" ideals of early Islam as they are believed to have existed. However, as we will see, not only Islamists or those engaged in Islamic activism hold these beliefs. The idealization of early Islam, particularly with regard to beliefs of moral incorruptibility, is one of the primary ways by which Islamic authority in the Qur'an, *hadith*, and *sunna* are perpetuated. Adequation is very much alive and well in economizing processes in Amman due, in no small part, to the reinvention of the tradition of morally, socially, politically, and economically idyllic life in early Islam (Eickelman and Piscatori 1996; Hobsbawm and Ranger 1983, 1–14).

As witnessed during Ramadan and with the *hijab*, attempts to Islamize economic processes, specifically, are complicated by the lack of an agreed-upon, systemic understanding of just what this entails. The Islamic bank employees often articulate widely diverse visions for a contemporary Islamic economy. This trajectory of uncertainty and disagreement continues, as there is very limited consensus at the Islamic bank as to whether such economic actions can or should be Islamized at all, and wide disagreement on many of the methods of Islamic finance that attempt to do so (Henry and Wilson 2004; Warde 2004, 17–36).

Islamic economics, banking, and finance demonstrate that everyday piety is not an economized consumptive act that occurs solely during Ramadan or in relation to the *hijab*. Everyday piety also a productive act. Because consumers are also producers, there is relatively little consensus and moral and ethical certainty about what exactly inheres in producing the real Islam in economic practices, the relationship to Shari'a, and how to bridge the gaps of adequation between a normative construction of the real Islam with the consumption of Islamic economics that is a convincing and appealing, everyday, practical reality.

## Shari'a and Islamic Economics: A Historical Overview

The general application of Islamic law to economic practices is not a new idea. In fact, it goes back to the very founding of Islam, the life of the Prophet Muhammad, and the *ahl al-salaf*, or first generations of Muslim scholars (Berkey 2003; Heck 2006; Kuran 2011; Rodinson 1978; Tripp 2006).

During the first two hundred years of Islam (approx. 610–820 CE), the divine revelation and the sayings and traditions of the Prophet Mohammed were collected, organized, and authenticated in the Qur'an, *hadith*, and *sunna*. To make sense of these, at times divergent traditions, a plurality of localized and Islamic jurisprudential and interpretive traditions, or *fiqh*, developed in a kind of decentralized "ethical imaginary" (Hefner 2011, 2). These volumes provided the new Muslims with localized bodies of knowledge and reference points for embarking on their everyday lives in new Muslim communities. Over time, the Qur'an, *hadith*, and *sunna* became consolidated and ranked for their reliability, truthfulness, and authenticity. Those same efforts put wind in the sails of a consolidated *fiqh*. As the third century after the advent of Islam passed, four primary *fiqh* traditions emerged for Sunnis (*madhhab*, pl. *madhaahib*). The four schools, named after founders Maliki, Hanafi, Shafi'i, and Hanbali, offered interpretations on everything "from prayer, diet, and dress to commerce, taxation, and warfare" (Hefner 2011, 11). Rather than practicable law, Shari'a offered general ideals for a good, Muslim life in a community. For example, professing the faith in community prayer made an early appearance, as did dealing honestly in business transactions and supporting a woman's right to own property—a practice that was already occurring in Mecca at the advent of Islam (Ahmed 1992, 53).

This process of Shari'a consolidation and codification began with Islam's early traders and artisans (Zubaida 2003, 4). From the very beginning Shari'a spoke to economic practices (Berkey 2003, 61–69; Lings 1994; Vikor 2005; Zubaida 2003), promoted entrepreneurialism (Nasr 2009), and began as a predominantly oral, ethical, and socially diffuse and informal process (Calder 1993; Zubaida 2003, 21). Within the context of ethnoreligious pluralism that characterized early Islam, an urban, middle-class bias emerged, and what would be considered contemporary ideas of individual privacy, responsibility, and initiative (within the limits of the community) are present in the *fiqh* of early jurists (Berkey 1992; 2003, 119–21). Fostering honest market dealings was of early interest, and the *muhtasib*—those tasked with "commanding right and forbidding wrong" (Cook 2000)—were its enforcers (Berkey 2003, 121). In fact, much of Shari'a is designed to promote entrepreneurialism and a commercial spirit.

In contrast to contemporary concerns, most of these early Islamic responses to economic practices did not greatly emphasize more productive aspects of banking procedures, investment methods and types, or entrepreneurship as the means of Islamizing economic realities. Rather, Islam developed in an early capitalist society (Rodinson 1978), supporting trade and a massive commercial empire that eventually spanned three continents (Heck

2006, 3). A distinctively Islamic approach and early responses by Muslim so-cieties focused on ethics of consumption and certain lifestyle developments, including prohibitions against alcohol and pork, the purification of animals for eating, and the regulations of modes of dress. In fact, many of the early developments of an "Islamic economy" would be better characterized in terms of the development of a "moral economy," which grew out of a need for the "ethical regulation of human transactions" as a means to protect against the fracturing of society (Tripp 2006, 31).

As the centering and development of Shari'a occurred, so too did the understandings and applications of it on economic transactions. It assumed a conventional form on a limited range of topics such as bans on usury and interest, implementation of inheritance law, and the enforcement of some technical aspects of rule of law in contractual arrangements (Heck 2006; Henry and Wilson 2004; Kahf 2004, 18). These emerging points of consen-sus, however, did not directly determine or regulate all aspects of economic life. Accommodations and variability, particularly during a long and extensive period of Empire growth and economic flux, were common (Heck 2006).

Where there were conflicts between Islamic precepts and market demands in the large-scale Islamic empires, the "Books of Ruses and Circumventions" or *Kutub al-Hiyal wa al-Makharij*, enabled accommodations (Heck 2006, 6, 93–98). In short, the Hanafi school of law developed a series of ruses or "special exercises in juridical sophistry whereby the promulgators sought to craft legal circumventions of certain practices, that, on their surfaces, seem-ingly violated their religion's ban" on certain transactions (Heck 2006, 93). This was particularly true for interest-based *riba'* transactions (Henry and Wilson 2004; Kahf 2004, 18). These *hiyal*, or ruses, were legalistic accom-modations made to promote certain economic transactions without violat-ing Islamic law, at least technically speaking. Even in the early days of Islam and through the Ottoman Empire, Shari'a was a "flexible anchor" invoked in legal transactions when it might be particularly financially fortuitous, but not always.

These early utilizations of Shari'a to enable and foster economic transac-tions continue. One of the more prominent examples of this maneuvering in early Islam occurred in the 'Araya contract, which allows for the barter of unripened dates on a tree against their value as calculated in terms of edible fruit. Such a speculative contract can be considered—technically speaking—in violation of Qur'anic injunctions. However, the technicality was generally overlooked in order to provide for the livelihood of the growers; it was a pragmatic alteration, but not an arbitrary one (Zubaida 2003, 16). This ar-rangement demonstrates that the early work of *fiqh* served to inject religious and ethical content into commonly occurring practices, not to establish a structure against which Muslims were to measure themselves and their actions. As a result, local customary conduct in economic dealings was injected with an Islamic scriptural and prophetic ethic, even above and in opposition to strict interpretations of Qur'anic injunctions (Zubaida 2003, 18). In its origins, Shari'a's ethical orientation enabled Muslims to utilize established alternatives and bypass unfavorable transactions.

Today's Islamic banking practices still utilize many of these early accommodations. For example,

> Ubida b. al-Samit reported the Prophet Mohammed (Peace Be Upon Him) said, "Gold is to be paid for gold, silver for silver, wheat for wheat, barley for barley, dates for dates, and salt for salt, same quantity for same quantity and equal for equal, payment being made on the same spot." (Cited in Sahih Muslim, Book 9, *Hadith* 3853; Muslim ibn al-Hajjaj 2000, 1007.)

One popular means around the conditions of quantities, equities, and spot payment was to engage in two separate contracts that each does not, in and of itself, violate the terms of the *hadith*. In collaboration, however, they accomplish desirable outcomes that a single Islamic contract would not make possible: person #1 sells a bushel of wheat to person #2 in exchange for, say, two bushels of barley. Then person #2 sells two bushels of wheat to person #1 in exchange for, say, two bushels of barley at a later period. This arrangement effectively enabled person #1 to buy one bushel of wheat without spot payment and without violating the terms of the *hadith* above. This "double exchange contract" was used in the medieval period to "sell gold for gold" without spot payment, which is expressly forbidden by this *hadith*. This is the basis for today's liquidity-raising and somewhat controversial arrangement, *tawarruq,* or Reverse *murabaha,* described below. This early proviso was the subject of much creative juridical work (Heck 2006, 94–95).

By the Ottoman Era, Muslims "entered into contracts that followed an Islamic template and were enforced through Islamic courts" (Kuran 2011, 7). This integration of Islamic law into legal-economic orderings has been well documented (Masters 1988, 2004). For example, the *mudaraba* contract (discussed below) explained and justified the example of the early economic relationship between the Prophet Mohammed and Khadija, the woman who became his first wife. *Mudaraba,* once legitimated and popularized, continued. It is found throughout the Ottoman Era, and is, in fact, present throughout the Mediterranean basin during the sixteenth through eighteenth centuries

(Masters 1988, 50). Historically speaking, Islamic economics was anchored in Shari'a to the degree that it endorsed certain preexisting, customary, and technical contractual arrangements rather than serving as a primary force in the production of new financial methods and instruments.

During the Ottoman Era, Islamic contracts expanded to included provisions for social justice, protections for personal and privately owned property, limitations on the abuse of wealth, and fortifications for a sacredness of contract (Masters 1988, 187) and the perpetuation of wealth through enforcement of Islamic inheritance laws (Kuran 2011, 7). The *Mejelle* (Tyser, Demtriades, and Ismail 1967) and works by Edhem Eldem (1999, with Goffman and Masters 1999), Timur Kuran (2011), and Charles Wilkins (2009), among others, point to these systematic applications of Islamic law in the enforcement and regulations of certain economic transactions during the Ottoman Era. In fact, as Kuran points out, during the mid-nineteenth century, the world entered into the period of modern economic growth, characterized by self-sustaining economic expansion as well as "rapid technological change, the doubling of life spans, massive urbanization, and the means of mobilizing abundant capital through complex organizations" (Kuran 2011, 13, 23). Nevertheless, much of the Muslim—particularly Ottoman—world lacked the institutional capacities and transformations necessary to accommodate the new financial needs prompted by this modern economic growth (Kuran 2011, 13–14). Furthermore, many of the institutions and processes of economic production, consumption, and distribution came under the influence or direct control of non-Muslims (Heck 2006; Kuran 2011; Masters 1988). Muslims and Shari'a contracts were neither keeping up with the changes sweeping the economic world during the nineteenth century, nor regulating them. During the Ottoman Era, Shari'a as a tool for an Islamic economics was largely passed by.

Therefore, it was relatively late in the Muslim engagement with Western economic powers—namely the latter part of the twentieth century—a broad-based and self-conscious concern with formulating a systemic Islamic response to complex, modern economic challenges emerged, one that emphasized the production of distinctly Islamic goods and services. This contemporary movement, therefore, differs from the earlier vetting of "Islamicness" in the realms of consumption or through earlier ethical-contractual regulation or enforcement.

The tensions and opportunities created by the penetration of modern advanced capitalism and, most recently, consumer capitalism and neoliberal reforms into Muslim-majority societies such as Jordan have presented new and unprecedented demands for altered economic arrangements (Guazzone

and Pioppi 2009). These were defined not only by the strength of Western
economic ascendance but also by twentieth-century events including the
Islamic Resurgence (as discussed in chapters 1 and 2) and heightened expectations for public piety and orthopraxy (as discussed in chapters 3 and 4). In
fact, it is well-documented that the "surge in Islamic banking and finance
is part of the much larger phenomenon of Islamic reassertion" (Henry and
Wilson 2004, 2; Vogel and Hayes 1998, 21, 25–26, 29). In these large-scale
programs of change, actor-oriented assertions of authentic Islam are both
accessible and important.

## Islamic Economics in the Twentieth Century

In the 1940s Indian Muslims launched what became today's Islamic economics out of a desire to define an Islamic civilization that was set apart from
foreign cultural influences (Kuran 2004, 39). Later on, the writings of the
Pakistani ideologist Sayyid Abul-Ala Mawdudi established the term "Islamic
Economics" (2009). *The Islamization of Knowledge Debates in Saudi Arabia*
(Abaza 2002) describes the push for a new methodology for the discipline
of economics, envisioning it as a vehicle for establishing and recentering Islamic authority in a domain that was increasingly falling under the influence
of Western ideas (Kuran 2004, 39; Maurer 2005, 29). In the first half of the
twentieth century, the impulse and agitation for an Islamic economics was
found throughout the Muslim world.

The cultural meanings in an Islamic economics as an intellectual tradition and revivalist form of knowledge were intentional from the beginning
(Tripp 2006, 103–18). Islamic economics was "Islamized" knowledge that
carried economic, developmental, and social goals (Warde 2004, 40; Henry
and Wilson 2004). The movement rejected a Western, value-free approach to
social science, and it strove to develop the discipline of economics while still
upholding ideological, cultural, and political ends that remained distinctly
Islamic. These values and interests became important when some producers
aimed to bring an Islamized abstraction into contemporary methods and
applications, namely in the form of Islamic banking and finance. In fact,
the principles informing the methodology manifest into two distinguish-
able elements that became the basis for the technical development of Islamic
banking and finance methodologies: the prohibition of interest and regulation of the religious injunction on almsgiving and taxation, or *zakat* (Kuran
2004, 39).

Islamic banking and finance, in its most recent expressions, asserts that the
laws and institutions put forth by Shari'a provide a "just and equitable model

for economic growth" by creating a "third way," which balances the social justice and equality underpinnings of socialism with capitalist entrepreneurialism and the commercial traditions of Islam (Hefner 2006a, 2000b). In other words, contemporary capitalist practices that are often categorized as neoliberal have put wind into the sails of a morally oriented Islamic economics. The latter is an intellectual, cultural, and economic "invented tradition" that upholds terms for an alternative approach to the dominant capitalist system. In accordance with the idea that Islam is a "total way of life," Islamic economics—in its most abstract and rigorous form—is an ambitious project of reforming all economic practices (Kuran 2004, 2).

At the same time, the most recent expression of Islamic economics in the form of Islamic banking and finance is very much reliant upon new technologies, contemporary forms and styles of implementation, and the steady growth of public ethics and consumer demands—including neoliberal technologies and ethical projects—that continue to fuel their shaping and reshaping. This socioreligious shift has brought forth unanticipated results: economic power now also generates the implementation of Shari'a (Henry and Wilson 2004; Kahf 2004, 32), which serves as a prompt for neoliberal piety. Rather than being passed by in the global economy, Shari'a is being turned into a tool to promote distinctly Islamic banking and finance methods, with highly inconclusive results. Islamic banking in both aspirational and practical forms is experimental, relatively untested, and often fails to inculcate individuals with the intended values and symbolic meanings, instead appearing as an Islamic veneer or window dressing on otherwise conventional practices. Islamic banking, at least in Jordan, remains a niche, alternative market with an uncertain future.

## Islamic Banking and Finance Methods: Technicalities and Justifications

Since the late 1980s, widespread consensus has emerged on one of Islamic banking's basic contractual and technical principles, the Qur'anic injunction against *riba'*,[6] which translates literally as "increase" but is most frequently understood as "interest." It is frequently interpreted as a universal prohibition against both usurious and non-usurious rates of interest (El-Gamal 2006; Hefner 2006a, 2006b; Kuran 2004; Maurer 2005; Tripp 2006; Warde 2010, 2001). By extension, many also believe there to be a prohibition against profit without risk (Kuran 2004, 8; Warde 2009, 2004, 2010, 2001). Islamic banking developers and practitioners define this as interest, which is calculated when there is a guaranteed increase on one's capital over the passage of time. A prohibition against profit without risk really means that there should be no increase in capital without potential loss. Thus, risk is required as a guarantee against interest. This idea is extended to banks where the notion that lenders can receive increase in the form of interest on their capital loans, without taking on risk, is widely rejected.

Such prohibitions and interpretations of interest have resulted in three primary forms or methods of banking and financial services, which approximate the venture capitalism and lease financing found at conventional, or non-Islamic, banks.[7] The first form is *mudaraba*, in which an investor or group of investors entrusts an entrepreneur with capital, who then invests in a particular productive or trade venture for a share of the profits or a commission. Upon completing the venture, the entrepreneur returns the principal and a prespecified share of the resulting profits to the investors (Kuran 2004, 8). This is the model that the Prophet Mohammed and his first wife, Khadija, are said to have exemplified in their joint commercial enterprises.

According to the *hadith* and historical sources (Lings 1994, 33–35), Khadija bint Khuwaylid had inherited wealth from her father, a successful sixth-century merchant, and had managed it quite well. A wealthy woman in pre-Islamic Arabia, Khadija had married and been widowed twice before Mohammed, and had received many other offers of marriage. Khadija's business strategy was to send out trade caravans from Mecca to areas as far north as Syria. She relied on the traders to make profitable sales on her behalf, compensating them with commissions. At the end of the sixth century, Khadija, then forty years old, needed a reliable trader to bring a caravan to Syria. Family members recommended Mohammed, a twenty-five-year-old relative of Khadija's who had gained a reputation as honest and trustworthy. In fact, his reputation was so outstanding and the need for this trade caravan to be successful was so high that Khadija offered Mohammed twice the normal commission. Her investment paid off: based on Mohammed's business savvy, profits doubled and business flourished. The endeavor was successful enough that Khadija and Mohammed became endeared to each other and married the following year.

Whether this story is an example of divine intervention or merely good business sense, the fact remains that this relationship is often upheld as the first model for an ideal Islamic business relationship. In this method, Khadija was the *mudarib* and source for capital, and Mohammed was the entrepreneur entrusted with capital for trade. Though this arrangement existed prior to the revelation of Islam, because this was the Prophet Mohammed's model economic relationship it served as the first *halal*, or permissible, financing practice in the Islamic tradition.

*Musharaka* is similar to *mudaraba*. However, in this second form the entrepreneur exposes her own capital for both profit and loss, rather than solely the capital of the *mudarib*. This second model is based upon the relationship established between the Muslims from Mecca and the Prophet Mohammed's *ansaar*, or helper hosts in Medina. For many Muslims, this the most important story in the history of Islam. In 622, Mohammed and his early followers were warned of an assassination plot in Mecca. Over the course of two weeks, the Muslims left Mecca in the Hijra, a series of movements designed to help them escape capture and ultimately find safe refuge in Medina. There, the Muslim *ansaar* offered up their resources to assist the Meccan emigrants.

Initially, the group directed their energies toward building the first house of worship in Islam, the Quba Mosque, which exists today. To further solidify the shared work and shared outcomes model for a new, integrated life between the Meccans and Medinans, Mohammed set about matching Meccan emigrants, or *muhajerun*, with host Medinans, or *ansaar*, in shares of work, land, and capital far beyond the mosque construction. These "brothers" and fictive kin shared their labor, and profits and losses were incurred together at a prescribed ratio. As Martin Lings explains:

> In order to unite the community of believers still further, the Prophet now instituted a pact of brotherhood between the Helpers (*ansaar*) and the Emigrants (*muhajerun*), so that each of the Helpers would have an Emigrant brother who was nearer to him than any of the Helpers, and each Emigrant would have a Helper brother who was nearer to him than any Emigrant. But the Prophet made himself and his family an exception, for it would have been too invidious for him to choose as his brother one of the Helpers rather than another. (Lings 1994, 128)

This arrangement comprises the earliest justification and incorporation of *musharaka* into Islamic tradition and Shari'a.

The third form of business relationship involves cost-plus or lease financing. *Murabaha*[8] is a cost-plus form of ownership transfer for goods and is the most popular financing or sale mode in Islamic banks (Kuran 2004, 10). Again, following the idea that banks should not profit without taking on some risk, a producer or trader tells them about the types of goods she is interested in purchasing. The bank purchases the items, marks up the price by a known margin, and then physically and/or contractually transfers ownership to the client, who pays the elevated amount either on the spot or in scheduled payments.

Despite this financing mode's popularity,[9] there is no singular Qur'anic or *hadith*-based example after which this is modeled. *Murabaha* is believed to have existed prior to the advent of Islam; it was folded into the economic practices of early Muslims and later documented and explicated in the *hadith*.

In a departure from *mudaraba* relationships, there is no sacred story rendering this arrangement distinctly "Islamic." It was a part of "the tradition" in a vague way that persisted without direct reference in the Qur'an. In the first formally coded book of the Prophet Mohammed's traditions, *Al-Muwatta*, Imam Malik reports:

> The generally agreed on way of doing things among us about a man buying cloth in one city, and then taking it to another city to sell as a *murabaha*, is that he is not reckoned to have the wage of an agent, or any allowance for ironing, folding, straightening, expenses, or the rent of a house. As for the cost of transporting the cloth, it is included in the basic price, and no share of the profit is allocated to it unless the agent tells all of that to the investor. If they agree to share the profits accordingly after knowledge of it, there is no harm in that. (Book 31, *Hadith* 36; Cited in Ibn Anas 1989, 271)

This *hadith* models two important facets of *murabaha* transactions. First, the seller discloses his cost—narrowly defined—to the buyer. Second, the profit is transparent, known to and agreed upon by both parties. The disclosure of cost and profit in sales and financing assumes transparency and honesty in dealings, which lends itself to discussions of the role of Islamic ethics in such transactions. This cost-plus financing becomes legitimate from an Islamic standpoint because there is technically no interest involved in the sale, and the banks or traders have taken on ownership and exposed themselves to risk for some time. Physical or contractual ownership for even a fraction of a second can legitimate this, exposing the bank or trader to a measure of risk.

The Shari'a grounds for this arrangement is retroactively legitimated with Qur'an 2:279, in which "Allah has permitted trade and forbidden *riba*'," which scholars have interpreted to mean that trade with a profit (*ribah*) is valid, but a trade with interest (*riba*') is not. In addition, the goods sold must meet some basic criteria for sale; for example, their condition must be clear, transparent, and known before the sale, in order to avoid *gharrar*, or speculation, which is also forbidden (Warde 2010). The goods must exist in tangible form, and they cannot be used in a "buy-back" arrangement in which only two parties contract to buy, sell, and resell them to each other.[10]

## Islamic Banking and Finance: Shari'a-Derived Understandings

These three types of Islamic financing remain the center of technical and methodological efforts in Islamic banking and finance. Most Islamic banks offer these services and most Shari'a committees would agree on their Islamic "soundness." Beyond this point, however, the Islamic underpinnings for transactions and financing have more variability and lack strong consensus. In the case of *mudaraba* or *musharaka*, the average consumer educated in basic Islamic history may consider the Qur'anic examples of Khadija and Mohammed as well as the socio-economic relationships between the *muhajerun* and *ansaar* in Medina striking, clear, and understandable. However, when moving into types of *murabaha*, the rulings and establishments of the methods are based more clearly upon extrapolation from guiding principles in Shari'a rather than a more direct imitation of Qur'anic examples.

One means by which extrapolation and inference occurs when examining the permissibility of Islamic banking and finance arrangements, rather than a more strict modeling found *mudaraba* and *musharaka*, is by way of systematizing, categorizing, and then approving or disallowing the products and services for investment; they are considered technically *haram* (forbidden) or *halal* (permissible). This expansion of audit culture (Strathern 2000) into Islamizing products and services demonstrate that assessments of the processes of economization in Islamic banking and finance are highly rationalized. Products and services have now been vetted for investment in accordance with nine categories or "screens" (Alchaar and Sandra 2006, Warde 2010).[11] The industry forbids:

1. Committing business with conventional banks in such a way that violates Islamic fundamentals such as through interest payments or debts; derivatives, futures, or securities; and Foreign Exchange for fixed-terms.
2. Engaging in conventional insurance or accompanying activities.
3. Profiting from alcohol production, consumption, selling, and marketing.
4. Dealing in illicit drugs.
5. Profiting from gambling, even if it falls under a name like "lotto," sports betting, or financing the structures for that purpose.
6. Profiting from pork production, processing, or sales.
7. Financing any sexually explicit entertainment, prostitution, nightclubs, or other related activities, which usually include pornography but not beachwear or lingerie sales.
8. Making any transactions that lack appropriate levels of knowledge and awareness, or take on excessive risk, or involve interest.
9. Transacting any business involving weaponry.

This last item, "Any business involving weaponry," is highly debated. Some sources do not reference this at all. Some say that investing in weaponry is acceptable as long as the weapons are not used against Muslims (Salam 2009). One member of Shari'a Compliance at the International Islamic Arab Bank indicated that weaponry should be avoided and would not be approved in a number of Islamic banks with which he was familiar.

Clearly, there are items missing from this list that would constitute a measure of consistency with the "spirit" of Islam as derived from Shari'a. The lack of desire to pay employees a fair wage and a disregard for environmental concerns are frequently referenced in critiques of the priorities for Islamic banking and finance. For example, while at the Islamic Council of New England Conference in the fall of 2009, I asked a keynote speaker the question, "How is it *halal* to hire South Asian workers for Islamically funded real estate projects in Dubai, paying them less than a livable wage? Or to invest in Exxon, which was a responsible for one of the largest environmental disasters in recent history?" The speaker replied,

> The inverse is also true. You could invest in Anheuser-Busch, which is known for paying and treating its employees well, and probably for some environmental consciousness, but that doesn't make it *halal* either. The bottom line is that they produce alcohol and that is *haram*.

As this case shows, an elaborated, marketized logic holds true: these eight (or nine) screens are the principal means by which the industry examines the soundness of assets and investments. Other values and priorities, including those that may violate the spirit of Islamic banking and finance, such as treating employees unjustly or committing acts that damage the environment, are outside the current set of ethics and threshold criteria in the industry for establishing investment soundness.

Adequation reveals tensions between the abstract aspirations for concrete and convincing Islamic financial institutions, the daily challenges of sorting through the technical requirements of Shari'a, and the often-conflicting interpretations required to enact such aims. Certainly, it would be difficult to find someone—particularly an Imam or other Islamic leader—who would agree that paying a livable wage or protecting the environment is *unIslamic*. In fact, it would likely be possible to find a religious leader who supported such endeavors as distinctly Islamic and coherent with the spirit of Islam, if not directly derived from Shari'a.[12] However, when put into a position of competing Islamic values and priorities—such as prompted by working at Anheuser-Busch—those that are more clearly in consensus take priority, such as the aversion to alcohol. These Islamic values and ethical injunctions exist in a set of competing priorities that shift depending on how consensus changes with context and circumstances. I have also heard it argued that typically less-agreed upon values for Islamic banks, such as fair pay for work and ethics of environmentalism, are not given priority because of their "Western origins." Whether this construction of a genealogy of values as Western is factually true or not, this kind of statement works to marginalize many "competing Islams" and prompt Muslims in Amman to build and rebuild attempts at consensus with select interpretations and understandings of the real Islam based in a localized authenticity.

## History of Islamic Banking in Jordan

Within a few decades of Mawdudi's development of the term "Islamic Economics," and at approximately the same time that Islamic banking gained traction in Saudi Arabia, Jordan was emerging from a civil war in which King Hussein and the allied Muslim Brotherhood won over the Palestine Liberation Organization, sending their leaders and followers into exile in Lebanon (Anderson 2005; Robins 2004; Salibi 2006; Schwedler 2006). The resulting political and military alliance between the Muslim Brotherhood and the Hashemite Family proved vital in the establishment of the Islamic banking system in Jordan (Kahf 2004; Malley 2004).

The individual who carried the most influence for Islamic economics in Jordan was Sami Hamoud. Hamoud was an economist, a former employee of the Jordanian National Bank, the son of a prominent Islamic scholar, and a major proponent of the Islamization of economic practices. His doctoral dissertation, published as *Islamic Banking* in 1976, was considered the "most substantial academic piece on Islamic banking that had been written until that time" (Kahf 2004; Malley 2004, 192).

Potential investors at the Arab Bank initially denied financial and technical support to Hamoud for Islamic banking in Jordan. He was also denied legal and operational permissions by Jordan's Central Bank. Shortly thereafter, members of the Muslim Brotherhood became involved. These members of the Muslim Brotherhood, who were also members of the Royal Family, began pushing for the establishment of an Islamic bank that maintained an appearance of independence from both the government and the Muslim Brotherhood. After investors were found in Saudi Prince Mohammed Al-Faisal and Sheikh Saleh Kamel, the Jordan Islamic Bank was established in 1978.

It took another twenty years before the second Islamic Bank was given licensing from the Central Bank—the Islamic International Arab Bank—in

1998 (Malley 2004).[13] A third institution, the Investment House for Financial Services, provides no banking services per se, but is registered as providing investment services in "corporate finance, mergers and acquisitions,
private placements and public offerings, brokerage, financial advisory and
research."[14] Because the Investment House is not a bank, in the sense that it
does not reach the Central Bank's threshold criterion of accepting deposits,
it is not required to be licensed and registered as an "Islamic bank." Another
institution, the Industrial Development Bank, was a government bank that
had aims of privatizing and becoming an Islamic bank. The Dubai Islamic
Bank acquired its assets and took over operations. In 2010, the new Jordan Dubai Islamic Bank began operations as a publicly held institution and
Jordan's third Islamic bank. In 2011, the Saudi-based Al Rajhi Bank began
operations in Jordan. Beyond these, no other conventional or foreign banks
have been granted license by the Central Bank to become Islamic banks or to
offer Shari'a-compliant financial services through an Islamic "window." The
expectation was that three or four more Islamic banks would be licensed in
the upcoming years, due primarily to the increased demand. As is discussed
below and in later chapters, however, the context for formal institutionalized Islamic banking changes rapidly. In an effort to avoid the licensure
difficulties, other institutions such as microfinance organizations have taken
on Islamic methodologies and are able to do so without license as a "bank."

## Contemporary Islamic Banking in Jordan

Of the twenty-five financial institutions in Jordan as of 2012, thirteen are
publicly owned conventional banks, eight are foreign, and four are Islamic.
Despite this diversity, the Arab Bank and the Housing Bank for Trade and
Finance effectively control more than fifty percent of the market share.
The other twenty-three institutions compete for the rest of the market by
identifying and reaching "niche markets." The four Islamic banks have
garnered their niches as religious institutions; other banks, such as Standard Chartered, cater to corporate clients. Standard Chartered, Citibank,
and HSBC have attempted to enter the realm of Islamic banking through
Islamic "windows," hoping to reach large industrial and corporate Islamic
clients, but have not been granted licensing for Islamic operations by the
Central Bank.

Customer satisfaction with the Jordan Islamic Bank and the Islamic International Arab Bank remains relatively low, although the latter has a better
reputation. One informant described the buildings at the Jordan Islamic
Bank as "dark and drab, with nothing but a rusty ceiling fan for ventilation."

Corruption is considered common, and management poor (Malley 2004, 210–12). Cynicism that the Islamic banks and their financial services are not altogether different from the traditional banks is high, and not wholly unjustified. As a former Jordan Islamic Bank employee informed me, "We used to take the contracts, print them out on paper with green trim and put a '*Bismillah*'[15] at the top and—wham—it became 'Islamic!'"

Such negative impressions of the Islamic banks do not go unnoticed by the competition. The CEO of HSBC in Jordan expressed a confident interest in his bank's ability to provide quality Islamic banking services to individual customers because "we could show them [the Islamic banks] how to do it." Standard Chartered has expressed interest in providing Islamic services to large industrial and corporate clients. Clearly, the appeal to these banks for entering a poor-performing niche market by providing competitive financial services to all customers is strong.

The overt and covert ties between the ruling government, the Islamic banks, and the Muslim Brotherhood, as well as a governmental fear of growing Islamization, is often speculated upon (Malley 2004, 210–12; Wilson 1987, 1991) and has been discussed as a primary reason for the denial of further licensing by the Central Bank for new Islamic banks or for Shari'a-compliant services in non-Islamic banks (Wilson 1987, 210). To the contrary, when I interviewed the Deputy Governor of the Central Bank of Jordan, she denied that any political or religious considerations are regarded when licensing new banks. She added, "We actually prefer to work with foreign banks because they tend to have higher levels of knowledge, experience, know how, and experience outside their own country." Regardless of the real or perceived fears of Islamic fundamentalism or relationships that link the government to economic functioning in Jordan, the Jordan Islamic Bank and the Muslim Brotherhood have attempted to use the bank's economic and political positioning to create innovative adequations and to allow certain normative ethics in economic behaviors for a modern Islam to penetrate. Dahiyat Al-Rawdah is a case in point.

## Islamized Spaces: The Case of Dahiyat Al-Rawdah

Dahiyat Al-Rawdah, or "Neighborhood of the Garden," is the result of investment efforts by the Jordan Islamic Bank in 1981 (Wilson 1987, 220–21). Previous to this experiment, Jordanian law did not allow banks to participate in non-banking practices such as selling buildings or buying cars, which are now common practices of Islamic banks. Altering this arrangement required a change in the law, which is not a particularly expedient process and was cited at the Central Bank as one of the reasons why Islamic banking has been somewhat slow to grow. In this investment endeavor, the Jordan Islamic Bank acquired approximately ten acres of land in north Amman as the minority stakeholder, but full owner and controller of the project. The scheme, aimed at the Jordanian middle class, included thirty villas, 213 apartments, a mosque at least colloquially termed "Masjid Al-Bank Al-Islamy Al-Urduny," or "the Mosque of the Jordan Islamic Bank," a three-story shopping center, a community hall, a school, and a drive-up ATM for Jordan Islamic Bank account holders. Recently a hair salon for women and a comprehensive medical center have also opened. As of 1998, approximately 1,460 people lived in this complex (Abu-Ghazzeh 2002).

According to one informant, the complex was established as the "ideal Islamic community," and was referenced by a number of the people I interviewed as "Al-Hay Al-Ikhwaan," or "the Muslim Brotherhood Neighborhood." It was also, ironically, the area in which I received the highest levels of sexual harassment, which one day culminated in a chase by two men in front of the mosque and around the Jordan Islamic Bank ATM, where I found a taxi driver willing to drive me out of the neighborhood.

The notion of the Jordan Islamic Bank becoming involved in the construction of a shopping mall and ATM alongside a housing and community complex is not foreign to banks in general. Financial institutions have a long history of corporate social responsibility in various forms. As the CEO of Standard Chartered Bank in Amman told me, "Banks *do* community service." However, investing in the construction and operations of a mosque or an "ideal Islamic community" is not the norm at conventional banks. The Jordan Islamic Bank has taken a structure and tradition of bank involvement in communities and in community service, and attempted to "Islamize" it by building its own mosque. Such comprehensive community service and community planning enables the bank to push a singular, comprehensive notion of an authentic Islam, the *real* Islam.

In addition to building, promoting, and sustaining a community who, at least in theory, could live every day in this "total way of life" and attend to all needs within walking distance, the Jordan Islamic Bank's advertising and self-promotion in the neighborhood are everywhere. This is both an Islamic and a highly commercialized neighborhood. The mosque is named after the bank. The open-air shopping mall is organized around a story-high Jordan Islamic Bank logo. The drive-up ATM is conveniently located just below the mosque's sign at a busy corner across the street from the largest newspaper in Jordan, *Al-Rai*, and its English equivalent, *The Jordan Times*. Green is the color of Islam, and it is also the color of the Jordan Islamic Bank.[16] Sign letters and trim are painted in the same shade to reflect a consistent—and Islamic—theme throughout the neighborhood (see figure 10).

The notion that a neighborhood could somehow become adequately Islamic and "Islamized" into a comprehensive, complete Islamic community appears to be met with the same skepticism and cynicism that Sharifa expressed about Dr. Hamid: there is no singular way to produce "the *real* Islam" in economic practices. As an architect at a local firm in Amman indicated,

> I think Islamic architects who want to create "Islamic space" try to find ways of spatially codifying "Islamic values." So they might pay attention to single-family privacy, for instance, or space for women. But a lot of times it becomes just putting arches around [the complex] or dropping a big ol' mosque in the middle.

In addition to the skepticism and cynicism of the Islamic nature of Al-Rawdah, the space itself is neither particularly aesthetically pleasing nor comfortable for the tenants. As two residents described,

> The elevator always smells like urine and is run-down. There are all these weird inclines instead of stairs. The kids are always outside

**FIGURE 10**    Dahiyat Al-Rawdah shopping mall and mosque, 2014. Photo by the author.

roller-blading, and people gather in the hallways because there aren't any good places to sit outside. The contrast between the areas outside the apartment and inside the apartment is really amazing. It's so nice inside the apartments, but a total disaster outside.

The neighborhood of Al-Rawdah fails to adequately embody and transmit Islamic values from the intent and physical structure of the community to the residents. It does not bridge the gap of adequation, bringing together an Islamic abstraction with the reality. Furthermore, the exterior aesthetics are devoid of the modern touches demanded by the Ammani public, instead pushing unorthodox architectural styles with inclines and lacking sanitary upkeep.

The same is true for the knowledge transmitted from the neighborhood mosque to the community, which also does not provide for a believable or adequate Islamized message for Islamic living with a modern aesthetic. Wizarat Al-Awqaaf wa al-Shu'oon al-Islamiya, or the Ministry of Islamic Affairs and Endowments, is the governmental section responsible for the management of all mosques in Jordan. Although a donation of land, materials, and labor will bring forth a mosque named after the donor, most typically a local family, the organizational maintenance and staffing of the mosque is taken over by the government. The Mosque of the Jordan Islamic Bank (Masjid Al-Bank Al-Islamy Al-Urduny) is no exception. Although it offers classes in Qur'anic recitation, or *tajweed*, the primary knowledge coming from the mosque is the publicly broadcast Friday *khutba*, or religious address. The Imams, under the employment and legal rulings of the Ministry, are given a list of appropriate and acceptable topics for each Friday's *khutba*, straying from which can and does lead to imprisonment. As such, any messages about "acting rightly" in economic practices are neither radicalized nor outside of the realm of the Imam's personal insertions into authorized *khutba* topics. When the Imam seeks to make some reference to "acting rightly" in economic practices, his comments reflect perspectives such as the following:

- "The message of Mohammed (PBUH) is great and a cure for many problems—economic, social, and so on."
- On the opening *aya*, or verse, of the *sura*, or chapter of the Qur'an on the Israa, or night journey of Mohammed to Jerusalem: "The *aya* is the logo and the trademark of the *sura*."

In the first example, the overall message of the Imam reiterates and glosses over the larger message of Islamic economics and Islamic banking: that Islam is a total way of life that will rightly guide you in your economic pursuits. One should, he asserts, turn to the message of the Prophet for answers to economic questions and uncertainties in practice. In the second example, the language of the consumer economy—"logo" and "trademark"—is used as a reference point and icon to orient the story of the Prophet Mohammed's night journey. It is a message that highly promotes the valuation and marketization in Islamic practice. The analogy is that to understand marketing is to understand the Qur'an.

The opening verse of the chapter titled Israa in the Qur'an (17:1) reads,

> Exalted is Allah who took His Servant by night from al-Masjid al-Haram [the Sacred Mosque in Mecca] to al-Masjid al-Aqsa [the Farthest Mosque in Jerusalem], whose surroundings We have blessed, in order that we might show him of Our signs. Indeed, Allah hears and sees all things.

The Qur'an then goes on to describe the *Israa* of Mohammed from Mecca to Jerusalem. Mohammed woke in the middle of the night to visit the *ka'aba* at al-Masjid al-Haram, the most holy space in Islam. During this visit, he fell asleep. He was awakened three times by the Angel Gabriel, who led him out of the mosque. At the gate was Buraq, a "white animal that was smaller than a mule and bigger than a donkey . . ." Its "step was so wide that it reached the farthest point within the reach of the animal's sight" (cited in Sahih Bukhari Book 63, *Hadith* 3887; Bukhari 1987, 132–36). The story goes on to describe Mohammed riding Buraq and traveling with the Angel Gabriel from Mecca over Medina and Khaybar, until they reached Jerusalem. There, Mohammed tied Buraq to the Western Wall, where the Prophets Abraham, Moses, and Jesus met him. They prayed together, with the Prophets lined up behind Mohammed.

Both of the statements from the mosque quoted above demonstrate moments of co-production that also constitute attempts at adequation in Dahiyat Al-Rawdah. In the first, Islam is a "cure-all" for economic ills. In the second, economic orderings of a logo and a trademark become metaphors for organizing and understanding the relationship between the opening verse of the Qur'anic chapter and the rest of the story. In these moments, the Imam reproduces messages of Islamization and of Islamic economics structurally, rhetorically, and without additional commentary. The assumption is that the typical *khutba* listener knows enough about both Islam and economics to understand and conceptually organize the references.

As these examples show, attempts at making "adequately Islamic" the physical and discursive spaces around individuals can be met with simultaneous cynicism and demand. The physical sections of the complex—the interiors versus the exteriors—are each judged on different merits rather than in sum. These same discursive attempts at knowledge production and reproduction of something deemed "adequately Islamic," however, are more complex. This is particularly true in light of restrictions such as government regulations and a wider set of cultural, social, and rhetorical references, such as those found in the consumer economy. Ultimately, the combined symbolic weight of the Jordan Islamic Bank and the Muslim Brotherhood in Dahiyat Al-Rawdah was not enough to bring about a comprehensive, singular and convincing Islam to the community, as this was the only investment attempt that I found.

The adequation of certain Islamic values, economization, and Islamization are often reified by the producers as a simple and straightforward process with wide appeal: in discourses of status claims ("We have Islam"); in discourses of conversion ("I invite you to Islam"); in technical and methodological arrangements of *mudaraba, musharaka,* and *murabaha*; and in the architectural arrangements of Dahiyat Al-Rawdah. Producers of an Islamic economics undertake these transformations as an overt and obvious alteration of spaces, symbols, meanings, and knowledge with what they hope will be a singular outcome.

Both historically and in the contemporary economy, however, translating abstract ideas of "an Islam" into "this particular Islam" by way of Shari'a is a much more subtle and implicit process. It is complex, and, as this chapter also demonstrates, meanings and knowledge are not produced and consumed directly or in identical ways; they are subject to all kinds of individual interpretations (Barth 1993). Try as Dr. Hamid, the Jordan Islamic Bank, and other producers of Islamic economics and banking and finance might, variation between and among individuals on meanings and knowledge will persist and are revealed in adequation. The fact that there is some consensus on normative notions of Islamic economics does not necessarily imply that the bundle of symbolic meanings and ideas will always confer. A closer examination of the Islamic banks reveals the levels and types of sophistication being brought to bear on attempts to realize abstract and Islamized ideas for economic practices. These processes revealed in adequation further fragment consensus in constructions of a singular Islamic economics in the banking and finance industry. Most interestingly, we see that the sources for the fragmentation in consensus are the very producers of Islamic banking and finance: the employees. This is explored in-depth in chapter 6.

# CHAPTER 6

# Uncertainty Inside the Islamic Bank

## *"Is This the* Real *Islam?"*

Over the course of nearly two years of research, I engaged in participant observation and conducted interviews on perceptions of Islamic banking and finance. Beyond interviews, one of my goals for this study was to gain first-hand experience in an Islamic bank. I spent months trying to find someone who worked at one of the banks and could provide me with an introduction and point of entrée. I asked teachers at the Arabic language school where I studied. I checked with Jordanian and international staff members at the Fulbright office. I sought out local friends and their families, but all lacked any connections. After months of searching without result and exhausting my list of local contacts, I brainstormed new ways to connect with people outside the traditional face-to-face contact that is highly valued in Amman. I logged onto my Facebook account and messaged all those in the Amman network who had an Islamic bank in their profiles. The responses astounded me: All of the people I messaged at the International Islamic Arab Bank offered assistance. One young female replied, "I'll help you. You're an American, and many of my family members are American." After meeting with me several times and getting to know and trust me, she introduced and recommended me to the director of Human Resources. He, in turn, arranged for a five-week internship.

The internship was devised so that I would spend one week in each of the five major departments and with Shariʿa Compliance: the first week was spent in Risk Management, the second in the Treasury Department, the third in the Retail Services Department, and the fourth in the Corporate Services Department. The fifth week was to take me to one of the local branches. Shari'a Compliance, which is not a formal department but rather part of the Auditing Section in Risk Management, was intermixed with my experiences throughout the five weeks.

Toward the beginning of the fourth week, however, when I was with the Corporate Services Department, the head of Human Resources called me into his office. He sat me down and said:

> Sarah, you know I understand you. I understand Americans. I am an American! I have an American passport and I lived in California. I love the Lakers! But, you know, things here in Amman are different. Not everyone knows Americans like I do. The people here, in the head-quarters of the bank, they understand you. They are educated. They are open-minded. They know you.
>
> But next week, you're scheduled to be in the branch, and we can't allow it. We can't allow you to sit with the customers. You're an American. You're white and have blonde hair and blue eyes. You speak Arabic with an accent. Everyone will know you're a foreigner. And you're not a Muslim. This is a reputational risk to our bank. People will think that you're stealing their account information and giving it to the U.S. government. Maybe they'll think you work for the C.I.A.
>
> All these customers will come into the bank, and everyone will see you. You're going to make everyone ask, "Is this bank *really* Islamic? What kind of Islam is this? Is this the *real* Islam?"

On the one hand, many of the employees I encountered at the Islamic bank disagreed with the head of Human Resources that this would be the cus-tomers' perception of my presence at the branch office. Many found the idea of C.I.A. affiliation ridiculous, and they were embarrassed that Human Resources would have suggested it. On the other hand, many of my infor-mants who are customers of the bank agreed: customers would see me in the branch with access to their accounts, wonder about my affiliations, and doubt the credibility of the Islamic bank as sufficiently and authentically, "really Islamic." Despite my best and continued attempts to negotiate the week of training in the branch—including offering to significantly alter my dress and comportment to include wearing the *niqab*, or face veil—I was ultimately denied. Though I was able to spend one month researching in the bank in four departments and with Shari'a Compliance, I was not permitted to conduct research in any of its branches.

As discussed in chapter 5, through adequation we see that there is a tension between abstract aspirations for convincing Islamic financial institutions to embody "the *real* Islam" and the daily challenges of sorting through the technical requirements of Shari'a, their presentation, and their often-conflicting interpretations. This chapter examines the tensions between abstract Islamic aspirations and the technical realms of producing Islamic banking and finance found in these four departments and in Shari'a Compliance. They play out in interesting, revealing, even surprising ways that underscore the fundamental difficulties of producing Islamic banking: the aims of Islamizing banking processes in an everyday sense are complicated by the lack of an agreed-upon systemic understanding of just what Shari'a banking entails and what an authentic Islam looks like in economic actions.

Consensus here is highly fragmented and largely indeterminate. This is because there is a penetrating moral and ethical uncertainty about what exactly inheres in "the *real* Islam" in banking and finance. It revolves around how to bridge the gaps of adequation between a normative construction and the production of an Islamic banking and finance that is a convincing and appealing, everyday, practical reality. This chapter examines the moments of coproduction of Islamizing economic practices and economizing Islamic practices in the heart of these spaces of production—the Islamic bank—and examines the strategies used to create authenticity and modernity. Furthermore, the bank employees themselves both embody and transmit these tensions and uncertainties, as their own understandings of orthopraxy and normativity meet their personal self-interests and practical demands in everyday piety, personal practices and understandings, and hopes and dreams.

As these employees reveal, "the real Islam" in the bank is vague, yet highly debated. It is through these debates that "the real Islam" is constructed. For example, bank policies become established as "Islamic" not through a declaration by one employee, but rather through an interactive, complex, and distributed web of actors and technologies in which individuals exercise power (Hutchins 1995a, 1995b), culminating in something that is simultaneously more than—and different from—the parts any single individual could accomplish. In these moments, marginal interests drop off and cancel out (MacKenzie 2008), which raises consensus and agreement. One employee's input is unlikely to create much of a difference in the outcomes of a policy or procedure, but this remains necessary as part of the larger process. More specifically, the practice of not charging bank customers late fees to avoid the appearance of *riba'* (discussed below), while clearly eliciting individual

employees' dissent, were solidified as "Islamic policies" through commu-
nitarian debates and discussions. More and more powerful employees supported the decision. The strongest of points of consensus—whether achieved
in flat, democratic consensus or by discursive force on the part of those with
greater influence—materialize in the form of public facts and policies without necessarily reflecting individuals' interests, but requiring them nonetheless. "The real Islam" is highly debated and very tenuously discussed, even as
those are the processes and conditions required to construct it.

## Risk Management: Spiritually Pure, Financially Secure

During my week in the Risk Management Department, the discussions often
turned to defining risk, limiting it, and managing it. Although I received
several days' training in physical and structural risk and the bank's emer-
gency management plans, I was most intrigued by the discussions about
defining and managing its financial exposure given the alterations of daily,
routine methods and investments according to Shari'a guidelines, as discussed
in the previous chapter. Specifically, the employees in the Risk Management
Department asserted that Shari'a compliance actually reduced the financial
exposure of the bank. They considered the Islamic bank to be a lower-risk
option than the competing conventional banks, and therefore more appealing
to customers. After all, they were "following the tenets of Islamic banking set
forth by Shari'a," and were therefore authentically or "really Islamic." Shari'a
compliance was deemed an Islamic solution to the technical problem of risk
and a potent combination of better banking and better religion (Tobin 2009).
My time in the Risk Management Department highlights the degree to
which fiscal and discursive accommodations are made to define something
as distinctly and authentically Islamic. The International Islamic Arab Bank
used Shari'a-derived alterations to construct its reputation as a lower-risk
option in several ways. First, the Rate of Return Risk on private customers—
that is, the likelihood of losing anticipated gains from private customers—
was low. According to the staff in the Risk Management Department, the
bank was in this favorable position because its customers were interested in
practicing Islamically informed ethics; as a result, the numbers of delinquent
or default borrowers were minimal. As one bank employee said, "We attract
'real' Muslim clients."

One way to measure this claim of lower risk is to examine the rate of late
payers, or delinquent or default borrowers. When I asked to see the numbers or be given some sort of comparison, I was told that "there are no late
fees or interest charges as penalties; it doesn't work like that here." In fact, a

member of the Shariʻa Committee indicated that non-interest-based late fees "too closely resemble interest-based fees, so we avoid them." Nonetheless, borrowers were given a notice of "late" status after thirty days. After sixty days the Credit Department began calling the now "on notice" borrower for payment, much as a collector would. After ninety days, the account was marked as "delinquent," then as "default," and turned over to the government as a criminal case. At no time was a late fee assessed at the International Islamic Arab Bank. Therefore, the threshold criteria for judging the clients as "delinquent" or "default" borrowers was kept high to limit the risk.

Conventional banks may charge an interest-based fee if a payment is even one day late and aggressively pursue clients within the first three months of non-payment. The Islamic bank did neither of these. There, paying one day late was financially the same as paying eighty-nine days late. I jokingly noted that such a structure could be taken advantage of by borrowers who simply wanted to extend the period of time for repayment: in theory, one could pay the monthly amount every eighty-nine days without consequence. My joke was received with pursed lips and silence, which leads me to believe that perhaps I was not the first one with this idea. Because of this lenient construction, the rate of return risk at the International Islamic Arab Bank was low; most people made their payments within eighty-nine days, and only the most seriously "delinquent" clients were referred to external collections.

Without recourse to strict payment structures or late fees, the bank relied on rigorous prescreening of customers to try to assess their personal sense of moral duty to pay on time and in full. One employee in the Risk Management Department summarized:

> Delinquent clients can get lines of credit at the Arab Bank but not at the International Islamic Arab Bank. This is because their delinquency is less costly to the bank when you can charge late fees and interest than when you won't and can't. This is the problem with the Islamic bank. Our clients cost more, but they're never considered delinquent. Our clients hold a lot of power.

Not charging late fees of any kind is costly. Therefore, prescreening clients for their ability—and expressed desire—to pay on time, had to be considered when monitoring costs. The Islamic bank needed to account for this and placed the responsibility squarely on the shoulders of its employees. "KYC," or "Know Your Customer," was the mantra when setting up new accounts and working with existing customers. It also guided fund transfers, with bank employees responsible for knowing the purpose of each one.

Prescreening and knowing customers' moral dispositions for timely repayment was tied primarily to reported perspectives on debt and a person's
financial ability to repay it. Bank employees often discussed customers' quo-
tation of verses from the Qur'an and *hadith* as markers of the seriousness
with which they approached debt and repayment. The longest such Qur'anic
verse (2:282) speaks to transparency and accountability in writing contracts
about debt repayments:

> O you who believe! When you deal with each other in contracting
> a debt for a fixed time, then write it down; and let a scribe write it
> down between you with fairness . . . And if he who owes the debt
> is weak of mind or body, or, is not able to dictate himself, then let
> his guardian dictate with fairness . . . and be not averse to writing
> it [whether it is] small or large, with the time of its falling due; this
> is more equitable in the sight of God, more reliable as evidence, and
> more likely to prevent you from having doubts later. And remain
> conscious of God, since it is God who teaches you—and God has full
> knowledge of everything.

Customers also recounted stories from the *hadith*. In one example, Sahih
Bukhari documents a frequently retold story about debt repayment that
legitimates both the power held by the creditor and the need for Muslims to
repay debts "handsomely":

> A man came to the Prophet Mohammed and demanded a camel that
> the Prophet owed him in such a rude manner that the companions of
> the Prophet intended to harm him. The Prophet Mohammed said,
> "Leave him, for no doubt, he—the creditor—has the right to demand
> it harshly." The Prophet Mohammed then told his companions to give
> the man a camel. They said, "We cannot find any camels available ex-
> cept an older, better camel than what the man demands." The Prophet
> Mohammed ordered his companions to give the man that camel. The
> man said, "You have paid me in full and may Allah also pay you in full."
> The Prophet said, "The best amongst the people is he who repays his
> debts in the most handsome manner." (Cited in Sahih Bukhari Book
> 43, *Hadith* 2393; Bukhari 1987, 331.)

Debt and repayment reportedly weighed so heavily on the Prophet Mohammed that he ended his prayers with supplications for Allah to provide refuge
from it:

The Prophet Mohammed used to invoke Allah in the prayer saying, "O Allah, I seek refuge with you from all sins, and from being in debt." After prayer, someone said, "O Messenger of God! I see that you often seek refuge with Allah from being in debt." The Prophet replied, "If a person is in debt, he tells lies when he speaks, and breaks his promises when he promises." (Cited in Sahih Bukhari, Book 43, *Hadith* 2396; Bukhari 1987, 334.)

I witnessed bank customers explain their perspectives on debt and repayment through such references to the Qur'an and *hadith*, after which the employees assessed their financial ability to sustain an account and to repay debts. The minimum amount required to open and maintain an account was 200 Jordanian dinars ($282.00), about a month's salary for most people. "Bonuses," typically in the form of waived or lowered administrative fees for loans, were given when customers opted for direct deposit of their monthly salaries, when they were employees of reliable institutions such as the Jordanian government, and when they could show a history of income. The most unreliable customers were those who were self-employed or had erratic incomes; for example, earning a small amount one month and a large amount the next. Here, employing Islamic discourses from Shari'a and the ability and willingness to part with one month's salary as a deposit and consistency in one's financial history were primary markers of ability and willingness to repay debt on time. By extension, these were also markers of one's moral and "real Islamic" character. Shari'a compliance altered the methods by which the bank limited risk and determined a customer's commitment and ability to repay. This reorientation shifted the responsibility for proving one's authentic Islamic practice to qualities that emerge in account prescreening, rather than in a history of actual payment practices.

Shari'a compliance, as a process that creates and imbues value, ultimately limited the bank's rate of return risk by setting an ambiguous but morally charged "authentic Islamic" threshold, which was met by private customers in prescreening and by the bank in the discursive categorization of late payments. In these moments, Risk Management demonstrated the ways in which Islamic ideals are concretized and materialized in a number of policies. Those policies revealed the tensions that exist between a financial institution's abstract aspirations to embody "the real Islam" and the daily challenges of enacting and presenting it. The added difficulty was that, despite the attempts to fix the meaning of "the real Islam" into one's likelihood of loan repayment, there was no standardized, singular, and comprehensive way to assess customers' claims of authenticity. These thresholds are vague, discursive, and highly indeterminate.

This resulted in what I refer to as a "consumptive risk." That is, the risk shifted from the financial rate of return to a discursive assessment at the point when the customers presented themselves to the bank as potential consumers.[1] How would the customers respond to the bank? Would they view its products and methods as "really Islamic?" Would they become consumers of what the bank had produced? Why or why not? And how did one account for this given the complex influences of other interests such as gender and class? The head of the Risk Management Department commented to me that his resolution to this tension resided in a tautological turning to "the real Islam":

The problem with coming up with a model for understanding consumption at the conventional bank is that there is a split in Jordanian society with the wealthy and the poor. You know, the people who can come to a conventional bank and those that can't. So in order to capture that split, I would need to develop two models of consumption—one for the bank customers and one for the others. However, one Islamic banking system can capture the needs of Jordanian society in its entirety. Islamic banking is simple, and everyone can find what they need in it.

The notion that one banking system—an *Islamic* banking system—is able to envelop and "fold in" the different classed variables highlights this uncertainty. This employee is presenting the hope and aspiration for one Islamic banking system to meet the needs of all Jordanians, both rich and poor. At the same time, and within the same department, some customers would be technically delinquent or default, and therefore too costly to maintain. Some would not meet the discursive threshold of being "Islamic enough." Some would be unable to come up with the 200 Jordanian dinars required to open an account. All of these customers would be refused access to the Islamic bank. How the customers perceive this tension, presentation, and the impacts is explored in greater detail in the next chapter.

Risk Management at the International Islamic Arab Bank was concerned with monitoring these risks in light of the Shariʿa-derived parameters for contracts and methods established by Shariʿa Compliance. Technically many of their methods were not widely divergent from those of conventional banks. Certainly, conventional banks screen customers who seek credit lines. At the Islamic bank they reconfigured these processes under a "moral banner" and Islamic framework that the conventional banks lack. Though the Islamic bank does not typically provide services or take on risks that conventional banks also refuse, these additional arrangements do explain how an

Islamic bank becomes considered, at least to some degree, a less risky under-
taking than a conventional one.

As discussed in the previous chapter, interpretations of Shari'a also limit
moral and spiritual risk in terms of prohibitions against interest and speculation. These interpretations and their applications create tensions between
the hopes and realities for convincing Islamic financial institutions. Despite
the construction of risk aversion at the bank, however, the kinds of contracts
and financing that Islamic banks do undertake are often the subject of much
debate about their "true Islamic nature" among the employees, further highlighting the lack of consensus. This is best explained by my experiences at
the Treasury Department.

## Treasury Department: Making Islamic Banking "Islamic"

I spent a considerable amount of time in the Treasury Department during
my week-long training there and during breaks from training in other departments. In addition to learning about the various facets of investments
and financing that occur in the Treasury Department, I found the staff there
to be particularly friendly and open to discussing and debating larger questions about what, exactly, makes Islamic banking "Islamic."

In the Treasury Department there are three primary forms of transaction, each conducted by a different member of the department. Shireen was
responsible for the Foreign Exchange Desk; Sameer for Money Markets and
*murabaha* contracts for lending and borrowing money; and Laith for Capital
Markets.

Shireen explained her job to me:

> I can hold one million Jordanian dinars' worth in any currency, and
> four million Jordanian dinars worth of U.S. dollars to cover accounts
> in both short and long terms. Currency rates don't change very often.[2]
> Because they are already at set amounts, they tend to be profitable.
> They come from the Central Bank anyway. So, I don't really do any-
> thing with the rates. I don't have to watch them. Not paying attention
> to the market is boring. I was trained at the University of Jordan in
> traditional banking. I would love to work at a conventional bank be-
> cause it's more exciting.

In this passage, Shireen adds an intriguing element to the tension between
the abstract Islamic aspirations of Islamic banking with the everyday realities
of the practice. She does this by framing her views in terms of "boring" and

"exciting." In this case, conducting foreign exchange in an Islamic way, without speculation, is not engaging; it does not capture her interest and attention because she is required to use published rates and cannot watch the market. It is "boring." Simultaneously, Shireen believes that working in a conventional bank would be "exciting." The contrast here symbolically links "Islamic" with "boring," and "conventional" with "exciting." She conveys a sense of disappointment because the symbolic associations are not inverted. Her practical realization is that foreign exchange in the Islamic bank is not engaging in the way she had hoped. It fails to capture her attention and imagination.

Later in this conversation, Shireen added that she only applied to work at an Islamic bank because of a desire to work in an "Islamic" environment with a dress code that she liked. She added, "Anyway, I don't really think that the International Islamic Arab Bank is Islamic because it charges a margin as an 'administrative fee' on top of loans. We're just like the other Islamic bank, The Jordan Islamic Bank. And we're both just like the non-Islamic banks." Islamicness, for Shireen, is indexed more by the *hijab* than by the institution of *murabaha*. In this case, the Islamic bank is able to gain an employee due to its overall religious environment, even if the specifics render its methods not authentically or convincingly Islamic.

Prompted by Shireen's high regard for a *hijab*-friendly environment and her low regard for Islamic banking instruments, I discussed with Shireen, Laith, and Sameer a variety of banking methods and the threshold criteria or conditions that fix their meaning as sufficiently Islamic. In one conversation, Laith—who had previously worked at an Islamic bank in Dubai—shared the example of a soccer player who had been purchased by the Al-Jazeera Sports Club in Abu Dhabi from a Spanish team by way of a *murabaha* contract through an Islamic Bank:

LAITH: It was considered *halal* by the bank and able to be executed without any trouble. But, I guess it was unclear if it was because it was the player's contract that was being bought and sold, or if it was the person, or what exactly was on the table.

ST: It strikes me as strange that it wouldn't have been made clear in an Islamic contract what exactly is being purchased. Aren't Islamic contracts supposed to make that clear? But the idea of buying a person is also weird to me. It seems inconsistent with the ideas of Islamic banking. I mean, can you even do that at a conventional bank?

LAITH: Maybe it was his work, his labor, as a player that they were purchasing.

SHIREEN: I agree with Sarah. I think it's weird.

> SAMEER: [ambiguously half-joking and half-serious]: I am trying to get an Islamic contract to fund the startup costs for my friend, who's a singer in Jordan. She's really good and I want to arrange her financing and get her career started. I'm not sure which would be better, *murabaha* or *mudaraba*. [Laughing, turns to me]: What do you think, Sarah?

As this example demonstrates, there are frequently no clear-cut demarcations of "Islamic" and "non-Islamic" arrangements. There is often a tension between competing visions for how to implement Shari'a and the modes for enacting such visions, which are fraught with debate, uncertainty, and confusion. In this case, the Al-Jazeera Sports Club was able to use Islamic methodologies to move a player to their team from Spain. How such arrangements were considered Islamically sound remained a mystery, even among these producers of Islamic banking. It hinted at ethics that made them all uncomfortable: Laith tried to justify how it would be possible, Shireen commented that it was "weird," and Sameer extrapolated the concept to justify startup costs for a similar example. This conversation and the employees' responses reiterate Shireen's earlier comments, which indicate that any self-proclaimed Islamicness of the bank was not entirely or even primarily convincing to the very producers and implementers of the financial instruments.

Furthermore, this example illustrates the challenges to valuation that come into play when the precise terms and the meaning are not sufficiently fixed and concretized. *That* it was an Islamic contract was not questioned. *How* it was an Islamic contract was the primary point of debate. These employees were looking for ways to fix meaning to the contract as distinctly Islamic, but were not able to do so in relevant and convincing ways, rendering consensus elusive.

Time and time again, our conversations in the Treasury Department would center on debates about the threshold criteria for something to be *halal*, or permissible, in Islamic banking, and how. We oftentimes debated the most problematic cases, such as how to fund a hotel with one-third of its profit arising from alcohol sales, the differences between tobacco for *argeelah* and cigarettes in Islamic business models, and financing the purchase of weaponry. These conversations revealed that the employees were frequently skeptical of the bank's practices and Islamizing attempts, even as they composed contracts and enacted transactions using Islamic methodologies. In the end, Laith, Shireen, and Sameer concluded that there was very little that was unambiguously *haram* and totally cast out from financing possibilities. The employees' position was typically to bring possibilities into the realm of

Islamic law, banking, and finance, rather than exclude them. There appeared to be something I would call "Islamically redeemable" about all types of investments and contracts. Even restaurants and hotels that serve alcohol are able to apply for funding for the nonalcoholic portions of their establishments, and profits made from such *haram* ventures can be "purified" and redistributed to appropriate charities. In the name of good business, moral and legal hoops are often jumped through, even in ways that make bank employees deeply uncertain and uncomfortable.

## Retail Services: Balancing the Modern Economy and an Islamic Way

My time in the Retail Services Department focused primarily on internal bank politics, in particular, employees' views of the bank's newest method of direct car title transfers and of human resources policies for dress. Internal politics on the part of the bank employees revealed much tension between the realities of running and managing a bank in light of the abstract aspirations for a truly Islamic banking experience and the methods by which this vision is realized. The case of the car title transfer demonstrates this well.

In February 2009, the bank's Shari'a Committee ruled that customers were able to transfer vehicle titles directly from the seller to the buyer. Previous to this ruling and announcement, two title transfers were required, the first transferring ownership from the seller to the Islamic bank, the second from the Islamic bank to the buyer.

This change in policy had two major implications. First, it meant that the buyer was no longer responsible for paying for two title transfers. This is an expensive endeavor in Jordan, requiring a tax payment of ten percent of the vehicle's value with each transfer. This took a substantial financial weight off the shoulders of the customer.

Second, this new method analytically separated the concept of "ownership" into one of two types: 1) title-based and contractual and 2) physical. This policy and definitional change required the bank to draw up two separate contracts. The first stipulated the terms of the contractual sale by the first owner directly to the second. The second declared the bank's "physical ownership" of the vehicle. This change was justified because someone from the bank would go out to purchase the car and bring it back to the bank, where the buyer would retrieve it; the bank maintained physical ownership and took on risk, as required by Shari'a. For those few minutes—or hours, depending on traffic—the bank "physically owned" the car, but not the title. This analytical and policy-important separation of physical from contractual ownership, authorized by the bank's Shariʻa Committee, enabled the bank to avoid requiring the customer to pay for two title transfers, while demonstrating the bank to be Islamic, and, they hoped, opening up the market to a wider audience.

However, this is a technically complex set of arrangements that the average customer may have difficulty following. Even employees sometimes struggled to understand the concept as authentically Islamic and to convey it to the customers. In response to everyone's confusion and uncertainty, the Retail Services department set up a call center—staffed primarily by fresh-out-of-college 22- and 23-year-old females—to answer customers' questions about the new product. I observed the call center during its first week. The phones rang constantly, with each of the women taking turns answering the phones and discussing, in their most polite, professional, and frequently flirty voices, how this new arrangement was both important to the customer's financial position and really Islamic.

I interviewed the director of the marketing subsection at this time and asked her more about the new title transfer arrangement and call center. This was her response:

> Sometimes we're not very good at marketing these Islamic methods. Do you know what happened when we introduced the credit card? We called it the "Islamic credit card" on the radio and in the newspapers. Our phones rang off the hook! People called us wanting to know what was unIslamic about their current credit cards. They wanted to know if you can have an unIslamic credit card. It caused us a real problem. We had to be careful not to tell people that what they were doing was *haram*. You can't tell people that.

Here, the director of Marketing described a fundamental and technical difficulty in communicating Islamized banking methods to non-experts and to potential customers who might be offended by the characterization of their current economic practices as "unIslamic." In this moment of a concretized and objectified "real Islam," customers began questioning their credit card practices for the first time. It reveals the challenges and contestations of "commanding right and forbidding wrong," particularly when the ethics have not yet been fully established in consensus (Cook 2000). Further, the difficulties in communicating technically complex Islamic methodologies are pronounced, which adds yet another dimension to the processes of solidifying "the real Islam"; how can one know if this practice is "really Islamic" if one cannot understand it? Some attempts at concretizing meaning and claiming authenticity in the creation of Islamic banking and finance are more straightforward than others. Some policies are complex and their promotion and clarification constitute a major effort and portion of daily work on the part of many bank employees. Furthermore, because marketing strategies are not easily subject to Shari'a rulings or codifications,[3] they are fodder for a whole host of approaches and views, most of which derive from the professionals' experiences with Islam, their job-based knowledge, and their own personal visions for the bank.

Frustrations in communicating Islamized methods to the customers and external audiences are not the only challenging aspects of balancing the tension between aspirations for Shari'a-based banking and the difficulties of materializing it. Communicating the material realities of banking and finance back to the Shari'a Committee and to those internal audiences who are the gatekeepers to expanding the Islamized banking services is also difficult. The Marketing director explained:

> I have been trying and trying to get the Shari'a Committee on board with some of these new products. Like this title transfer change was my idea. I just suggested to them that they should make a real credit card, so that people can carry a balance. They refused my suggestion. They said it couldn't be done *Islamically*. But I am sure it can. We just have to teach these *ta'alim* [educated ones] to understand banking.

Here is a fundamental difficulty in communicating banking methods to non-experts in the field: the bank's Shari'a Committee is made up of Islamic scholars rather than bankers. The difficulties in communicating Islamic methodologies, both internally and externally, are due to the underlying differences and outlooks that exist between the Islamic scholars on the Shari'a committee and the bankers and financiers who also might happen to be Muslim, along with a diverse public (Sloane-White 2011; Warde 2010).

The difficulties communicating among the realms of the managerial, operational, and "Islamic" were most noticeable in the Credit Department. Most of the conversations I had with the women working in the Credit and Quality Control sector, for example, centered around issues of Human Resources. After describing to me the functions of the Department, the employees took advantage of my "outsider's ear" to candidly express their feelings about working at the bank. The most frequent comments had to do with women and their appearance in the workplace. These opinions highlight the challenge raised by Shireen: not even the employees who are drawing up contracts and selling the bank's services necessarily believe that what they are doing is Islamic. Nonetheless, many of them find the atmosphere of the bank and interpersonal connections meaningful enough, or Islamic enough, that they continue in their jobs.

Although discussed in chapter 4, women's appearance in the bank is worth elaborating upon here. As one employee in the Credit and Quality Control sector described:

> The best benefit to working here is that I can wear anything I want. I dress like this anyway [pointing to her brightly colored headscarf and layers of fashionable clothes], but it's not restrictive like over at the Jordan Islamic Bank. There the women have to wear a black *abaya* and white *hijab*. They can't wear makeup over there. At non-Islamic banks, they only hire Christians because they can wear anything [pointing to short sleeves and revealing necklines]. It's like marketing for the bank for women to dress like that. It is here too. It's like marketing that we dress like this.

In fact, wearing the "right" amount of cosmetics is one of the female employee's duties. If they apply makeup too heavily—or too lightly—they suffer a reduced score on their performance appraisals.

The notion that women's dress serves as a representation, an index, or even a marketing strategy for the bank was not lost on the staff. I came to discover that it was actually Dr. Hamid, discussed in chapter 5, who spearheaded the movement to keep me out of the branch during my fifth week of training. It was a curious dynamic. The head of Human Resources—a completely separate department from Dr. Hamid's Retail Services—had originally suggested this aspect of my training, but then changed the training plan upon the rather strong recommendation of Dr. Hamid. One employee said to me, "Dr. Hamid wants to tell you no [about training in a branch] in a nice way. Because he doesn't want to tell you that it's about your look." By "your look" the employee was referencing my blonde hair, white skin, and blue eyes.

The employees articulated a strong separation of orthodoxy and orthopraxy in their employment practices, with little to say definitively about normative doctrine in such a field with relatively limited consensus. On the one hand, employment with an Islamic bank is a convenient means of expressing orthopraxy, whether for the Islamic methods for financing or the ability to wear a *hijab* and a pantsuit to work every day. Much like the case of Ramadan, one is required and compelled by strong external factors to comport one's external, public piety in a certain way, which are in turn reproduced by other actors. In this case, production and reproduction of normative expectations

occur through employment contracts and employee evaluations and by vir-
tue of laboring every day to further an Islamic economics.

Employment at the Islamic bank is not, however, necessarily an expression
of orthodoxy; nor is it necessarily an expression of one's doctrinal affiliations
and affections. Piety here is not driven by the quest to subordinate oneself
to a transcendent or divine will (Mahmood 2005, 2–3). Nor is it typically
for more ideological ends of Islamizing economic practices. There is a very
pragmatic sense that working at the Islamic bank is "just a job" rather than a
fundamentally orthodox endeavor. As a result the employees strive to make
it meaningful in ways that cohere with their understandings of Shari'a and
of Islam. For many, this is articulated as a means to be a part of a Muslim-
majority office and to enjoy being both fashionable and Islamic. These are
meaningful forms of pious expressions, and Islamic authenticity here does
not assume a predetermined inward state. Piety for bank employees does
not require actually believing in the banking methods or products in order
to perform them. In these instances, an Islamization of economic practices
goes beyond banking and sets its aims on Marketing and Human Resources
policies. These areas have historically remained outside of the purview of
Shari'a, yet constitute the two most important economic and Islamic realms
in employees' everyday pious and professional lives.

## Corporate Services: "Too Religious" for the Islamic Bank

The week in Corporate Services was primarily defined by my being the
lone single woman among a group of university-educated men in their mid-
twenties. Only one was married, and the rest became attentive quickly to a
female in the department. When I first walked in, a sense of order and propriety was quickly established as the young men straightened their ties and
organized their desks. The married member of the four-man office took me
under his wing for the week, introducing me to the employees who worked
with the corporate clients and translating and describing some of the more
complex topics, such as licensing or an Islamic Certificate of Deposit. He
had just recently completed his master's degree at a university in England.
He had written a thesis on the banking industry in Jordan and was keen to
trade chapters and share experiences.

The member of Corporate Services who was most often a topic of conversation, however, was Ali. Previously, Ali had been employed by a conventional bank and considered himself a "typical" Jordanian youth. He smoked
occasionally and abstained from alcohol and girls, but flirted with them both.
Ali said that religious life had not been of primary importance, but it was not

completely absent. At some point, his religious life and piety changed, and then he started working at the Islamic bank:

> You know, I started spending time in the mosque. I started reading the Qur'an. I started to think about my life, "Is this what I wanted? To just live every day?" I realized that I was doing things that weren't bad; I wasn't a bad person. But I wasn't a *good* person. I could do more for Allah. I discovered "the real Islam." So, I started sleeping in the mosque during Ramadan, I grew a beard, and I stopped talking to girls. This was important. I have a fiancée now, and we're doing it the *halal* way. She's the only girl I talk to. Well, you know, outside of my work at the bank.

Ali was similar to Dr. Hamid in that he held high aspirations for a singular and robust Islam that would and could be expressed in concrete and convincing Islamic institutions. In many ways, his personal story is similar to the one about Asma's Islamic awakening that opened this book. Ali's description of the process of becoming pious raises a few behaviors and practices as markers or symbols of an authentic piety: reading the Qur'an, visiting the mosque, fasting during Ramadan, growing a beard, and ending extraneous interactions with members of the opposite sex.[4] These characteristics, among the others described in this book, rise again and again as primary, yet contested and negotiated markers of "the real Islam." In the case of Ali and in contrast to most other employees, however, we can also add an employment change to an Islamic bank as a marker of altered and heightened piety.

Ali's case is interesting because other bank employees—in a way that echoed the critical statements of Dr. Hamid—frequently described him as "too religious." He had, one of his coworkers indicated, become largely irrelevant and "extreme" in his beliefs. I asked one woman where the line was between "being religious, in a good way, and being 'too religious.'" She answered, "It's really up to each person. There's no 'line' that says this is good and this is too much religious. But it's there. The women here, we see it. His Islam is not for us." Perhaps because Ali was relatively more withdrawn from women in the bank, his female coworkers were not at all fond of him.

The discourse of individual choice in religious practice—even if such choices are denigrated—reinforces this kind of piety as neoliberal. Ali's response to prompts for heightened religiosity is highly rational. He is engaged in a series of practices that are externally and publicly marked while carrying an internal framework that suggests such actions are individually selected.

"I could do more for Allah" and the resulting actions reveal Ali's pious Islamic practice as highly economized with calculative agency in thought and action.

Furthermore, as the female employee's statement indicates, even among employees at an Islamic bank—where Islamic symbols, meanings, and debates were part and parcel of one's professional and personal life—becoming "too religious" was both possible and looked down upon. It was not, of course, about his internal beliefs in orthodoxy, but rather the associated behaviors in orthopraxy that were considered "extreme" or "too much." The consensus was that Ali's Islam was unnecessarily severe to live as an authentic and pious Muslim, too rigid in the types of symbols and behaviors it embraced, and exclusionary against those—particularly women—at the bank who were also pious and producing Islamic banking. In their eyes, one did not need to go that far to be a *real* Muslim. It was not a modern, authentic Islam in the eyes of many bank employees.

When my father came to visit me in Jordan, I was keen to show him a mosque during Friday prayers, and had asked around at the bank if anyone knew of one that would be particularly appropriate. Ali, who never shook my hand and avoided looking me in the eye as part of his religious practice,[5] volunteered to take us. He picked up my father and me and drove us to the mosque. I retreated to the women's section, where I was the only person there for most of the evening, and could hear my father and a number of men downstairs talking, laughing, and enjoying the time together. After the prayers, we were invited to the house of a nearby Sheikh, where we sat in completely segregated environments: me with the Sheikh's wife, Imam's wife, children, and household help in the living room around the television, while my father, the Sheikh, the Imam, and Ali were served course after course of Middle Eastern salads, foods, and desserts in the formal sitting room.

After we left, I explained to my father that these were among the most religious Jordanians he had met, and some of the most conservative that he would meet during his visit. My father looked surprised and said, "Like the kind of people they call 'extremists' in the news?" I answered that sometimes, yes, the very pious and the "too religious" are considered such. My father laughed, "Well, these guys sure weren't going to hurt me. They would have been more likely to feed me to death than to shoot me." Although Ali, the Imam, and the Sheikh were exclusionary to women and conducted gender-segregated social interaction, they were not this way with other men, even foreigners and non-Muslims. The day after Ali and my father met, Ali stopped me in the bank and said, "Your father's hilarious. I loved meeting him."

This story demonstrates that the claims of the Dr. Hamids and the Alis of the comprehensiveness of Shari'a-derived understandings and realizations in Islamic banking efforts need to be taken seriously and are not easily dismissed. The hopes and aspirations for a singular and irrefutable Islamic banking based in Shari'a are grounded in the notion that this is consistent with the vision for an Islam that is singular and irrefutable. Ali also demonstrates that it is possible and, in his eyes, preferred, to envision a serious Islam that also reaches out to foreigners and non-Muslims as visitors, friends, and economic partners, and in ways that are influenced by normative Islamic ethics of gender and class. In many ways this is in contrast to the more illiberal constructions of a religiously charged society envisioned and as described in chapter 3.

This complicates the impressions both in Western communities and among some women at the bank that the "too religious" are "extremist," and discussed as a threat, ready to strike Westerners, to exclude and downgrade women and their roles, and to push other Muslims into their kind of Islam. Even within this Islamic bank—where being highly religious and pious *could* be valued—such an attitude was considered "too much." The ethics of being personally pious in an orthodox fashion at the bank and promoting piety in Shari'a banking and orthopraxy were clearly not simple, uncomplicated matters about pursuing one's devotion to Allah. There are community-wide implications, and falling outside the normative frame even in the field of being "too religious" could cause consternation and conflict.

## Shari'a Compliance: Practical, yet Pious

Each Islamic bank has a Shari'a Supervisory Board or Shari'a Committee. This comprises three or more Shari'a scholars, typically men who have received training in jurisprudence at universities and institutions for Islamic learning around the world. The Shari'a boards and committees determine the details of Shari'a compliance of banking products and services in six important ways. First, they review the concepts for new products as described and created by those who develop them (such as the director of Marketing, who pushed for a credit card that could carry a balance). Second, they assess market conditions. Third, they review the product developers' views on the Islamic principles on which the proposed projects are based. Fourth, they review the product developers' proposals and issuing opinions (*fatawi*). Fifth, they listen to the product developers' responses to these opinions. Finally, they discuss with the developers the rulings and outcomes. (Alchaar and Sandra 2006, 7).

In my time designated for the Shari'a Committee, I met with Faris, the liaison to the Shari'a Committee and the Compliance Auditor. His job was to make sure that the methods used by the bank continued to meet the Shari'a Committee's guidelines.[6] Faris's desk was in the Auditing office, which was shared with two other young men, Mohammed and Hussein. Faris was the first person to explain to me how the new vehicle title transfer fit the Shari'a Committee's threshold criteria for consideration as "Islamic." He also spent much time with me explaining, from a Shari'a-based, jurisprudential perspective, why some methods were considered Islamic and others were not.

Not everyone at the Islamic bank who was noticeably "religious" was considered "too religious." Faris was a self-reported Salafi.[7] He was a family man with a wife and children, and was always very professional and personable with me. Unlike Ali, Faris shook my hand and looked me in the eye. He sat next to me to diagram various methods and accounts. He did not have a beard, was active in connecting me to the only other known Christian working in Islamic banking in Jordan at that time, and encouraged me to pursue the Islamic Finance Qualification. His personal religious beliefs in a conservative religious movement were belied by his gregarious and personable presence in the office. He was always appropriate and professional with me.

When I asked Faris about Dr. Hamid and his belief that the bank need not worry about being competitive, as discussed in chapter 5, I figured that he would have insight since he was considered the Shari'a Committee's representative and the leading authority in the bank on issues of Islam in its methods and products. He revealed to me the tension between his position and Dr. Hamid's with regard to the future of the bank:

> Sarah, you have to understand that Dr. Hamid has this old mentality. He does. He's from the original Islamic banks, where, yes, you could say that Islam would sell the bank. The religion would sell itself. But it's not like that anymore. If we're not competitive, the new bank [Jordan Dubai Islamic Bank] will take us under. We are a better bank than the Jordan Islamic Bank. This is true. But we have to be competitive to keep that edge and to face the new bank. We're going to lose employees and we're going to lose customers. It's true. I know all the employees are going to leave. Why wouldn't they? Dr. Hamid is going to have a shock when he sees all his employees leave.

It became clear to me in this and other conversations with Faris that there was a major division between the senior management of the International Islamic Arab Bank. On the one hand were those such as Faris, who supported

Islamizing new banking methods and products in ways that would be convincing to both employees and customers. They supported a vision of Islam and Islamic banking that was open to Christian customers and American academic researchers. They were keen to put a modern and moderate face forward, one that acknowledged that Islamic banking was ultimately a business and needed to be approached as one. The surprise was that this relatively progressive and innovative approach came from one of the most religious men in the bank.

The other side of senior management included Dr. Hamid and was supported by employees such as Ali. They held the belief that *Islam* was the selling point rather than the bank, that women's appearance was a means to promote a certain kind of Islam, and that the aesthetics of what kind of Islam was promoted was often more frequently presented by bearded Ali than by clean-shaven Faris. Such perspectives among the young employees were widely unpopular and considered outdated, but still powerful.

A bifurcated construction oversimplifies the reality. As a Salafi, Faris preferred a strong personal devotion to Allah and personal piety that many could have considered "too religious." However, he did not embrace the austere lifestyle of the Salafis. He pursued friendly and professional relations with women, did not sport a beard, and remained an affable character at the bank. It appears that any disagreement with Faris' personal piety as "too religious" was easily tempered by his collegiality. Being easier to work with, especially through the eyes of women, was a defining characteristic when assessing someone's religiosity and piety.

Dr. Hamid was often the one that employees pointed to as "outdated." He utilized religious rhetoric in ways that the employees found offensive. He was considered part of an "old guard" who was inattentive to employee needs and too conservative in his approaches to bank management. Yet, Dr. Hamid supported the typically popular human resources policies that required women to wear colorful *hijabs* and cosmetics. The employees' profound disagreements were primarily with his management style. They only disliked his personal piety when it negatively informed his working affairs.

As each of these individuals demonstrates, the analytic separation of orthodoxy, highly divergent normative ethics, and orthopraxy in the bank further reveals the complicated understandings of everyday piety and the wide variety of symbolic and practiced pairings and groupings that it can prompt in banking and finance. They challenge a simplistic understanding of the relationship between their internal pieties and external representations in the bank, and defy simplistic bifurcations and explanations. These ethics are very much under construction.

These ethnographic sections also demonstrate that the production of Islamic banking is fraught with tensions between something resembling aspirations for Islamic banking and the practical challenges of its embodiment and implementation. The economic and Shariʿa-derived behaviors that accompany *murabaha* arrangements, for example, articulate hope for a kind of Islamic economics, in this case, one that places Islam in the atmosphere of the bank, in the Human Resources policies, and in the marketing plan, even as the specifics remain debated and indeterminate. Without a more agreed-upon, systemic understanding of just what the Islamization of economic practices might entail in these spheres, such tensions will continue to undermine consensus and reorganize the myriad ways of envisioning and enacting everyday piety by the industry's visionaries as well as its practitioners and producers.

What the Dr. Hamids and other producers of the Islamic banking movement are espousing is not a cultural or moral hoax. He and those like him take seriously the immense hopes and aspirations that they place in Islamic banking and the self-referential value of a singular "true Islam." In a way that mystifies many of the employees, Dr. Hamid and his ilk do really believe that Islam will sell the bank, and that the products and services offered are authentically Islamic. This chapter takes these ideological, pietistic, and highly personal hopes and aspirations seriously, because they are a major thrust behind the materialization and concretization of a work force engaged in classifying, organizing, and bringing to market the meanings of an Islamic economic practice in banking and finance.

In the Islamic bank, the tensions between the variety of understandings of Islamic banking, of management, and of Islam itself are important—and incomplete—distinctions. Lines are blurred between otherwise seemingly cohesive factions, making alliances and consensus between individuals incredibly difficult and rendering the distributional aspect of creating consensus an important sociotechnical arrangement. At the same time, other elements of everyday life play a vital role in constructing Islamic banking, including aesthetics and the issue of appearing a certain way—as a Muslim woman, as an American, as not Muslim enough, or as "too religious." These other elements complicate any constructions of consensus and unified understandings. What we see is that there is not a clear and uncomplicated movement from the structural intents of Islamic economics to its manifestations in Islamic banking and to the producers and practitioners of the industry. The actors complicate the transfer of symbols, ideas, and objectives with their own interpretations and visions for its implementation and transfer to others.

Amman's social and cultural climate is one in which attempts to Islamize economic practices are occurring. However, this is no longer as simple as printing contracts on paper with green trim and *Bismillah* at the top. Islamic banking is a primary means by which such attempts are occurring in the monetized markets, but they are not happening without the inputs of the economic actors—namely, employees and practitioners of Islamic banking— along the way. Authenticity in Islamic orthopraxy is debated at every step. Nonetheless, despite Islamic banking's position as an institution very much "under construction," it provides an "alternative market" that is accessible to Muslims who seek to Islamize aspects of their everyday piety, even as the exact methods for doing so are still being negotiated.

A major critique of Islamic banking articulated by the employees themselves is that such efforts more frequently result in cosmetic changes to otherwise non-Islamic financial service offerings rather than some kind of large-scale, Islamic economic revolution. In many ways, Islamic banking is an "Islamic veneer" on otherwise conventional economic practices (Kuran 2004). This critique is rampant among Islamic banking customers and potential customers, and is explored in depth in chapter 7. Despite providing what is, to some, an appropriate and favorable alternative, the production reforms that Islamic banking and finance would propose are not fundamentally altering conventional economic systems. Rather, what we have witnessed are the processes by which "the financiers and their religious boards will make compromises with financial markets because these banks enjoy one major underlying competitive advantage: popular demand among pious Muslims for an alternative to interest-based savings accounts" (Henry and Wilson 2004, 5). The need to meet customer demand—albeit in a niche market and in fits and starts—makes Shari'a Compliance more flexible and potentially "democratic," even when customer demand for Islamic methods is not always straightforward.

Furthermore, there is a disconnect between the Islamic bank employees and Shari'a scholars and committees about how to convince consumers of the merits of Islamic banking. Certain actors make efforts to construct an institutional and ethical reality in an Islamic public sphere that embraces the notion that Islamic banking is a constituent part of doctrine in the *real* Islam. These efforts are only moderately successful, eliciting, by any measure, an array of responses in Amman. Despite some systematic attempts to convince the public through strategies that align Islamic banking with other "*halal*ized" practices and malign the institutions and people outside the sphere of *halal*—all signs of the construction of an Islamic public sphere—considerable disconnect still exists between the producers of the movement and its consumers.

The hopes for Islamic banking remain high. Perhaps this also explains the intensity of the debates. Bank promoters and some employees hope that Islamic banking can do things as radical as "end poverty" or as simple as provide a kind of religious safe space for the fulfillment of one's pious practice. Islamic banking is often freighted with a socially transformative or even utopian weight that it is incapable of fulfilling (Hefner 2003; Tobin 2009). This prompts a Muslim public to go through a process of social realization or cultural reframing, whereby many come to understand that Islamic banking is not the great transformation they had expected, but something that may yet provide useful services in what is thought to be an ethical way. If the hopes were not so high and the investment (on the part of supporters such as Dr. Hamid and Ali) not so personal and intimate, the loftiness of the hopes for Islamic banking might be reduced. However, given such hopes, how to define and interpret "failure" becomes an issue fraught with tension.

The bank employees use two methods to sustain these notions. First, they are quite concerned with how to present themselves within the bank. To present the modern, Islamic self requires that women pay attention to their cosmetics and dress so as to appear sufficiently Muslim to pass their employee evaluations, but not "too religious." Men, too, adopt professional dress and comportment, which is particularly pronounced in a mixed-gender setting. People are careful not to violate the ethics of those in their midst who are "too religious," even if they do not agree with them. Secondly, the employees themselves enact Islamized economic practices through their consumption, a fact that is often ignored in the discussions of a productive Islamic banking and finance. The front line of employees' engagement with economic practices is located more centrally in dealings with ethical constraints or issues of lifestyle—the everyday lives and everyday pieties of Muslims—than in what type of financial services they may produce or promote in their offices.

The latter point becomes an important link between producing Islamic banking and finance and the consumptive behavior of Muslim economic actors discussed in chapter 7. Islamic banking and finance serves a "peripheral portion of the Muslim world economy" (Hefner 2006a; 2006b, 21) and has very little to say about the primary points of debate on an ethically informed, modern Muslim lifestyle, as explored in the chapters on Ramadan and the *hijab*. Many typical customers consider Islamic banking too abstract, inaccessible, and obscure. In fact, in Amman, beyond interpreting and regulating interest prohibitions, Islamic banking and finance says very little of import for most subjects' everyday pieties.

Still, a broader, more abstract idea has emerged in consensus: that Islamic banking is a moral option in a sea of potentially immoral but highly desirable conventional banks (Tobin 2009). Whether or not individual employees or customers agree, the banks have established a certain sense of being "Islamized." They avoid interest, take on risks before making a profit, have their services and products approved by a Shariʻa Committee, and invest in objects that adhere to Islamic law and eliminate *haram* elements such as smoking, alcohol, gambling, pork, and morally reprehensible acts. At the same time, new methods are constantly being demanded and then legitimated as "Islamic." This is where further points of divergence begin.

When Muslims face differing Islamic understandings and debates as they attempt to engage in ethically informed economic practices, the resulting consumption is not at all simple or straightforward. Tracing the development of the points of negotiation and value-shaping of Islamic practice and piety by way of consumption helps to demonstrate that identities are neither simply cultivated by the powerful forces that produce Islamic knowledge (Mahmood 2005) nor the result of *homo economicus* in a free-market society (Hefner 1998a, 1998b). Instead, the complex processes by which Islamic markers of identity are produced in the context of economic practices can be held together despite contradictions and hostilities. They can also be hybridized and negotiated in very specific ways that, in turn, shape the culture, communities, and consumers' everyday practices, particularly in neoliberal ways.

Chapter 7 takes on many of the same questions regarding the possibilities for "adequation" or realizing hopeful and aspirational beliefs about Islamic banking given the practical realities of negotiating Shariʻa in a complex modern economy. It does so from the perspectives of people who became the customers of an Islamic bank and those who chose not to. By rounding out the discussion of everyday pieties with the production and then the consumption of Islamic banking, I hope to highlight the tremendous variety in outcomes of interaction, even if intentions are more singular.[8] Consumption of Islamic banking, the field with the least amount of normative consensus of those examined in this book, is a subject for high hopes and intentions. However, examining these intentions is insufficient to understand the complexity of negotiations in which subjects engage to make meaningful their Islamized banking and finance practices for their personal piety.

# CHAPTER 7

# Consuming Islamic Banking

*"They Say They're Islamic, So They Are"*

> *I don't understand the Islamic banks. I want to do the right thing and practice the real Islam. I know the Qur'an says, "Those who consume interest won't stand on Judgment Day. Allah has forbidden interest." But I just don't understand how the banks are Islamic. They don't feel Islamic, and when you compare the Islamic banks with the others, they look and feel the same. But, you know the Islamic banks. You know, they say they're Islamic, so they are. But I'm still not sure that I want to bank there.*
>
> —Male informant

As this quote indicates, there is deep confusion and uncertainty on the part of many Ammanis regarding Islamic banking. As discussed throughout the book, while there is a generalized, orthopraxic interest in adhering to some idea of a modern, authentic Islam in economic practices, there is very little consensus as to how, exactly, one does this. Furthermore, economizing one's Islamic practices occurs in moments of coproduction with Islamizing economic practices, which is undergirded by neoliberal ethics and logics.

The reference to the Qur'an that opens this chapter is a truncated version of 2:275,[1] which gives only vague guidelines that Allah has forbidden interest and permitted trade. Avoiding all interest is difficult in contemporary economic practices that rely on it in technologies such as credit cards or student loans. As a result, actors often turn to neoliberal logics as a means to resolve these tensions and amplify individual choice. In these cases, actors are considered to be reliant upon their own knowledge, experiences, and resources for vetting an authentic Islamicness that works for them. Given that Islamic banking is a recent institutional development, as described in chapter 5, individuals often struggle to find trustworthy sources of authority, and they rely heavily upon their own knowledge and experiences to make sense of Islamic banking and finance and its implications for their Islamic practice. Ultimately for many customers of the Islamic banks, there is an orthopraxic resignation to the claims of Islamicness by the banks, even as skepticism and uncertainty prevail in normative ethics and doctrinal statements as well as in personal belief.

When customers reference Islamically infused notions of morality and economic performance in the banks, they use a wide variety of complex discourses for assessing "Islamicness." These discourses are contingent and responsive, rather than static and monolithic. "Islamicness" in Islamic banking is continuously being constituted and reconstituted in alternative, highly personalized ways. This further fragments consensus in Amman.

## Assessing the "Islamicness" of the Islamic Bank

Customers of banking services apply three conceptual categories to the question of whether Islamic banking is really or authentically Islamic, and to what degree it may be deemed sufficiently so:

1. *Affective responses.* These are sometimes understood as "Islamic" but are not justified with explicit reference to Shari'a norms as much as by a sense of propriety or aesthetics, often invoking a "sense" or a "feeling." This constitutes a bundle of interpretations, judgments, feelings, and personal moral experience as a Muslim. Here, people indicate that Islamic banking does or does not "seem" or "feel" *really* Islamic.
2. *The pressures of orthopraxy.* The perceived mandates of orthopraxy and orienting one's behaviors in line with consensus in Islamic injunctions are weighed against a feeling of satisfaction or dissatisfaction with a bank's more explicitly managerial or operational measures such as capabilities to meet customer needs, efficiencies and timeliness in service provision, and range of services provided.
3. *Consensus and agreement with Shari'a norms.* More accurately, these are Shari'a norms agreed upon by much of the local public and the ways they fit into the person's intellectual understanding of Islamic banking, Islam and its required practices, and the demands of contemporary society.

Each of the three categories presents potential obstacles to a successful inculcation of subjectivities that perceive Islamic banking as authentically Islamic. First, the evaluations of Islamic banking that are based on affective responses emerge as important reasons to refrain from banking there. The way Islamic banking *feels*, based on personal and moral experiences, may prevent people from doing business there.

There is a debate in moral and social psychology about the causes, role, and influence of affect when it comes to questions of morality. While most experts agree that emotion is an "understudied yet powerful contributor to the decision-making process" (Loewenstein et al. 2001; Monin, Pizarro, and Beer 2007, 99; Vohs, Baumeister, and Loewenstein 2007), some have argued that affect and emotion play a primary causal role (Haidt 2001; Monin, Pizarro, and Beer 2007). As Monin et al. assert, one's conceptions of the moral dilemma often determine the degree to which affect plays a causal role. "If one conceives of the typical moral situation as one in which we must judge others' moral infractions, one may conclude that morality involves quick judgments that have a strong affective component and are not necessarily justifiable by reasoning" (2007, 99; Pizarro and Bloom 2003). One of the reasons that affect plays out so strongly in assessments of "the real Islam" is that actors see the judgments and assessments of others' moral behaviors as part of "commanding right and forbidding wrong" and also as part of being a savvy Islamic consumer themselves.

Secondly, customers of Islamic banks and conventional banks raise questions about orthopraxy by way of satisfaction and dissatisfaction with the bank's more managerial or operational aspects. This criterion is often a means for skeptics or cynics to legitimize their lack of participation in the Islamic banks because of their dissatisfaction with elements such as long waits, difficulty in obtaining cash loans, or having to go inside the bank to withdraw cash. In other words, non-Islamic bank customers may offer up the idea that they do not patronize the Islamic bank because "a really Islamic bank would offer free checking" or "a really Islamic bank would have a cleaner waiting area." In their perception, Islamic banks are simply not as good as the conventional competitors, and they couch their dissatisfaction in terms of an authentic Islam. Others, who also have deep reservations about the Islamic banks but still choose to become customers there, may rely upon the pressures of orthopraxy and defer to the banks' discursive self-legitimacy, as in "the banks themselves say they're Islamic." They may also use an explicit Shariʻa-derived evaluation to justify their orthodoxy and practice. Often, the bottom line is that customers evaluating a bank's Islamic elements utilize neoliberal calculative agencies to weigh the costs and benefits and their positive and negative evaluations about its managerial and operational practices.

Customers may opt to bank at an Islamic bank because it is simply better at providing the banking services they need. Conversely, they may opt to bank at an Islamic bank *despite* having tremendous reservations about its services, choosing orthopraxy over the managerial and operational elements of the banking services.

Finally, consensus and agreement about Shari'a norms is a conceptual space in which people consider the intellectual consistencies or inconsistencies of Islamic banking and judge them against what they believe to be true about Islam, banking and finance, and their place in the world order. This is the realm in which Islamic scholars are most engaged in their efforts to convince people of the merits of Islamic banking; they often advocate for an enlargement of consensus in the publicly agreed-upon Shari'a norms and rulings people may access when they make their banking decisions. The guiding assumption is that a higher level of familiarity with Shari'a and other sources of Islamic knowledge can supersede other types of knowledge as a means of convincing potential customers of the merits of Islamic banking. Many producers of Islamic banking approach this as a question of higher-order calculations and intellectual reasoning rather than an affective obstacle (Monin, Pizarro, and Beer 2007). As such, their attempts to attract new customers rarely rely upon appeals to affective responses or to orthopraxy. Rather, they focus on building a Shari'a-derived public ethics that supports Islamic banking as the result of higher-ordered intellectual processes. The disconnect between reported personal affective dissatisfaction and producers' responses in intellectual debates is an important factor in understanding the continuous and unaddressed obstacles that keep potential customers from becoming consumers of Islamic banking services.

## Affective Responses

Time and again, I found that customers of both Islamic and conventional banks used a bundle of interpretations, judgments, and feelings—affect—to evaluate the Islamic bank. Frequently, those who did not do business at Islamic banks opted out because Islamic banking did not *seem* or *feel* any different from conventional banking. To justify their position, they cited a general, vague affective sense. People who did use an Islamic bank attributed their decision to the feeling that the bank's employees, policies, and customer service put forth something resembling "Islamic values," which often remained ill-defined and unclear. When opting to become a customer of an Islamic bank, or not, some affective sense of "Islamicness" was the threshold criterion for deciding where to bank.

This vague set of affective experiences was frequently the context for discussions of Islamic banking rather than the subject. The most commonly recited comment in conversation was, "*Al-kharaji Islami, wa al-dakhali riba'wi*" ("The exterior is Islamic and the interior is interest"[2]). The common perception was that the Islamic method for giving a loan without interest, *murabaha*, and a conventional loan with interest, *riba'*, are essentially the same thing. According to the logic, simply assigning one an Islamic name does not render it *really* Islamic. This veneer carries a particular sting of deception: Islamic banking lacks an internal essence of Islam, even while it promotes itself as Islamic (Kuran 2004, 7).

This disconnect is an obstacle for many people when deciding where to bank: the bank's name is Islamic, but the general *sense* or *feeling* is that it is not. The institution's "ethos" (Geertz 1973, 2000) does not fit a more normative, if ill-defined, understanding of a *truly* Islamic business. The Islamic bank feels like a conventional bank because it does not single out or promote Islamic values and structures the populace finds convincing. Islamic values may include attention to women's desire to avoid interacting with male employees or customers, an accessible prayer room, structures that protect women's modesty and privacy when waiting in line or conducting business transactions, a prioritization of the family unit in physical and symbolic space, the encouragement of deep trust that comes from "good business" norms of predictability and transparency, and highly personalized business transactions. In fact, in Amman one can find all these elements at the aptly named Mecca Mall or Barakat [Blessings] Mall, but would struggle to find them at the Islamic bank.

Furthermore, Islamic banks require Shari'a rulings for institutionalization and legitimation (as discussed in chapter 6). However, to require the backing of the Shari'a Committee also detracts from a clear sense and obviousness of Islamicness. In other words, if the bank has to keep saying, "It's Islamic, it's Islamic, it's Islamic," the repetition undermines the very discourse of affirmation. As such, it confirms the notion of an Islamic veneer and raises questions as to why the banks continue to repeat it.

A rather complex process of perception and affective judgment is at play here. Affective judgments occur quickly and decisively (Monin, Pizarro, and Beer 2007), so much so that without positive affective experiences and evaluations of the Islamic bank, the customer could desire to, and in fact does, turn to a conventional bank. In particular, customers weigh the notion that the Islamic banks are required to uphold a better banking standard and to carry the moral burden of Islam, as is characteristic of the neoliberal environment discussed in chapter 1. One informant described the experience:

I asked for a checkbook and they gave one to me right away at the Islamic Bank. The Cairo-Amman Bank [a conventional bank] made me wait so long. This is the main issue. It's the order of things. At the Cairo-Amman Bank they said you need to own a shop or be a businessman or own a school or something like that. A simple person cannot get a checkbook. I heard that in Jordan there's like 200,000 checks without any account. So the banks are afraid all the time for embezzlers. But I felt like the Islamic bank trusted me. They gave me a checkbook right away.

"The order of things" here refers to a perceived violation of class-based affiliations, where the conventional banks prioritize wealthier customers over "simple," everyday customers. Considering how many bad checks are rumored to be in circulation, the fact that the Islamic bank would issue a checkbook upon request is seen as an example of its personal, even Islamic, trust in people. In this case, this informant's evaluation is based on two sets of feelings. First, there is a normative assessment that things "should" be a certain way, one in which the Islamic middle class is prepared to trust a "simple" person to not commit a crime. Second, the informant interprets his receipt of a checkbook upon request as a gesture of this trust. Here, a structural problem of class bias is resolved through personal avenues, which is consistent  with neoliberal structures of shifting responsibilities and the amplification of the individual (Ong 2006).

In these processes, we see that the Islamic banking experience is highly constructionist. That is, identity and interactions are not predetermined as distinctly "Islamic" or "unIslamic," and are subject to change. What is meaningful as "Islamic" in this instance is both social and rhetorical, and interpreted as highly personal. At the same time, instances such as these indicate that the Islamic banks and at least some of their customers are keen to see a growth in the normativity that surrounds the way that things "should be" for the typical, even "simple" Muslim banking experience. The informant highlights "trust" as one of these vague values. At this ethnographic moment, "trust" is a personally meaningful, yet vague concept within the technological realm of banking.

Another informant indicated a perception that the Islamic banks are limited in the degree to which they can refuse a customer's request, for fear that it will reflect poorly on both the bank and Islam:

The Islamic bank is very good. You know, if someone goes to the bank and asks for money, and they say no, it will make [the customer] think it's about Islam. That it is Islam that is refusing to trust him, not the bank.

In this case, the informant believes intertwining Islam with business practices that are not favorable for the customer's needs might lead people away from the bank and away from Islam. Trust, as a vague ethical value and affective experience of banking, becomes elevated as a defining characteristic of the *real* Islam. The informant is indicating that feeling good about the Islamic bank's practices will also lead to good feelings about Islam. The affective experience of *Da'wa*, or a kind of Islamic evangelism (Mahmood 2005) here becomes intertwined with good banking.

## The Pressures of Orthopraxy

As Timur Kuran (2004) has pointed out, there is no evidence that implement-ing Islamic economic policies has "brought about the behavioral changes envisioned in Islamic texts" (47). In fact, despite enhanced access to Islamic banks and pressures to abide by some measure of Islamic orthopraxy in eco-nomic practices, many people still resist becoming customers because they are dissatisfied with the managerial and operational practices of the Islamic banks. Many of those who do participate do so out of a desire to adhere to the perceived mandates of an Islamic orthopraxy, despite their reticence or objections. As one informant, Khalid, articulated:

> I have three bank accounts. One is at the Housing Bank, and then I have one at the Jordan Islamic Bank and one at the International Islamic Arab Bank. I am a practicing Muslim. You know, I pray, I fast for Ramadan, and I try to live my life like a good Muslim. So, I go to the Islamic bank too. I keep the account at the Housing Bank because they have better specials and discounts and better service too. But the Islamic banks say they're Islamic, so, *khalas* [that's it], I have to bank there.

Unlike the previous informant, Khalid looks at the lower managerial and operational appeal of the Islamic bank not as a tainting of Islam, but a justi-fication for his reticence for banking there. He then invokes the notion that how he feels and what he thinks—his dissatisfaction—is not the most press-ing priority. He hedges his satisfaction in the "better specials and discounts and better service" at the conventional bank by also going to the Islamic banks because the banks say they're Islamic, "so I have to bank there." Here, the pressures for orthopraxic behaviors outweigh the interest in more appealing managerial and operational measures.

This passage illustrates the tension between perception of better services found at the conventional bank and the orthopraxic desire to fulfill Islamic duties. At least for Khalid, the Islamic banks gain him as a customer because the current environment makes it difficult for him to choose otherwise; there is a sense here that a religious discursive justification can be more heavily weighted than individual and personal opinions and ideas of preferred banking. But Khalid also holds multiple bank accounts, including one at a conventional bank, demonstrating a tension and hedging between his feelings of satisfaction with the conventional banks and his need to fulfill his Islamic duties. He is hedging the pursuit of orthopraxy in religious life at the Islamic bank with his personal preference for conventional banking. In this case, the Islamic banks gain him as a customer because religious authority and the pressures for orthopraxy are more heavily weighted than individual and personal opinions about economic or managerial efforts.

Islamic bank customers are sometimes openly, even strongly, critical of these institutions, despite the fact that they bank there. This exchange is a case in point:

> ST: Why do you go to the Islamic bank?
> INFORMANT: It's just the name, no more.
> ST: But it's *gheir riba'* [without interest].
> INFORMANT: Yeah, they said this, but they are, you know, liars. I have an account at the Islamic bank, but it's the same as the Arab Bank [a large, conventional bank]. The Islamic bank says to me, "This [one] is Islamic, that [one] is not Islamic." So I just go there now because of the name, for Allah.

In this case, the informant denigrates the employees of the Islamic bank as "liars" for what seems to be an arbitrary differentiation between what is and is not Islamic. This is particularly notable because the informant holds an account that is the "same" type he would hold at a conventional bank. Still, despite his seemingly arbitrary view of what "is Islamic," continuing to be a customer at the Islamic bank demonstrates a significant behavioral choice. His personal affect and feelings, as well as belief in orthodoxy about banking practices, are trumped by the commands put forth by religious authorities in the pressures for orthopraxy. That is, despite his rejection of the Islamic bank, the informant chooses to continue banking there out of a sense of religious duty "for Allah."

Not everyone who participates in Islamic banking out of a sense of religious duty harbors such cynicism and explicitly negative perceptions. I heard one informant say energetically that the process of vetting banks is "like shopping!" That is, banks and their economic or managerial measures are subject to a highly rational, systematic, and personal (even neoliberal) process of ascertaining which services and methods are preferred and better implemented. Conclusions are balanced against which Islamic or Shari'a-derived values are important to implement in one's life in orthopraxy and how they compare to the practical matters at hand. Customers evaluate which bank fits these highly fluid and competing priorities better. The notion of vetting Islamic banks as "shopping" is the exact kind of process that could imbue them and their practices with meaning and cultivate the subjectivity of the Islamic banking customers in a way that could build consensus. However, as these ethnographic vignettes demonstrate, this is not typically the reality.

These two points—a resignation to orthopraxy and the evaluative process that imbues meaning—represent differentiations in orthodoxy and ortho-praxy on the issue of contemporary pieties practiced in Islamic banking. On the one hand, the Islamic Resurgence and Islamization aim at a complete cultivation of a subjectivity that folds orthodoxy and orthopraxy into a single sphere; a "total way of life" that encompasses what one does, what one thinks, and even what one believes, all in the pursuit of deepening one's devotion to Allah (Mahmood 2005). This is the point when customers may assert that Islamic banking is *really* Islamic.

On the other hand, orthopraxy occupies a kind of middle ground, or what I call a "subjunctive compromise." I argue that a subjunctive compro-mise is a positioning indicating that although personal belief—informed, at least in part, by affect—is not fully in line with the Islamic authorities in normative ethics, practice is. This compromise is not unknown in other Abrahamic religious traditions. The historian Hugh Trevor-Roper (2010), in the context of Christianity, inquired of a friend how anyone could believe

> those quaint, superannuated doctrines of the Incarnation, Resurrection, Ascension, etc., which, in the Creed we solemnly say that we believe . . ." while sitting in church "as the various parts of the service follow one another among the fanatical Bedouin of ancient Judaea, the hooligan clergy of Byzantium or the Roman Maghreb, the scholarly Anglican bishops of the 17th and the sniveling Methodist hymnologists of the 19th century. (xviii)

Following resignation to and adoption of the practice of Islamic banking and finance, another set of meanings can emerge, not necessarily that banking is "Islamic," but an affirmation that one is actively pursuing one's faith in economic practices "for Allah." One just happens to be doing so through Islamic banking. The deeply personal and widely varying responses of pious, practicing Muslims to the banks' claims of "Islamicness" are diverse, yet all meet some subjective standard for personal religious identity: the informant self-identifies as a practicing Muslim. In fact, fulfilling one's duties in practice and in ritual—in orthopraxy despite uncertainty in doctrine and reservations in orthodoxy—is a means of engaging in everyday piety.

Jurisprudential guidelines for orthopraxy are further enhanced by the structuration of Islamic practice by the bank's staff. I witnessed Islamic bank employees enter into discussions with customers, clients, and each other about the difference between *haram*, explicitly forbidden; *maqruh,* disapproved according to analogy; *fi shobha,* or in doubt; and *halal*, or explicitly permitted. Orthopraxy, in this model, emerges as part of a moral gradation of religious practices, with some in a more Islamically preferred status. The employees utilized this method of structuring behaviors, adding, "Islamic banks take the conservative approach because you don't know when *haram* will start." In other words, avoiding *haram* means that one must also avoid the path to *haram*. In this "better safe than sorry" moment of a less-leveraged spiritual logic, customers need not release their skepticism about the bank's Islamicness. Rather, by appealing to those cynics and disentangling belief and orthodoxy, normative ethics and doctrine, and orthopraxy in the kinds of Islamic pieties at play—from "explicitly forbidden" to "in doubt"—the bank diffuses and deconstructs the question of whether the banking is really Islamic to such a degree that one no longer is required to answer the question in order to accept the prospect of banking there. This acknowledges a space for doubt and uncertainty, but still appeals to the bottom line with a neoliberal logic: if you seek, to any degree, to avoid *haram* things, you need to avoid the path to *haram* things. Therefore, you should bank at the Islamic bank in order to be spiritually safe rather than sorry.

Given this context and analytical possibilities, it could be quite difficult to resist these elements of an Islamizing and religiously engaged context for selecting a bank. The banks say you should become a customer at the Islamic banks, and the Shari'a says you should do it, so you do it. At this point, "the real Islam" can become an enveloping and encompassing discourse for consensus and limiting dissent. In other words, one needs to become a customer at an Islamic bank because someone smarter, better educated, more qualified, and likely more religious than you has said that it is not just better economically, but "more *right*," even if one does not believe it.

## Consensus and Agreement in Shariʻa Norms

For some Ammanis, the process of evaluating and measuring Islamic banking methods also includes a closer look at Shariʻa and the public consensus of the norms of Islamic banking. The latter is then measured against one's more personal experiences with other forms of knowledge, often highly intellectualized, and with one's understandings of the type and place for "correct religious practice." As it turns out, many people believe that not every sphere of economic life can or should be imbued with Islam.

Here, it is helpful to return to the discussion about the primacy of affect and the role of higher-level reasoning in decision-making processes of moral questions. As Benoît Monin and others discuss, when we judge others' moral infractions, we do so with a strong affective component that is not easily or necessarily justifiable by reasoning (2007, 99; Pizarro and Bloom 2003). Other scholars have argued that higher-ordered reasoning plays a causal role in moral judgments (Monin, Pizarro, and Beer 2007; Pizarro and Bloom 2003). They argue that when one "thinks of the typical moral situation as involving the resolution of a moral dilemma, one is likely to arrive at a model of moral judgment that heavily emphasizes the role of rational deliberation" (Monin, Pizarro, and Beer 2007, 99). On the one hand, there is a significant role for affect in assessing the moral infractions of others. On the other hand, intellectual reasoning is primary in situations in which an individual actor must resolve one's own stance on a moral dilemma. As a result, when the question shifts from "Is the Islamic bank really Islamic?" to "Should I bank at the Islamic bank in accordance with my understandings of Islam and Shariʻa?" the source of judgment shifts from affect to higher-level reasoning.

For those spheres that can or should be imbued with Islam, wide consensus exists that moral principles for righteous living are found in Shariʻa. What is contested is exactly which moral, guiding principles are best suited for universal application in some kind of Islamic public sphere and how they should be implemented. Not everyone agrees that the Shariʻa rulings and principles for Islamic banking currently emphasized by members of the ʻulama, or religious scholars, are the best-suited for highlighting and amplifying in a diverse, contemporary society. Furthermore, how those principles should be applied is met by even less consensus. This ultimately renders the moral consensus in an Islamic economics in the public sphere particularly fraught with tension and uncertainty.

This process constitutes the third mode for evaluating the Islamicness of the Islamic banks. Customers and non-customers of Islamic banks approach the question of real Islamicness in a highly intellectual, cognitive approach that seeks to measure Shariʻa-derived understandings of Islamic banking against knowledge that they have attained elsewhere, such as in the formal educational system and universities, and in their lived experiences as Muslims. This mode differs from the pressures of orthopraxy described above as it often involves a more intellectual approach characterized by esoteric and abstracted debates about Islam and Shari'a, as well as one's knowledge of banking methods in general. Still highly personal in terms of implications and outcomes, such discussions are frequently couched in terms of the alignment of one's personal understanding of the economic issues at hand with Shari'a. Such knowledge and intellectual understanding is often considered objectified and abstracted by the person contemplating it.

Participation in Islamic banking and in building public consensus, and resignation to the authority of the Islamic bank and its Shari'a Committee, are often concomitant with other sources for religious authority in the public sphere, such as an outside imam or sheikh. Consensus here requires a "web" of reinforced affirmations. Alternatively, rejecting Islamic banking due to a lack of intellectual convincing can rise concomitantly with the authority one finds in other sources of knowledge, such as local universities or other sources for religious education, even tradition or highly localized sources such as a parent.

To highlight this third category for assessing the Islamic banks, I quote an informant, Mohammed, at length:

> My B.Sc. was in Engineering but I took courses in Economics. What I think about Islamic banking is that, nowadays, it's very difficult to apply. . . . So, on the issue of interest rates, it's impractical to think that you can do this. The world is interconnected and there are always money transactions that require interest. My Engineering Accounts professor who taught at Northwestern University for twenty-five years, in Chicago, he's a Christian Jordanian. He was telling us, okay, "Islamic banks, they don't do interest. But they actually do." First of all, they have to abide by the rule legislated by the Central Bank of Jordan. The Central Bank of Jordan has a certain interest rate. To call it *murabaha* is a loophole for interest. So you call it *murabaha*, but it's interest. So that actually makes a difference.
>
> I like the pro-Islamic banking arguments sometimes because I get in arguments with them about it. "Why are you putting your money in an Islamic bank?" I ask. They're like, "You know. It's *halal*." I'm like, "Well, not really. It has interest and they take interest. They give you interest. They call it *murabaha*." They're like, "Yeah, but I mean, I'm not an expert on what counts. If it's *haram*, well, I'm not a religious expert.

The religious experts are the ones that said it's *halal*. So it's their fault. God's problem is with them and not me because they're the ones that said this to me. The other banks are explicitly *haram*. Therefore, if I go to them, I knowingly am doing something *haram*. When I go to the Islamic bank, I might be doing something *haram*, but not knowingly."

In this example, Mohammed is appealing to an intellectual, academic experience and knowledge. He uses his degree and courses in economics and the reputation and know-how of his well-reputed Jordanian professor for a framework of understanding Islamic banking as not authentically Islamic. Mohammed uses another powerful intellectual tradition—that of a non-Islamic education and the State's academic system—to legitimate this discourse.

In recounting conversations with Islamic banking customers, Mohammed paints himself as the more knowledgeable conversant, due to his academic credentials and experiences. He takes issue with two main points. First, that the Islamic banking customer demonstrates a measure of unwillingness to examine the fullness of the intellectual, ethical-legal, and normative issues at play is a point of contention. Mohammed has "arguments" with people over their lack of knowledge of economics, the rulings of the Central Bank, and the concept of interest, as well as how it is used in the banks. He challenges people for not being experts and for not educating themselves on the same topics he has invested his time and efforts in studying and for "ignorantly" engaging in Islamic banking, when he has already found the answers himself. Second, he appears to take issue with the degree and readiness with which one's personal intellectual and spiritual "responsibility" is being jettisoned in these discussions. The larger point of this story is, of course, that he sees the people with whom he argues as willfully ignorant of Islamic banking methods and legal issues and quickly deny their spiritual responsibility and pass it off to the religious experts while remaining uninformed. The people with whom he converses are part of consensus-building endeavors for Islamic banking, and Mohammed finds them insufficiently informed.

Both the conversations of which Mohammed speaks and his responses are representative of this third mode for evaluation. People examine and evaluate the popular perceptions of Shari'a and Islamic scholarship on Islamic banking, and then use their own experiences with other, external sources of knowledge to choose whether to become a customer of an Islamic bank. It is a kind of rationalization of religious practice that balances the norms for Shari'a compliance in everyday life with competing knowledge on the subjects garnered from other institutions and experiences.

Interestingly, this highly intellectualized conceptualization and approach is the one most frequently addressed by the religious authorities. Their approaches are rife with an "if people only knew" strategy: they campaign and debate in efforts to convince people intellectually that the principles from the Shariʻa are the right ones to focus on and that they are being implemented correctly. In other words, they typically do not approach the idea of obtaining new banking customers by appealing to their affective responses or by overtly pressuring people in orthopraxy. In fact, in this mode how people *feel*, perceive, or intuit their Islamic banking experience is considered highly irrelevant. Rather, the religious authorities appear to invest large amounts of time and energy in appealing to an intellectual understanding, using metaphor and analogy to amplify the place for *tawhid*, or the oneness of Allah's creation and law, and grow consensus and agreement in ethics and Shariʻa-derived norms for "Islamicness." This is, in fact, the only category for understanding the Islamicness of Islamic banking that has developed a systematic campaign to "win" people over to Islamic banking.

As one imam told me, it is not the substance and methodologies of Islamic banking that need to be altered. He indicated that the argument by critics of the Islamic bank that *murabaha* and *ribaʼ* are only different in name represents a kind of cognitive and intellectual confusion and a misunderstanding about Shariʻa. To remedy this confusion, he drew a parallel to *halal* meat:

> Islamic banking is like how we make meat *halal*. Everyone knows that the meat is the same. The cows all eat the same food. But it is how we kill it that makes it pure for Allah. It's the same with the banks. *Murabaha* might feel like a regular car loan to the customer. But what he doesn't understand is that we're doing it in the real Islamic way, from Shariʻa. He needs to understand the process. If he understands the process, then he will see that this is Islamic.

In this quote, the imam confirms that it is not intuitive for customers to understand how Islamic banking is, in fact, Islamic. By saying that *murabaha* might "feel" like a regular loan, he acknowledges that evaluations based on affective responses are important. However, the imam does not address the "experiential deficiencies," or experiences that do not make the customer *feel* that the Islamic bank is actually "Islamic." He does not respond with a call to alter Islamic banks' physical and symbolic spaces and structures to improve the "Islamicness" of customers' experiences. He does not call on people to disregard their consciences and engage in orthopraxy anyway. Rather, the imam invokes a justification based on consensus and agreement in Shariʻa norms. That is, he creates an analogy and a metaphor for Islamic banking that is rooted in Shariʻa and intellectual approaches. He engages in this work of cognitive "convincing" even though the deficiency is frequently based on customers' affect or perceptions of better economic and managerial practices in conventional banking. This reveals a significant disjuncture: using a knowledge-based approach to educate customers about Islamic banking by convincing them that it is *halal*, when their reticence is often operating in a different sphere of experience, that of affect.

Still, the comparison to *halal* meat is an interesting strategy for expanding consensus and agreement in Shariʻa norms in the Islamic public sphere. Because the Shariʻa-derived norm for *halal* meat exists widely in consensus, this metaphor could enhance the likelihood that Islamic banking would gain credence in the public sphere as well. If the populace believed that Islamic banking is like *halal* meat, consensus and agreement on the Shariʻa basis for Islamic banking would grow. To effectively link these subjects would also limit dissent because people would rarely argue against the merits and justification for *halal* meat, as they do about Islamic banking. The debates would lessen and the adoption of Islamic banking methods would grow. These purposeful attempts to create an Islamic public sphere require crafty and creative techniques, as the use of metaphor and analogy here demonstrates.

It is within this conceptual space that many banking practitioners and proponents of new bank management and methodologies could find success. If bank employees can alter people's affective experiences and meet customers' sense of gendered propriety, for example, participation in Islamic banking might grow. Islamic banks outside Jordan often do take steps in this direction, such as designating space and staff for "women's banking," or prioritizing single families, or building gender-segregated prayer spaces, or advancing other forms of "Islamic values." Nonetheless, the banks are faced with the nearly impossible task of altering the banking experience in such a way that customers have a positive affective response based upon ill-defined ethical and localized notions of feeling sufficiently "Islamic." Regardless of Islamized structural intents and alterations in physical space (as discussed in the case of Dahiyat Al-Rawdah in chapter 5, for example), these attempts alone are not sufficient to inculcate a sense of being truly Islamic. As a result, the message that the Islamic banks are implementing "the real Islam" is not deeply penetrating the populace.

The Islamic banks and religious authorities would benefit from these points. Dr. Hamid's notion that "Islam will sell the bank" will only do so much to build public consensus and a stronger customer base. There are strong limitations to this approach across many sections of society. As described in chapters 5 and 6, it is not a strategy that is particularly successful with the bank employees. Nor does it convince the customers that Islamic banking is anything more than a threshold requirement for one's religious duty, much less a pleasant experience or one that invokes a compelling feeling or belief in its methods' Islamic authenticity.

In contrast to the scholars and religious authorities, bankers and practitioners of Islamic banking need to work creatively to reach customers and their subjectivities. For the banks, promoting Islam means that customers need to experience "it"—this ill-defined sense of "Islamicness"—in moments of successful customer service encounters with personnel or technologies such as ATMs, or in structures as they wait in line or interact with employees on technical aspects of their accounts. For the religious authorities, there is a disconnect between their lack of acknowledgement of the importance of these experiences and their attempts to counter such subjunctives by invoking consensus and agreement in Shari'a norms. This disconnect does not appear to remedy customers' frustrating or offensive interactions at the banks. Nor does it seemingly appeal to people such as Mohammed, who are utilizing a well-informed, highly intellectual approach in their understandings of an authentic Islam in an Islamic bank. Religious authorities, such as the ones referenced here, are largely unconvincing.

## Profile of an Islamic Banking Customer: Raniya

One of the difficulties in understanding people's perceptions of Islamicness in Islamic banking is the degree to which the three modes of evaluation are fluid and easily applied at any given moment and in changing circumstances. The case of Raniya demonstrates this fluidity and responsiveness to altered contexts. A single female in her mid-twenties, she was one of the few committed Islamic banking customers I encountered. Ethnically a Palestinian, Raniya was a serious Muslim. She expressed her piety in modest, but contemporary and stylish fashion, a lack of cosmetics, and a strong sense of propriety when dealing with the opposite sex. She refused to shake hands with men or be alone with them, and would only "go out with the girls" when her mode of transportation did not put her into a vehicle with men. That meant she drove herself or had her father drive her. When we spent time together, I drove. This seriousness of her religious practice also emerged in her banking perspectives and practices. Raniya described her initial impressions and reasons for choosing an Islamic bank:

> My bank is the International Islamic Arab Bank. I have had an account
> for two years. I transfer my salary to it. I have ATM cards, for example,

so I don't have to go inside and see people and talk to them. This is Islam. This is good. But in general there is kind of a reputation for the Jordan Islamic Bank that their customer service is not so good. But at the International Islamic Arab Bank, it's not like that. When comparing it to the Jordan Islamic Bank, the International Islamic Arab Bank is much better. I went once to the Jordan Islamic Bank to cash a check and it was horrible. They don't talk to you because they have so many people to deal with. And I'm not talking here whether you are a girl or a man, it's just that they don't have time and it's crowded. But the International Islamic Arab Bank is a branch of the Arab bank. It's much more, let's say, proficient.

Here, Raniya begins her discussion by invoking the idea that the bank is "good" because of the affective experience prompted by the availability of ATM cards and ATMs outside of the bank. Although the bank's reputation frames the larger experience, the access provided by the ATM enables Raniya to keep some privacy from men and to manage her accounts on her own. Women often cited the ATM as a service that they preferred, as it enabled them to obtain their cash without compromising their modesty. They were not required to talk to male employees or other customers standing in line, or to interact with them in public in order to obtain cash. The system for accessing one's bank accounts by way of ATM cards is interpreted by Raniya and others in terms of Islamic values of privacy and modesty.

Raniya contradicts herself by citing the inability to access employees and get them to "talk to you" as a dissuading, affective factor. She appears to like the privacy of the ATM, but also wants access to gender-appropriate customer service on her terms. Furthermore, when she discusses the crowded conditions of the Jordan Islamic Bank, she makes a point that this frustration is not gendered. It is not about "whether you are a girl or a man." In fact, denying the gendering of the negative experience constructs it as a more universally negative experience: all customers would be frustrated with the crowdedness of the Jordan Islamic Bank.

Raniya invokes the English term "proficient" as her adjective of choice throughout the interview to describe the positive attributes of the International Islamic Arab Bank. In this instance she uses the term to underscore the bank's total services and capabilities to meet customer needs, such as limiting the amount of time spent waiting in line. This is another ethically informed idea of what an authentically Islamic bank does, which becomes important again later.

Next, Raniya expresses the values at play in assessing and evaluating her experience of Islamic banking, referring to the idea discussed earlier in the chapter that *murabaha* and *riba'* are the same thing. Following this, she moves into a framework that articulates that her choices are based on the notion that there is pressure for orthopraxy because religious authorities have endorsed Islamic banking, and that this is sufficient to explain the "Islamicness" of the banks. She explains:

> People are saying that the Islamic banks are just using the title but underneath they are just as other banks. But for me, even if that's correct, at least for me, I know that they are Islamic. There are two points here. For me, when I intended to open an account, the Jordan Islamic Bank and the International Islamic Arab Bank were the only two options for me. I didn't want to open an account at any other bank. So I chose the International Islamic Arab Bank.
>
> In terms of whether they are Islamic, first, there is *riba'*. You know *riba'*? In the International Islamic Arab Bank, they call it *murabaha*. At the Islamic banks it is *murabaha*. Some are saying that it is the same thing, and the Islamic banks just change the words. But for us, since some of the sheyukh say it's *halal*, it's ok. We go with it. My mom has an account at an Islamic bank. She used to work as a teacher and they used to transfer her money to this account. Now, what she does to avoid the *haram* money is, for example, there is a certain amount of profits each year, she just takes it out and gives it to charities.

For Raniya, the standards for orthopraxy put forth by the Shari'a committees and scholars that Islamic banking is *halal* trumps or supersedes the more personal, subjective sense or feeling that the methods might not be *halal*. In fact, from the outset, Raniya knew that she would use an Islamic bank and that there was no question that this was the best and right choice for her, regardless of the perceived similarities between *murabaha* and *riba'*. In fact, in a fashion similar to Mohammed's above, Raniya jettisons the argument entirely, relying upon the Shari'a scholars and sheyukh to justify her practice of banking "Islamically."

Most interestingly, there is a very gentle movement into the consensus and agreement of Shari'a norms, but in a way that reinforces and expands Islamic banking rather than tempering it. That is, the majority of Islamic scholars and Shari'a committees have issued *fatawi*, or Islamic legal rulings, that the profits gained at an Islamic bank from investments on deposits to savings and checking accounts are *halal*. However, Raniya's mother is turning her profits over to charity to avoid any hint of *haram* practices. She is going above and beyond, "avoiding the path to *haram*" by taking measures to make her Islamic practice at the bank as correct as possible.

In the next section of the interview, I pushed Raniya a bit about the oft-repeated notion that *murabaha* and *riba'* are the same, but with different names. Though she previously jettisoned the discussion by deferring to the scholars, she surprisingly shared a critical opinion. Here, Raniya uses the consensus and agreement in Shari'a norms, particularly by homing in on "the spirit" of Allah's message and Shari'a, as a means to justify her own position:

> ST: Some sheyukh say that *murabaha* and *riba'* are the same. Some say they are different, and *murabaha* is *halal*. What do you think?
>
> RANIYA: Honestly? I think they are the same. It's a kind of manipulation. The concept is correct. In *murabaha* they buy the thing you want to buy and they sell it to you for a higher price, and make you pay for it on the spot. In *riba'*? No. They will say "How much do you want?" "I want a thousand [JD]." Then they make you pay it back to them with four thousand. So actually it's the same: you end up paying more money than you took but with different ways. I don't think that Allah, when He said that *riba'* is *haram,* He didn't mean that only if you took the money from the Islamic bank He will give you twelve instead of ten. I think it's about the whole idea of taking money from people more than it costs you to deal with them. There is a rule in Shari'a that you can't buy money with money. Like for example if you took ten thousand you can't just buy it for twenty thousand. And the *riba'* is the same. And since I'm not involved in *quruud* [loans], then I don't care if it's *murabaha* or *riba'*.

By this point in the interview Raniya has already expressed cynicism about the Islamicness of the methods. In her personal experience and intuitive sense *murabaha* is not Islamic and is instead a "kind of manipulation." Raniya grounds this perception with a definition of *haram* financial transactions according to her knowledge of Shari'a: buying money with money. She is able to analytically separate the idea and the guiding ethic behind Islamic banking from the mechanism by which is its implemented, the former being "correct" and the latter, "manipulation." She expresses that, although she agrees with the critics that *murabaha* and *riba'* are essentially the same and critiques this aspect of the Islamic banks quite strongly as "manipulative," she sidesteps personally tackling the issue and ends the discussion by indicating that, because she does not utilize the loan services, she "doesn't care."

To probe this notion that Raniya avoids *haram* practices, particularly by avoiding loans, I asked her to explain her perspectives and understandings on moneylending. Here Raniya references consensus and agreement in Shariʻa norms. She said:

> The evil is in *quruud* [loans]. It's like, *"Al-shaytan ilathi taʻrifu ihsan min al-shaytan ilathi la taʻrifu."* ["The devils that you know are better than the devils you don't know."] So at least with the Islamic banks, the *sheyukh* said that it's *halal* and you can do it. You know we are not responsible for doing *fatawi* [sing. *fatwa*] and we don't know if it's *halal* or not. So, *khalas* [that's it]. We can do it. We can go to the Islamic banks.

Here, the notion emerges that individuals are not responsible for the kinds of knowledge and understandings for which the sheyukh are. Based on her knowledge of Shariʻa, Raniya is able to frame conceptually the issues of the "evil" found in Islamic banking in loans, and then to shift the responsibility for understanding it fully to the religious authorities and the sheyukh who issue the *fatawi*. Here, personal understanding and education only take Raniya so far: beyond her certain knowledge, she defers her actions and responsibilities to the Islamic scholars.

Raniya's discussion continues to be grounded in and justified by Shariʻa. She cites *hadith* and begins using her knowledge of Islamic history:

> *Ribaʼ* is a very big thing in Islam. You know that there is a *hadith* that "every penny you ate from *ribaʼ*, on judgment day your flesh will burn." [Speaking slowly] "With every penny you ate." Honestly we feel that it has very un-good [sic] or hard consequences. And *Subhan Allah* ["Praise God"], let's say that at the beginning of the Islamic *dawla* (state), we think that it was much better. People were, *yaʻni* [I mean], Saidni Amr Al-Khatab said that he couldn't find one poor man to give him charity or to give him *zakat* [charity]. There was no *ribaʼ* at that time. So they were helping each other out of *musaʻida*, because, you know, "I want to help you." But now they are just taking advantage of needy people.

This section of the interview is particularly important. Raniya uses the combination of Qurʼan and *hadith*,[3] Islamic history, and the recorded sayings of the Caliphate and companion of Mohammed, Amr Ibn Al-Katab, to justify her understanding that *ribaʼ* is *haram*. At the same time, she expresses a vision for a different kind of economy and a different kind of society that could be achievable through the avoidance of *ribaʼ*. The discussion is of a truly Islamic society that was achieved in the past, should be strived for today, and will be accounted for on Judgment Day. Raniya's comments reflect a highly informed and intellectual grounding of the principles that the Islamic banks are putting forth, even if she disagrees with the methods that the sheyukh themselves have found acceptable.

Based upon this theologically and historically grounded understanding of the role of *riba'* and the inconsistencies Raniya saw occurring in the administration of *murabaha* loans, she made a choice to bank with an Islamic bank. In particular, she opted for the International Islamic Arab Bank. She describes this process and the associations she has developed with conventional banking, particularly on the issue of marriage:

> So I felt that, ok, I'll go with the International Islamic Arab Bank. Even if the other bank is the Jordan Islamic Bank, I'll go with it. Even if they are not proficient like the regular banks and even if they're not like, you know, I don't mind. It's just that I want to be in the safe zone. And to be honest with you, I wouldn't accept [to marry] a guy who's working in a regular bank. [laughs] Because he's part of a *haram* system. It's the same thing as a guy who is working in alcohol even though he doesn't drink it. It's a *haram* system. It's the same thing. You know, they [potential suitors] call us at home and say, "We have a son who's working at the bank," and I'll say, "No. I don't want him."

Raniya's choice to "go with" the International Islamic Arab Bank over the Jordan Islamic Bank appears to be tied to her earlier evaluations based on affective responses to the latter institution, which she described as "crowded" and having employees who "had no time" and "don't talk to you." Again the economized and rational notion that an attractive bank is "proficient" or "capable" emerges. In fact, even if the International Islamic Arab Bank was "not proficient" she had decided that she would still bank there. Presumably this was based upon her understanding of religious injunctions and Shari'a norms, in particular her understandings of *riba'* and deference to the rulings of the sheyukh that Islamic banks are *halal*, and would have occurred despite any personal misgivings. This decision was, in a reflection of neoliberal piety, driven by a desire to be "in the safe zone" and out of harm's way come Judgment Day, and to avoid the path of *haram* in order to avoid all things *haram*.

This decision to bank at the International Islamic Arab Bank framed her decision to completely disassociate from the conventional banks and anyone affiliated with them. No longer would she consider marrying someone who deals in *riba'*, much as she would not consider marrying someone who deals in alcohol. This moral equivalence between dealing in *riba'* and alcohol represents a distinct affirmation of Raniya's piety. She attaches her personal preferences for both banking and marriage to a set of terms for righteous living that are based in Shari'a and have emerged with Islamic banking.

The development of moral associations constitutes another mechanism by which consensus in an Islamic public sphere could be established. In Raniya's conceptions, not only are the conventional banks *haram* but so too are the people within them. This physical and symbolic association enhances the means by which the *haram* aspects of life, including marriage engagements, can be further pushed out of publicly acceptable spheres. The public sphere, in this way, can be Islamized further and consensus expanded; Shari'a-derived consensus would no longer include only physical places and impersonal managerial and operational structures but also symbolic and social affiliations with persons.

As for why Raniya chose the International Islamic Arab Bank specifically, she goes on to explain that it is more "proficient" or "capable" for her personal economic situation when evaluated against more managerial and operational measures. She explains:

> From the Islamic banks in Amman we have two options. One is more proficient when comparing to the other one. So I'll go with that one. I used my salary for my transportation and my clothes, though I take money from my dad too. So I don't need, like, to have a loan to buy a car or very upscale things. *Al-hamdulilah.* I don't go into the bank. I went into the bank only twice. Once for opening the account and once for taking my ATM card.

A very subtle gendering of Raniya's experience merits discussion here. As described above, the ATM does not require women to go into the bank and enables them to have more privacy; this is a gendered expansion on her use of "proficient," which she takes to mean "capable" or "competent." Here, the term also means "convenient" and affirms her preferential, gendered experience at the bank. Raniya is able to count on two fingers the number of times that she has been inside the bank. In fact, the use of "*Al-hamdulilah*" ("Praise God") offers up a gentle affirmation that she is particularly pleased with the lack of requirements for physically entering the bank. The fact that her father is supplementing her economic position and this banking experience is notable. The positive evaluations of the International Islamic Arab Bank are based on very subtle feelings and affect, which include her father's cash contributions and the limited extent to which Raniya is required to access the employees and the bank's additional, "upscale" services.

Raniya ends her discussion of the Islamic bank by referencing again how her mother has decided to manage her returns received on deposits. This time, however, she discusses the practice as a means to express current engagement with the sheyukh. That is, Raniya's mother changed her treatment of profits after a discussion with the religious authorities:

> My account doesn't have any profits received [on the investments of deposits]. But my mom's does. And we talked to the sheyukh about it, and they said it's better to take it from the bank. We used to just leave it with the bank and say to them "*Khalas* [that's it]. We don't want it." But the sheyukh said it's better to take it so that the banks don't use it in *haram* things, but to take the money and give it to people that need it. They said that it won't be considered *sadaqa* or charity, but you will get the *tajrid* [a kind of spiritual "blessing" for doing something good] of taking the money to them. Like it's not a credit to me because it's not my money.

The family's original "impulse" or "instinct" was to refuse the profits and give them back to the bank as part of "avoiding *haram*." However, after talking to the sheyukh, they shifted from refusing the profits to redistributing them through charity. Although a less significant spiritual credit is given for this act, this quote demonstrates is that there is a tension, even disbelief, by the sheyukh that the Islamic banks would use the profits for *halal* things. Furthermore, by suggesting that Raniya's mother take the money out of the bank and give it to charity, the sheyukh are actually undermining previous *fatawi* that the profits are *halal* for customers to keep. This demonstrates that those who are ruling that these behaviors are *halal* mistrust the banks to do the right thing, and even mistrust *fatawi* that say they are sound.

Such undermining of consensus by and of the sheyukh also undermines the capacity to build consensus in an Islamic economics. This contradiction gets to the heart of the matter: even the promoters of something resembling an Islamic economics in the public sphere are unable to agree upon which Shari'a principles constitute the most important guiding ethics and how they should be applied. Though this could be attributed to a lack of knowledge by the sheyukh, an inability to convincingly pinpoint the most important principles at work, other than a vaguely understood injunction "to avoid *haram*," creates a significant obstacle to consensus in an Islamic economics and public sphere.

As Raniya's case demonstrates, deciding whether to become a customer at an Islamic bank, and at which one, has become one of the ways that Muslims in Amman today engage their religious beliefs in the economic sphere. The act comprises a complex negotiation of personal religious practice, an evaluation of the methods of Islamic banking, a use of background knowledge of Shari'a, the Qur'an, *ahadith*, and other historically grounded and authoritative texts, and a consideration for the contemporary religious environment within the context of the demands of everyday life. The level of satisfaction that one feels with the Islamic bank is subject to change during the negotiations that can also render Islamic banking authentically Islamic. Ultimately, customer satisfaction and effective "buy-in" to Islamic banking is not necessary if consumers like Raniya either refrain from participating in the aspects of Islamic banking with which they disagree or sidestep their personal reticence and cynicism by prioritizing the public discourse that "it's Islamic," and that this is enough.

Raniya's case demonstrates that these different layers of feeling, thought, belief, and action all coexist, overlap, and even contradict when negotiating religious practice in the economic sphere and in Islamic banking. Such experiences are also classed, gendered, contextual, and responsive to changes in one's environment and new forms of knowledge and experiences. Raniya's narrative also demonstrates that, even among people who are seriously pursuing Islamic banking as producers, legitimizers, or consumers, there is always debate, contention, and negotiation at play; though the sheyukh may have publicly supported a *fatwa* that profits on deposits are *halal*, privately they may offer other, even contradictory, advice. The notion by the religious authorities and some producers of Islamic banking that it is "really Islamic" does not hold true, even if the discourses and rhetoric of the proponents of the practice push this line publicly.

## Islamic Banking Methodologies Outside the Banks

It is not only individuals who are consumers of Islamic banking. Many other formal and semiformal economic institutions are adopting Islamic banking methodologies as a means to Islamize their own practices and to attract new customers and increase their customer base and profits. Through Islamized financial methods, individuals who support Islamic banking and finance can push for the growth of consensus and the enhancement of their agenda in spheres that lack the same level of government regulation as the formal Islamic banks.

The lack of governmental regulation offers these formal and semiformal institutions a promising method of promoting enhanced Shari'a-based consensus in an Islamic public sphere. That is, they offer a more casual and less regulated means for the populace to access and utilize Islamic methodologies. In theory the social distance between employee and customer at these institutions may be closer than those at the formal and systematized structures of the Islamic banks, and therefore may offer a more accessible venue for the inculcation of Shariʻa-based Islamic ethics. In reality, however, the customer demand and mechanics for administrating Islamic methodologies can become a kind of "ruse," which is more quickly exposed and revealed there than at the Islamic banks.

In Amman, many local, less formally organized associations and networks such as the *jamaʻiyyat*, or rotating savings and credit associations, are known for adopting Islamic methodologies. As one participant reported:

> In our *jamaʻiyyat*, we meet every two weeks. Mostly we get together to connect with each other and learn from each other. But, yeah, we have started Islamic methods for how we manage the money. We have a sheikh with us now in the *jamaʻiyyat*. He is the one who is managing all the Islamic aspects of the money. Now we use *murabaha* for the loans. He [the sheikh] says it's Islamic, so we agreed to it.

As this example demonstrates, it is not only individuals who must wrestle with the question of Islamic authenticity in banking and finance methodologies. Even among non–legalized and non–formalized institutions, the questions of Islamic authenticity come to the fore. This informant reveals that, as a group, the *jamaʻiyyat* agreed to limit personal dissent and objections and submit to the religious authority of a sheikh who is a member.

The Postal Savings System (Al-Sanduq Al-Tawfir Al-Barid) of Jordan is another example of a highly legalized and formalized institution that adopted Islamic banking methodologies. Similar to the *jamaʻiyyat,* it is not a bank and therefore is not subject to the laws put forth by the Central Bank of Jordan. The Postal Savings System was established in the 1970s. Similar to other such systems around the world, in the Jordanian Postal Savings System there is no minimum deposit. The deposits are held for a minimum period, typically one to five years, during which time they are put into *halal* investments. After the investment period is over, the deposit plus the returns are available for withdrawal or reinvestment. It offers no ATMs or other banking services.

I interviewed the director general of the Postal Savings System, Dr. Wael Akayleh, alongside the Jordanian economist who spearheaded the movement to Islamize the institution's investment methodologies, Dr. Baker Rihan. During the interview, they gave me a large number of electronic books, reports, and PowerPoint presentations, as well as paper brochures and flyers. In addition, I received a short lecture from Dr. Rihan[4] that modeled how moving away from a credit-based economic system prevents inflation and therefore stabilizes economic practices and creates opportunities for a more equitable society. After the lecture, Dr. Akayleh jumped in, extolling the values of using Islamic banking methodologies in the Postal Savings System:

> It makes a difference, you know? It makes a difference for our society, that's true. But it also makes a difference in the lives of the people who invest. They are making money *the Islamic way* [emphasis Dr. Akayleh's]. They don't have to have much money at all, two JDs, three JDs [less than $4.25]. They can deposit it. We take any amount. You know who this helps? Women in the rural areas. It's true. Women in the rural areas don't have much money and there's no Islamic bank in their village. But there's a post office, and they can invest it there. You know what else? The women who deposit their money are the only people who can take it out again. Their husbands can't take their money from them. We're giving women independence and freedom, and we're doing it *the Islamic way*.

As the quote demonstrates, not only are structural aims in place at the transformation of society away from credit-based interactions, but also the intent is to expand economic practices down to a financially vulnerable population—rural Jordanian women. In fact, Dr. Akayleh is promoting Islamic financial methods to support what is more frequently conceived of as economic development.

The social agenda here is also clear. Dr. Akayleh is promoting socially progressive ideas as mediated by an Islamic ethic: women can and should be financially independent from their potentially domineering husbands. They can achieve these goals because Islam provides for it. Islamic banking and finance, in this model, is also social and community development.

Other formal institutions and organizations that deal in money but have not yet crossed the threshold to become a "bank" are utilizing Islamic banking methods for more economically developmental ends. Such organizations sit in a different position than the banks: they are subject to alternative—and typically less stringent—laws than Islamic banking regarding the provisions of financial services. At the same time, they are subject to more pressure from clients, typically because they are not-for-profit and nongovernmental organizations that occupy intermediary positions as both producers and consumers of financial services.

## Conclusion: The Uncertain Experiment of Islamic Banking

Islamic banking and finance attempts to promote a "just and equitable model for economic growth" (Hefner 2006b, 17). In principle, its methods promote a public ethic of social justice and entrepreneurialism in accordance with localized interpretations of Shari'a, or Islamic law, and the Islamic injunction of "commanding right and forbidding wrong" (Cook 2000). In reality, the efforts of many Jordanians to construct a more Islamic public and economic sphere remain a work in progress.

Consumers of Islamic banking articulate a high degree of diversity in their understandings of a moral and Islamic economic life (El-Gamal 2006; Hassan 2008; Hirschkind 2006; Mahmood 2005; Starrett 1998; White 2003), which exist simultaneously with multiple, competing visions for a normative understanding of a real or authentic Islam (Berkey 2003; Eickelman and Piscatori 1996; El Fadl 2001; Hefner and Zaman 2007; Vikor 2005; Zaman 2002). This is because, although some scholars and some in the public remain convinced that the Shari'a guidelines for an Islamic economics are simple, clear, and irrefutable, a closer examination of Islamic banking reveals that, in social and cultural fact, they are not. The moral weight associated with banking in accordance with the mandates of Islamic law is an impossibly heavy burden for a bank to carry and extraordinarily difficult to transmit symbolically and technically to customers in ways that are both meaningful and convincing.

Islamic banking is a highly contested space in which a portion of the Ammani populace attempts to construct consensus that its actions are really or authentically Islamic. However, the construction is a rather experimental and uncertain cultural space. This chapter rounds out a demonstration of a variety of efforts by a diverse set of cultural players to construct a public perception of Islamicness in Islamic economics and banking and finance. Such efforts are widely divergent and invite a range of reactions. Although some Ammanis remain convinced that the Shari'a guidelines are simple and irrefutable, this chapter particularly demonstrates that even pious Muslims do not operate within a single ethical mindset. Rather, they often invoke a sense of affect, balance different interests, reference concerns of a less exhaustively Islamic sort such as "proficiency" when making judgments, and consider higher-level reasoning.

This chapter demonstrates that the message that the Islamic banks are implementing "the real Islam" is not deeply penetrating the populace. One of the reasons for this cynicism and disbelief is also the same reason many opt to become customers at Islamic banks: Islamic banks provide services that are strikingly similar to those of the conventional banks, and are evaluated according to those means and ends. At the same time, people are experiencing Islamic banking and evaluating its importance to their own piety. They are challenging the authorities that promote these rather unconvincing ideas as "Islamic." They do so all while evaluating their own experiences based on affective responses, pressures for orthopraxy, and consensus and agreement in Shari'a norms. In accordance with the amplification of the individual in neoliberal ethics, this is also a highly personalized and individualized process.

Building consensus for an Islamic economics and public ethics is a difficult project at best. The nature of such an endeavor, as a social and cultural "construction project," is also highly contingent upon the alignment of certain social, rhetorical, symbolic, even historical, values and arrangements. The challenge is that the results are more a diverse pluralism than a substantive, hegemonic hold on public space and public knowledge.

Because of the concerns and cynicism individual consumers express about Islamic banking, relatively low participation will likely continue in Amman. How the bank looks and feels to the consumer in affective judgments and the considerations for gendered experiences need to play a primary role in how banks carry the banner of Islam and in the ways Islamic scholars address the question. Certainly, "Islam" itself can be sufficient to convince some consumers to enact an orthopraxy and participate in Islamic banking. However this does not remedy the resulting disconnect in orthodoxy; customers are not internalizing the "Islamic" merits of Islamic banking, even if they support it with their money.

It is not surprising that customers of Islamic banks are less in consensus than customers of conventional banks about their satisfaction and the variables that comprise a "good" banking experience (Wilson 1991). When individuals consider their day-to-day needs for savings and spending, they are not looking for a conventional bank to solve global, moral, and social problems. At the bottom line, for the great majority of customers individual satisfaction relies on extraordinarily complex affective judgments and intellectual assessments of the Islamic nature of the bank in a context that promotes orthopraxy. The complexity indicates the influence of multiple standards for assessing Islamic banks, as well as a lack of consensus about which are the most appropriate. All of this suggests that, at least with regard to the ethics of Islamic economics, the ideas of the 'ulama establishment and promoters of Islamic law are far from hegemonic. Rather, individual customer satisfaction is a much more economic response that depends on whether the bank's services meet the customer's economic needs and whether the Shari'a committees have absolved them from accepting spiritual responsibility for their banking practices.

Ultimately, the great diffusion of variables customers use to assess their satisfaction indicates that Islamic banking in Amman is subject to evaluation and critique for a wide set of values, only a few of which are tied to anything explicitly Islamic. This reality renders Islamic banks subject to evaluation for their effectiveness both as banks and as carriers of Islam. The lack of consensus and extensive critiques of Islamic banking by its customers and by conventional bank customers reflects a wider cynicism about the agenda of Islamic economics in Jordan and the difficulties for the penetration of Islamized ideals and practices in economic practices.

At the same time, deference to people in authority—religious or otherwise—is contested. The self-legitimating discourse, "They say they're Islamic, so they are" is countered primarily by those with other socially recognized forms of knowledge, such as university degrees. This contestation of knowledge and legitimacy could be understood as a remnant of historical structures that have fragmented Islamic authority in other realms (Zaman 2002), and it is certainly part of the socially important process of deferring to the knowledge and experience of others, even if one does not agree with them. The bank's status as "Islamic" can be legitimized in this way. However, how the bank has achieved a certain threshold of socially-sanctioned Islamicness is established by a combination of the bank's self-legitimating discourses and the subjective experiences and knowledge at work within it. Banking can be rendered "Islamic" in title through relatively simple and self-reinforcing means; however, the degree to which it becomes Islamic enough for widespread buy-in and participation is held in each individual's experience and knowledge, and is not as easily subject to external legitimation. In Islamic banking and finance individuals are able to pursue their own religious practice and pieties while simultaneously contesting attempts to construct a unitary public ethic for an Islamic economics. This demonstrates a moral malleability and semantic versatility that renders the practice sometimes sufficiently Islamic for purposes of banking but rarely so for a convincing and meaningful engagement in one's personal pious life.

# CHAPTER 8

# Branding Islam

*Jordan's Arab Spring, Middle Class, and Islam*

## Jordan's Arab Spring

On January 25, 2011, I logged onto the Al-Jazeera website on my laptop and watched a live streaming video of Tahrir Square in Cairo with rapt attention. Like many people, I stayed up all night nearly every night that week, watching the news stories of protests erupting throughout the region. I could hardly believe what I was seeing: this was the end of Ben Ali in Tunisia, the end of the Mubarak regime in Egypt. Then leaders of other countries seemed to fall with surprising speed. My Facebook newsfeed featured story after story celebrating the great uprisings. The Arab Spring, they proclaimed, was the beginning of a real change in the region. Some believed that the protests were ushering in a new era for opposition parties, especially political Islamists such as the Muslim Brotherhood in Egypt and Al-Nahda in Tunisia, who proclaimed that they would replace the secular corruption, corporatism, and authoritarianism with equality, peace, justice, and—some hoped—a return to the ethics and norms of Islamic leadership witnessed at the advent of the religion. Islamic values and ethics—"the real Islam"—many asserted, would prove triumphant.

Commentators and Western analysts anticipated that surely Jordan too would fall to the Arab Spring. After all, the country was situated in between the most dramatic events in Egypt and Syria, was home to generations of

Palestinian refugees, and was one of the last bastions of monarchical rule. Journalists and analysts alike expressed excitement and alarm at the "the whisper of an Arab Spring" in Jordan (Farrell 2012). They wondered if Jordan would decide "To Spring or Not to Spring" (Sadiki 2012). They characterized Jordan as "Forever on the Brink" (Lynch 2012) of instability, revolution, and change. And yet, the Arab Spring never materialized in Jordan in the ways it did for its neighbors.

In fact, the Arab Spring of 2011 was relatively uneventful in Jordan and considered by some to be a "disappointment" or "washout," even a "failure" (Sadiki 2012; Seeley 2012). There were a number of protests calling for economic and political reform throughout the year, which were mainly planned, organized, and realized with little disruption and without mass mobilization. Though events of note such as the Dakhiliya protests in March 2011 were followed by both suppression and limited reform by King ʿAbdullah and the Hashemite Rulers, fundamental balances of power between the regime and populace remained overwhelmingly unchanged (Tobin 2012).

One reason for this is that protest is not a popular form of public expression in Jordan. According to one poll (Helfont and Helfont 2012, 90), "80 percent of respondents did not support the protests, 55 percent thought that protests led to chaos, and 15 percent viewed them as unnecessary and useless" (Barany 2013). The Hashemite regime, although not necessarily vested in the person of King ʿAbdullah (Yom 2009), carries some measure of legitimacy, religious authority, and prosperity (Adely 2012; Barany 2013; Clark 2004). Another reason is that political Islam, typically understood as present in the opposition parties of the Islamic Action Front and Muslim Brotherhood, has maintained that conditions of inclusive political plurality are, in fact, compatible with and defining of an Islamic moderation (Schwedler 2006, 2007). Furthermore, many Jordanians compared their situations favorably with their neighbors in Egypt, Syria, Iraq, and the West Bank. Because many people came to Jordan or descended from those displaced by situations of violence in these countries, their interests in security and stability were major obstacles to Arab Spring mobilization (Tobin 2012).

Most importantly, however, the Arab Spring in Jordan failed to mobilize the masses because a large and socioeconomically diverse middle class believed they were faring better than the most extreme cases domestically and those of most neighboring countries (Tobin 2012). Internal ethnic and religious differences and socio-economic cleavages were overlooked or ignored in favor of establishing a strong middle class ethic that embraced cosmopolitanism and rejected political instability or prospects of another civil war as a means to achieve political reform (Schwedler 2010; Tobin 2012). In many regards, the troubling political questions and engagements that fomented the Arab Spring in neighboring countries were trumped by "middle classness" and economic practices that are legitimized as really Islamic (Tobin 2014). As a result distinctive qualities to Jordan and Jordanian nationalism were revealed in the Arab Spring.

## Islam and the Nation: Post-Islamism

As demonstrated in this book, an authentic and modern Islam is asserted by way of style and aesthetic as well as cosmopolitanism. Benedict Anderson (2006) asserted that imagined communities are understood "not by their falsity/genuineness, but by the style in which they are to be imagined" (6). In Jordan, a stylized middle class Islam is key to a modern national identity. This is because Islamic practices cross ethnic divides and solidify a class-based form of socialization and affiliation, thus enabling a national identity. It is not the case, as Anderson argues, that national communities supplant "traditional" religious communities (2006, 7). The case of urban Amman demonstrates that Muslim modernity and cosmopolitanism are not necessarily the antithesis of national identity and in fact can be a constitutive component.[1]

As discussed in chapter 2, the Hashemites have attempted to sustain legitimacy by emphasizing the King's genealogical decent from guardianship of the Holy Places as well as his contemporary commitment to the welfare of the populace. King 'Abdullah embodies both an inheritance and a benevolence. This highly localized and contemporary construction of monarchal power "obscures both the monarchy's debt to British colonial powers in establishing its rule and the fact that, as a unified entity, Jordan has no historical memory before the twentieth century" (Schwedler 2006, 134). The shallow state-sponsored historical-nationalist narratives of tribe and natal geography resonate with less than half of the population who identify as ethnic Jordanians (Shryock 1997), and such narratives purposefully exclude ethnic Palestinians from national debates (Schwedler 2006, 134). These narrow nation-building attempts by the Hashemites left a large portion of Jordanian residents still seeking legitimate inclusion in the state.

Narratives of Islam and Islamic history, on the other hand, struck a chord with the ninety-two percent of the population who identify as Muslim. The Hashemite rulers utilized narratives of Islam "as an authentic expression of Jordanian identity against the spread of Arab nationalist, socialist, and communist movements" (Schwedler 2006, 139). They have attempted to reach ethnic Palestinians with claims of protecting the Islamic holy places in Palestine and struggling against Israeli advancement, invoking a language that the wider Jordanian citizenry find comprehensible through public displays of religiosity, speeches and public pronouncements. The carefully monitored messages broadcast from Amman's mosques, in turn, voiced support for the political aims of the regime, even promoting such ideals as supporting a national unity that supersedes political affiliation (Schwedler 2006, 140–41). By promoting a select, highly nationalistic version of Islam, the Hashemites sought to capture the Islamic Resurgence for its benefit, rather than allowing it to be channeled into political opposition (Boulby 1999, 98; Schwedler 2006, 140). By and large, it worked.

Political Islam has a primary concern of "building an 'ideological community'—establishing an Islamic state or implementing Islamic laws and moral codes" (Bayat 2007, 8). The Muslim Brotherhood and its political party, the Islamic Action Front (IAF), gained some traction in Jordan in the early 1990s, especially among Palestinians. The IAF's narratives of inclusion in the state have relied on carefully balanced, strategic relationships with the Hashemite rulers of support and nonviolence, along with the values of diversity and plurality and acknowledgement of women's rights. Despite this support, political Islam never ascended to the level of widespread popularity experienced in neighboring countries, and the Hashemite Rulers of Jordan are often upheld as the most successful in the region at managing its relationships with these actors and emergent institutions (Adely 2012; Brand 1994; Schwedler 2006; Tal 1995; Wiktorowicz 2001).

While the Islamic political institutions in Jordan may not be seeking a radical transformation of society, at least some of its participants are. For these Islamists, "Islam is more than a simple application of Shari'a. It is a synthesizing, totalizing ideology that must first transform society in order that Shari'a may be established, almost automatically" (Roy and Volk 1996, 39). As Janine Clark (2004) argues, however, rather than turning their efforts toward political activism in the state apparatus, the nation's Islamist interests engage primarily in the work of building and solidifying an Islamic middle class in Jordan. An Islamic middle class in Jordan has emerged as another narrative and a means for inclusion in the state. The outcomes, as this book has demonstrated, are plural, diverse, at times contested, and at times reach consensus.

Part of the reason for this, as is demonstrated ethnographically in this book, is that the Jordanian populace and its rulers simply can not agree on a singular Islam that serves as the standard for a total system of ideal, Shari'a-based political organization, public cultures of piety, and personal codes of conduct and morality. What "the real Islam" means politically in Jordan is simply too diverse for the Hashemites to control. The seeming contradiction is that it is through these conditions of Islamic plurality, rather than the processes of exclusion, the nation is generated and national sentiment is constituted. If political Islamism was "the Muslim middle class's way of saying no to what they considered their excluders—their national elites, secular governments, and those governments' Western allies" (Bayat 2007, 6)—then Jordanians were saying yes to living in a nation defined by diversity and plurality, in some cases more so than their counterparts in neighboring countries. This has not been unanticipated because "since the 1990s, against the backdrop of intensifying religious sentiment in the Muslim world, a nascent post-Islamist trend has begun to accommodate aspects of democratization, pluralism, women's rights, youth concerns, and social development with adherence to religion" (Bayat 2007, 188–89).

As a result, the Jordanian context much more closely approximates conditions of post-Islamism, which "represents an endeavor to fuse religiosity and rights, faith and freedom, Islam and liberty. It is an attempt to turn the underlying principles of Islamism on its head by emphasizing rights instead of duties, plurality in place of singular authoritative voice, historicity rather than fixed scripture, and the future instead of the past" (Bayat 2007, 11).

Post-Islamism as witnessed in Amman is, therefore, one way to characterize contemporary Islamic practice. The insertion of Islamic ethics and norms into economic practices and the economization of Islamic practices create a middle class that is pushing for contemporary, modern, market-friendly enterprises that dominate public religious life, civil society, and nationalist inclusions. Islamic nationalism in Jordan is contingent on economic practices and economizing processes with calculative agencies. As a result, we can see that the Arab Spring failed to materialize in Jordan in large part because of a lack of political interest in instability for the sake of anticipated rewards, which are derived from historical precedent, contemporary demography, and religious pluralism. Jordanians simply could not see the benefits when calculated in relation to the risks of instability, (another) civil war, and enhancing and deepening the cleavages that are already present. Accepting the Hashemite rulers during the Arab Spring, as an expression of nationalism, was an outcome of calculative agencies and processes of economizing. The idea that Islamic nationalism in Jordan is contingent on middle-class interests and economic practices is also made clear in the case of Jordan's attempts to join the Gulf Cooperation Council.

## Defining the Nation: Jordan and the G.C.C.

In early 2011, Jordan and Morocco submitted bids to become members of the G.C.C., or Gulf Cooperation Council, joining Bahrain, Kuwait, Oman, Qatar, Saudi Arabia, and the United Arab Emirates in an economic and

political cooperative relationship. The alliance brings with it a series of objectives such as regulatory consistency in economic, finance, customs, and
trade relations. Citizens of G.C.C. countries are allowed open movement
to other G.C.C. countries, as well as cross country investment and trade.
The Peninsula Shield Force, the unified military of the alliance, sent Saudi
Arabian forces to help quell Bahraini revolutionary uprisings in March 2011.
A common currency, the Khaliji, has been proposed. In an alliance that mir-
rors many European Union and Schengen State objectives, the G.C.C. holds
both short- and long-term promises for its members' citizens.

As Barany (2013) has pointed out, the citizens of G.C.C. countries
constitute some of the wealthiest in the world. In 2010, Qatar's per capita
gross domestic product in purchasing power parity was first in the world,
at $179,000. Saudi Arabia, the poorest of these member countries, ranked
fifty-fourth, at $24,200. The state-bestowed benefits in these countries often
include free housing, healthcare, education, and no income tax. By contrast,
Jordan would struggle to survive financially without aid from the United
States, European Union, and Saudi Arabia. Furthermore, living standards in
Jordan and Morocco are modest, with per capita incomes in 2010 of only
$5,400 in Jordan (142nd) and $4,800 in Morocco (149th). In relatively poor
societies like these—the rural poverty of Morocco and Jordan is particularly
conspicuous—regime legitimacy does not derive from people's sense of economic well-being. G.C.C. wealth, particularly in the wealthiest countries
of Qatar and the UAE, ultimately limited the interest of the populace in
participating in Arab Spring protests. "Rich people," it seems, "seldom take
to the streets" (Barany 2013, 15).

When Jordan submitted its bid in May 2011, it was the first time that
new members had been considered. The timing coincided with many Arab
Spring protests in the region, which raised eyebrows, concerns, and regional
support for political stability (Ramady 2012). Jordan, despite its status as a
poorer country, attempted to mirror the political strategies of the G.C.C.
countries to gain national support. By aligning themselves with the G.C.C.,
the Hashemites tacitly acknowledged a national importance to solidifying
and securing the Muslim middle class. Jordan's economic and political stability, it seems, would be best bolstered by way of patronage systems that secure
personal wealth rather than through the voting booths.

Reactions to the news of the bid by middle-class Jordanians were mixed.
Twitter, Facebook, and local blogs such as 7iber.com lit up with comments
that ranged from frustration and disgust that the Jordanian government
had unilaterally and undemocratically sought a political and economic alliance without polling the citizens, to joking and sarcasm about the deep
national differences between Jordan and the Gulf countries despite a general

similarity in characterizations as "Arab-Islamic." Many of the ensuing jokes displaying cynicism or uncertainty about the G.C.C. membership circled around differences in levels and types of consumption between wealthier G.C.C. member constituents and poorer Jordanians. References to Gulf cultural practices of austere dress, censorship, and extreme wealth dominated the Twitter responses. Multiple references were made to the *ghotra*, the red-and-white head covering associated with Saudi Arabian men, including how to wear it "correctly" and the amount of starch one must use when ironing it. One user posting on Twitter made reference to the lack of customs fees on otherwise cost-prohibitive cars in Jordan (which are in abundance in Saudi Arabia), stating that he had "just ordered my new white Chevrolet [C]aprice with the burgundy leather upholstery inside." Many other people expressed anticipation that gas prices in Jordan would drop to Saudi levels. As one tweeted, "Fuel prices to drop to pre-2003 prices and car prices to go down 50% #wishing."

At the same time, Jordanians on Twitter drew upon differences between the perceived and stereotyped austere, largely Salafi Islamic observance found in G.C.C. countries (particularly Saudi Arabia), contrasting this with the authentic Islam of Jordanians with questions such as, "Does this mean I can go up to any non-*khaliji* people and threaten them with *tafsir*?" *Tafsir* is the Arabic word for "critical interpretation" or Qur'ic exegesis. These questions attempted to turn the association of aggressive Saudi sheyukh back on them and "retaliate" with an interrogation of them and their religious practices. Another summed it up with, "I guess you will wear a *dishdash*, have 4 wives dressed in black and a few extra bucks."

These tweets and other social media responses all speak to a public dialogue about classed nationalism and do so in relatively antagonistic terms. Together, they amplify the notion that Jordanian nationalism through the Muslim middle class is one that prides itself on the values of diversity in dress and public representations, democratic processes of openness and some freedoms in expression, and a Shari'a-derived understanding of the role and purposes of wealth. At the same time, the assumption is that the cultures of G.C.C. countries and Saudi Arabia in particular are going to dominate Jordan's cultural landscape. These social media expressions, therefore, hint at a precariousness and an uncertainty about Jordan's Islamic middle class in the face of more singular expectations for public Islam. They also suggest an uncertainty within Jordan's borders. However, as long as middle-class Jordanians are able to continue consuming their symbolic markers of an Islamic middle class as distinct from other nationalist styles and austere aesthetics of an Islamic life and lifestyle, growing precariousness will be kept at bay. The

Hashemites will continue to secure their place as the political object of an Islamic middle-class, nationalist sentiment.

## Naturalizing Islam

As Robert W. Hefner wrote in the concluding chapter of *The Political Economy of Mountain Java* (1993b), "The 'self' at work in 'self-interest' about which economists speak is not something to be ignored, but is indeed both constitutive of and reconstituted by the very processes in which economic actors engage." As Hefner hints, a relegation of a "self" to that of the inevitable, taken-for-granted, Bourdieuian *doxa* (1977) overlooks the moments of tentativeness and unassuredness that are rife in religious practices and performances, in the education and socialization of ethics, and in the often public debates about what exactly it means to be an adherent of the "real" Islam in a contemporary Muslim-majority society. There is no assuredness in the transfer of ethics of practice and personal piety in socialization between parent and child, between religious authority and lay practitioners, or from belief to practice. Nor is there certainty in the transfer of ethics in the commanding of right and the forbidding of wrong (Cook 2000). The "self" here is on tentative ground, continually being pushed and prodded to think and rethink, to assess and reassess the rationales, logics, and aspirations of one's practices, and in turn pushing and prodding others.

The "self" at work here does not assume a predetermined, static, and pious "Islamic self." Even employees of the Islamic bank—the producers of Islamic economics, who, in theory, could have a singular vision for Islamic norms in economic practices—were altering and being altered by their work and interactions at the bank. Everyday piety in economic practices of Amman demonstrates that "inner states like sincerity or belief . . . may not always be relevant to the social and cognitive contexts of ritual action" (Seligman et al. 2008, 4). Although my informants sought to make meaningful normative practices and ritual performance, this study contains no assumptions of determinative linkages or even coherence between the external form of ritualized behaviors in orthopraxy, normative ethics and doctrine, and one's internal state in orthodoxy; orthopraxy, doctrine, and orthodoxy are analytically different realms for considering and engaging pietistic behaviors.

In urban Jordan these processes of economization are processes in which ethics and ideas become rendered as "Islamic," typically as they derive from the Qur'an, *sunna*, and *ahadith*, and are asserted in balance with competing demands, knowledge, and interests in everyday practice. These integrations of Islamic ethics and ideas in processes of economization and the logics of

neoliberal and calculative agencies in Islamic practice have become naturalized in the eyes of the actors. The injection of economizing religious ideals
is consistent, if not wholly expected. Mark Allen Peterson (2011) discusses
these phenomena in the context of children's magazines in Cairo, Egypt:

> Another important aspect of the imagined world of these texts is their
> naturalization of Islam. Although many of the countries in which these
> magazines circulate have large Christian minorities, there are few un-
> ambiguously Christian names among the readers. Articles emphasize
> Islamic history, and several magazines have regular columns on Islam:
> Majid's is four pages and is marked by a pastel orange and yellow car-
> toon mosque with pink minarets. Even where specific features about
> Islam are absent, *Islam is the unmarked normative cultural backdrop to most
> narratives.* (48; emphasis mine)

There is a seeming contradiction at play. On the one hand, throughout this
book we see Islam objectified and utilized for other, pietistic ends. On the
other hand, it works as an unmarked normative backdrop.

In naturalization processes "Islam" in an often abstract sense is injected
into economizing processes and vetted in competition, contest, and negotiation. In some spheres this results in resolution, and in others, greater fragmentation. That "Islam," in highly abstracted terms, *should* be present is largely
uncontested and constitutes the naturalized backdrop. Rather, debated in
these processes is *what kind of Islam* should be present. As "Islam" becomes
the "unmarked normative cultural backdrop," debates about right practice
can and do shift to differences in style, language, and temporal and spatial
arguments in objectified forms.

If one believes as one lives, then these debates are about life and lifestyle,
which are justified by way of Islam and references to Islam. The debates are
not about "Islam" per se, but rather about the style of the *hijab* or which Islamic bank to use. That Islam is present is the "unmarked normative cultural
backdrop," but what kind of Islam is still up for grabs. "Islam" is simultaneously naturalized, objectified, and functionalized.

As a result, a modern Islamic authenticity also carries significance for non-
Islamized ends. Islamic rituals and the acts of "consuming Islam"—including
fasting for Ramadan, wearing the *hijab*, working at an Islamic bank, or using
an "Islamic" credit card—are relevant for understanding human activities in
ways that go far beyond their seemingly religious meanings. For example, we
know that women balance the demands for an Islamic banking system with
gender and class-mediated preferences for "modesty" and "proficiencies."

Wearing the *hijab* may speak to internal debates about moral standing in the community and appropriate spaces for women's work as much as to one's personal devotion to Allah. We simply cannot assume it is only the latter. New forms for consuming Islam are also actions that speak to a whole host of symbolic meanings, many of which are tied to sex and gender, class, and idealized forms for contemporary middle-class living (Orlove 1989, Rutz 1989), with implications that will continue into the future.

## Branding Islam

Economizing logics and calculative agencies in pietistic practices are naturalized to the same degree as expectations for the presence of some visible and notable reference to Islam. As a result, Islamic piety can and does take on logics and motives of capitalism and ethical intentions of neoliberalism. Stylizing Islam as authentic and modern is also a way of "branding" Islam and oneself as a certain kind of Muslim.

It is no accident that Amr Khaled, perhaps the best-known of the Middle East's "self-help"–style televangelists, was an accountant before he became a preacher (El-Nawawy and Khamis 2009; Hardaker 2006; Moll 2010; Rock 2010). As his program *Life Makers* developed into a global phenomenon calling for action in local communities to promote socioeconomic development and equality, the economization of Islam became clearer. Hamzeh Hassouneh, the vice president of the *Life Makers* chapter in Jordan, said,

> Religion is used merely as our guiding force for a greater cause. Islam is our muse of inspiration though we are all here for the same reason. What *Life Makers* is about is the *nahda*, the revival, the potential for our nations to be more than they are. This isn't about politics or dissent; this is about utilizing the youth to make a positive change in their communities. (Tawarneh 2005, 41–42)

What Khaled called "development through faith and manners"[2] and what Daromir Rudnyckyj (2010) terms "development through faith" in Indonesia has struck a chord for Muslims around the world. The vision for Middle Eastern nations by middle-class participants throughout the region includes "jobs" and "women's empowerment" as its top priorities.[3] The future of Islamized economic practices and economized Islam reside in efforts at branding—branding oneself, one's community, and even one's nation. The movement is far from marginal: there is now a *Journal of Islamic Marketing* that published an article titled *On Islamic Branding: Brands as Good Deeds.*[4] The future of Islamic branding, it seems, is already here.

As this ethnography has demonstrated, building consensus on these features is not easy. Multireligious frameworks are necessary for life in any contemporary, global society. However, diversity in contemporary Amman is not defined simply in terms of Muslims and Christians. It is also defined by the varying practices of Muslims. Perhaps, however, branding an Islamic diversity is the next step for Muslims in urban Jordan.

# Notes

## 1. A Muslim Plays the Slot Machines

1. In Arabic, Ammanis discussed "the real Islam" using the literal translation, "*al-Islam al-haqqiqi.*"

2. This notion is quite pervasive in the literature, and analysts often point to the rise of political Islam as both the cause and the outcome. Nonetheless, the cultural expressions and underpinnings for post-Islamic Resurgent practices often reference dress, prayer, and ethics of consumption of and abstinence from food and drink. See also Tarlo 2010.

3. See also Adely 2012, Droeber 2005, Fernea 2011, Tobin 2013.

4. Much of the literature on Islam in the contemporary Middle East assumes a post–Islamic Resurgent and contemporary context in which "the public," broadly construed, is actively pursuing and deepening Islamic piety. This is my suggestion as to why this might be true.

5. When rendering decisions on "the real Islam," middle-class Ammanis did not typically use the Arabic term for authenticity, *asaala*. Rather, they invoked ideas of authenticity with claims and discussions of "the real Islam," or *al-Islam al-haqqiqi*, which indexes beliefs, values, and practices that are "assumed to constitute a normative and timeless 'Islam'" (Hefner and Zaman 2007, 51; see Bowen 2012).

6. '*Arabeezi* or *3rabeezi* is a word that mixes '*Arabi* and *Ingleezi*, or the Arabic and English languages, in a similar fashion to "Spanglish."

7. This is similar to trends in the neighboring countries of Egypt (Mahmood 2005), Lebanon (Deeb 2006), and pre–civil war Syria (Salamandra 2004).

8. My students referred to these agonistic relationships in terms of a combination of "friend" and "enemy," or "frenemy." The debates about the "real" Islam are often agonistic and even require such competition. This is described in more detail in chapters 3 and 4.

9. See Alam 2008, Jones 2011, Messick 1993, Metcalf 1982.

10. Many urban ethnographies take this approach, e.g. Bourgois and Schonberg 2009, Chen 2001, Gallagher 2012, Hartigan 1999, Salamandra 2004, Stoller 2010, Zhang 2002.

11. The anthropology and sociology of work literature is extensive. See Kondo 1990.

12. https://www.facebook.com.

13. The association of Saudi preachers with fearmongering appears to be shared throughout the region. In the first quote in Charles Hirschkind's ethnography *The Ethical Soundscape: Cassette Sermons and Islamic Counterpublics*, the informant says, "That preacher must be Saudi. They're the ones who really know how to scare you" (2006, 1).

## 2. The History of Amman

1. As translated from French by Austin Jessie Davidson.

2. These relationships continue today: the current King 'Abdullah protects the Abu Jabers, who own the largest alcohol production in the country with Amstel Beer.

3. There are conflicting reports between Kamal Salibi's and Eugene Rogan's accounts of the relationship between the Circassians and the Bedouin, and of the Circassians and the Ottomans. Salibi considers the Circassians "generally docile" and easily subject to Ottoman taxation and Bedouin attacks (2006, 44), while Rogan characterizes their local reception as "alien and menacing" and writes that they "were feared by the local inhabitants and accused of murder (1999, 75). However, both agree that the historical record indicates the Bedouin attacked the Circassians.

4. Christians comprised all kinds of ethnic groupings and could be found as "Palestinian-Christian" and "Jordanian-Christian." "Arab Christians in Jordan" has now emerged as a salient label in the literature, jettisoning the ethnic differentiations entirely (Sennott 2001), demonstrating the ways in which even a most basic religious identification trumps many other forms of identity and sociality.

5. The 1970–1971 Civil War, which most Jordanians are reticent to discuss even today for fear of heightening social differentiations and ethnic divides, can be seen as the violent peak to this contest for the "soul" of the new nation (Robins 2004, 3; see also Foucault 1991 on power contests in war).

6. A city in the south known as a prominent location for "Jordanian-Jordanians."

7. Amman's difficult agricultural origins are also considered to have been "an opening" for the attention of and investment by regional merchants (Rogan 1999, 94).

8. The Hussein Mosque was completed in 1927. Similar durability was developed in other, non-Muslim spaces for religious life. Rogan (1999) points out that the Orthodox Church in Salt became a "massive domed structure," and that a small mosque with a tiled roof had been constructed by 1921 (248). These events are both regional and important in the development of Amman.

9. As translated from French by Austin Jessie Davidson.

## 3. Making it Meaningful

1. Literally "Forbidden! Forbidden!"

2. As in, "It's obvious."

3. *"Iqra'a!"*

4. Qur'an 8:39.

5. Qur'an 2:144: "We have seen the turning of thy face unto the sky; and now we shall turn thee a way that shall well please thee. So turn thou thy face towards the Inviolable Mosque [the *Ka'aba* in Mecca]; and wheresoever ye may be, turn ye your faces towards it."

6. Quoted in Lings 1994, 149.

7. Qur'an 8:9.

8. Qur'an 8:12.

9. "'Ashura [i.e., the tenth of Muharram] was a day on which the the tribe of Quraish used to observe fasting in the Jahiliyyah [Before Islam]. The Messenger of Allah also used to observe *saum* [fast] on this day. So when he emigrated to

Al-Medina, he observed fasting on it and order [the Muslims] to fast on it. When the fasting of [the month of] Ramadan was enjoined, it became optional for the people to observe fast or not to observe fast on the day of 'Ashura" (cited in Sahih Bukhari Book 63, *Hadith* 3831; Bukhari 1987, 104).

10. "Ibn 'Abbas (Allah be pleased with both of them) reported that the Messenger of Allah (may peace be upon him) arrived in Medina and found the Jews observing fast on the day of 'Ashura. The Messenger of Allah (may peace be upon him) said to them: What is the (significance) of this day that you observe fast on it? They said: It is the day of great (significance) when Allah delivered Moses and his people, and drowned the Pharaoh and his people, and Moses observed fast out of gratitude and we also observe it. Upon this the Messenger of Allah (may peace be upon him) said: We have more right, and we have a closer connection with Moses than you have; so Allah's Messenger (may peace be upon him) observed fast (on the day of 'Ashura), and gave orders that it should be observed" (cited in Sahih Muslim Book 6, *Hadith* 2520; Muslim ibn al-Hajjaj 2000, 664).

11. Based upon the example of Mohammed as reported in the Sunnah, *tarawih* prayers are extra, optional prayers (in an order and number prescribed each by the various juridical schools or *madhaahib*) that take place during the month of Ramadan. The belief is that each night, one should recite a part of the Qur'an in prayer. Known to be physically exhausting, the nightly *tarawih* prayers contain up to forty series of prostrations.

12. Though this story was commonly recited by my informants as "true," I was never able to find a news article about it. Such rumors serve to reinforce the legal and ethical need to fast publicly and the potentially deadly ramifications if one opts against it.

13. This is a similar case to that of the arrest and death of a man who violated the Ramadan consumption laws described above. I heard women talking about the arrests and closure of Gloria Jeans, but was unable to find a written report or account of the events.

14. "*Al-amr bi'l-mar'uf wa-n-nahy 'an al-munkar.*"

15. A similar phenomenon is discussed by Lindsay Gifford in her dissertation (2009).

16. Prices for this affair often start at over 30 JD, or $42.00, per person, or roughly more than ten percent of an average monthly salary.

17. Other anthropologists have explored this theme (Jacobs 2002; Scott 2009, in the case of Thai Buddhism).

18. In fact, most popular shows in Amman are from outside of Jordan. This is primarily because the government's control of local media is as a "propaganda machine" (Moaddel 2002, 14). As my university students pointed out, they much preferred watching *Friends* on MBC from Dubai or news on Al-Jazeera than the mundane "news" of the Royal Family's comings and goings on Jordanian TV.

19. I had inquired as to how Aminah was able to be unveiled, while the rest of us were required to cover our heads. I was told that the *zawiyyah* is a space in which the rules of dress and sexual segregation were guided by the Sheikh, tradition, and localized norms, whereas those in a mosque were guided "by the Qur'an." In a mosque, the bride would not have been allowed to take off her veil, even in a women's section.

20. Maqlubah is a traditional Palestinian dish of flavored rice with some vegetables, often with fried almonds and other nuts, topped by chicken or other meats.
The dish is often served with a side of yogurt and salads.

21. Many of these authors examine the principle in Orthodox Jewish communities (as, for example, Schlussel 1982). While there are some similarities, the
competitive pieties on display in this Muslim community during Ramadan carried
distinctively different features because of the economizing self-interest in pious neoliberal formations and because of the temporality of the month.

## 4. Love, Sex, and the Market

1. The case of Egypt is particularly salient for this. HarassMap (http://harassmap.
org) tracks areas of Cairo where women report being harassed. Many if not most of
the victims wear the *hijab*.

2. McDermott (2010) cites 60 percent, roughly the same rate that Smith-
Hefner discusses in Indonesia (2007, 389–90).

3. See also Macleod 1993, Ong 1990, White 2002.

4. How the Islamic Bank can be considered an "intimate space" is discussed
later in this chapter.

5. Sunni Forum website: http://www.sunniforum.com/forum/showthread.
php?5741.

6. www.youtube.com/watch?v=f-UwS_XAcVE

7. Even the invoking of guarding men's spirituality in an appeal to a kind of
public ethic can be considered self-interest. Generally, women who wear the *hijab* in
Amman are assumed to experience less sexual harassment than women who do not.
Amman is not a place where veiled women frequently encounter public comments
about their looks or unwanted touching by men. Wearing the *hijab* protects against
the frequency of those experiences and, as such, can also be construed as an act of
self-interest.

8. The *mu'tazili* have been at odds with more mainstream Sunnis because they
hold the belief that human reason and intellect can be applied to Qur'anic revelation.
Therefore they tend to have a more metaphorical interpretation of the Qur'an. See
also Berkey 2003; Cook 2000, 195–226; Eickelman and Piscatori 1996.

9. Frequently cited for this was the *hadith* "'Ali reported that the Prophet (peace
be on him) took some silk in his right hand and some gold in his left, declaring,
'These two are *haram* for the males among my followers'" (cited in Abu Dawud Book
34, *Hadith* 4046; Abu Dawud Sulayman ibn al-Ash'ath 1993, 1133). Another *hadith*
supporting the idea that some materials are unacceptable for men but acceptable for
women is "The Prophet received some ornaments presented by Negus as a gift to
him. They contained a gold ring with an Abyssinian stone. The Prophet turning
his attention from it took it by means of a stick or his finger, then called Umamah,
daughter of Abul's and daughter of his daughter Zaynab and said, 'Wear it, my dear
daughter'" (cited by Abu Dawud in Book 34, *Hadith* 4223; Abu Dawud Sulayman
ibn al-Ash'ath 1993, 1175).

10. Unit of currency, expressed in coins, in the Ottoman Empire and many Persian states.

11. For details about these styles, see http://hijabfashionstyles.com/hijab-fashion/arab-hijab-fashion-styles.

12. Ammanis consider nightclubs places to especially avoid during the summer months because of the increased patronage by Saudis and other Gulf residents. In fact, the increased patronage of prostitutes in Amman in the summer has also attracted higher numbers of Arab female prostitutes from countries such as Morocco and Tunisia. However, female prostitutes typically dress in full *niqab* and *abayas* so as to protect their identities. This makes them nearly indistinguishable from other face-veiled Arab women such as most "Gulfies," and further complicates the notion that the more covered a woman is, the more religious or pious she is likely to be.

13. The *Sheyukh* from Saudi Arabia are particularly notable for advocating the most austere forms of the *hijab*, which is often locally seen as "illogical," "impractical," and even "absurd." On October 3, 2008, the BBC published an article in which a Saudi cleric, Sheikh Muhammad al-Habadan, argued on the Muslim satellite channel Al-Majd for a veil that only reveals one eye, because the *niqab* that reveals both eyes is too seductive and encourages women to wear cosmetics. http://news.bbc.co.uk/2/hi/middle_east/7651231.stm.

14. It is important to note that I never once heard anyone say that it was acceptable to put on the *hijab* in public. This is presumably due to the operating definitions of 'awra at play in a consistent and responsible manner: if you believe that your head is part of your 'awra, why would you ever display it? By covering your hair in front of people, you signal to them that they just saw your 'awra. It would be something akin to seeing a person in America zipping up their pants while walking down the street.

15. However, this did arise as an issue in my time at the bank and is discussed in chapter 6.

## 5. Making it Real

1. *Hadritak* is a formal salutation, roughly meaning "Sir." I rarely heard it used in Jordan. It is much more frequently used in, e.g., Egypt.

2. The Arabic verb used for "to invite" is *da'wa*. It also means "to call" someone.

3. The working theological assumption I heard frequently is that everyone is a Muslim, and becoming a Muslim is "returning" or "reverting" to one's true nature. The evidence I heard for this was from Shari'a: "Mohammed said, 'No child is born except in *fitra* (the innate state) and then his parents make him Jewish, Christian or Magian (Zoroastrian), as an animal produces a perfect young animal'" (cited by Sahih al-Bukhari Book 23, *Hadith* 1385, Bukhari 1987, 267).

4. This was the most polite way of saying "no" that I knew.

5. While it is true that such a divide between "real" and "abstract"—and a seemingly absolute one at that—is the result of "the economy," which Mitchell (2002) demonstrates as "a set of practices for producing this bifurcation" (82, 116–17), this is precisely how it appeared to my informants.

6. *Riba'* is literally "increase" and is most commonly understood as "usury" and/or "interest." It is widely considered forbidden in Islamic banking and finance. *Ribah* or *ribha* is literally "profit," which is widely considered acceptable and important in *halal* transactions.

7. Anwar (2003) cites twenty-one different modes. There are likely many more.

8. In *murabaha*, the origin of the word is *ribah*, or profit, not *riba'*, or interest. Confusion in the English literature—as *riba'* is very frequently written as *ribah* or *riba*—often results in misunderstandings as to the permissibility of interest.

9. Its pervasiveness has been called colloquially "*murabaha* hegemony."

10. The buying and selling of goods between two partners is now generally forbidden. However, as a liquidity-raising activity, the introduction of a third partner can legitimate the contracts as *tawarruq* or Reverse *murabaha*, as was described above. In contemporary financing through *tawarruq*, three parties are involved. Put simply, the first party needs cash, and buys something on credit from a second party. Then the first party sells the items to a third party for spot payment in cash. Effectively, this gives the first party an influx of cash and a scheduled credit payment. Technically, this is Islamically sound, although many see this as a violation of the "spirit of the law."

11. See also Warde 2001.

12. The Interfaith Worker Justice Organization (http://www.iwj.org/resources/islam) uses both the Qur'an and the *hadith* to demonstrate compatibilities between Islam and livable wage movements: "And O my people! Give just measure and weight, nor withhold from the people the things that are their due" (Quran 11:85). Another verse quotes Abu Huraira as saying "The Prophet Muhammad, peace and blessings of God be upon him, said, 'I will be the opponent of three types of people on the Day of Judgment . . .'" one of whom "hires a worker, but does not pay him his right wages owed to him after fulfilling his work'" (cited by Sahih Bukhari Book 37, *Hadith* 2270, Bukhari 1987, 258).

13. Kholoud Saqqaf, Deputy Governor of the Central Bank of Jordan, explained to me that the Central Bank had received only one other application for licensing as an Islamic Bank during that twenty-year period. It was from the Islamic National Bank, which shut down operations before it opened. Since 2005 the Central Bank has received thirty applications for licensing for Islamic banks, but has kept licensing approvals low in order to "maintain the strength of the Jordanian economy."

14. As one member of SABEQ, the USAID-funded Business Development Organization, commented to me, "If it operates like a bank and invests like a bank, why is it not a bank?" This raises an important question about the operations and working definitions found within the banking industry in Jordan.

15. "Bismillah al-rahman al-rahim": "In the name of God." This invocation to Muslim prayers appears in the opening to this book.

16. It is also the color of the Muslim Brotherhood. Another neighborhood in Amman, A'bdali, houses the Jordanian headquarters of the Muslim Brotherhood, a series of "Islamic" stores—clothing, media, and convenience stores, and a large branch of the Jordan Islamic Bank that is attached to the substantial Islamic Hospital, or Mustashfa Islamiya (which is frequently referred to by Jordanians as "Mustashfa Jaramiya," or the "Criminal Hospital," in reference to the notably high prices they charge).

## 6. Uncertainty Inside the Islamic Bank

1. This shifting of responsibility for individual account holders to individual bank employees' subjective judgments of customer "worthiness" represents another way in which neoliberalism is penetrating the Islamic banks. The privatization of risk and responsibility is very much at play here (Ong 2006).

2. The Jordanian dinar is pegged to the U.S. dollar, which explains the limited fluctuation between these two currencies.

3. This is primarily because claims of an ancient tradition of "Islamic Marketing" are much more spurious than claims of an Islamic Economics. While ethics can be readily applied, the early texts make very few references, if any, to something we might think of as "marketing."

4. Ali's statement also supports the earlier point raised that the Islamic bank is an "intimate space." Here he makes exceptions for talking to women when they are colleagues. As will be shown later, however, Ali's claims about his interactions with women in the bank are not consistent with how women viewed his interactions with them.

5. The fact that Ali volunteered to take my father and me to the mosque demonstrates that he was quite welcoming of non-Muslim men and relatively withdrawn from but not wholly avoidant of women. These behaviors are not an "all or nothing" construction; rather, they are contextual and depend upon other variables.

6. Unfortunately, I was unable to secure any meetings with the Shari'a Committee. It was never exactly clear to me why this was the case. Everyone I asked thought that it was a good *idea*, but I could not find anyone willing to introduce me and set up a meeting—even Faris, who seemed most enthusiastic.

7. Salafi Islam is an austere, fundamentalist movement that aims to emulate the life and lifestyles of the earliest Muslims, or *Salaf*. They are often considered related to *Wahhabis*.

8. The idea of more singular intentions resulting in a wider degree of outcomes is explored in Barth 1993, 105, 170.

## 7. Consuming Islamic Banking

1. The full verse reads, "Those who consume interest cannot stand on the Day of Resurrection except as one stands who is being beaten by Satan into insanity. That is because they say, 'Trade is like interest.' But Allah has permitted trade and has forbidden interest. So whoever has received an admonition from his Lord and desists may have what is past, and his affair rests with Allah. But whoever returns to dealing in interest, those are the companions of the Fire; they will abide eternally therein."

2. In Arabic, the phrase has a rhyme and rhythm to it that the English translation lacks. *Islami* and *riba'wi*, "Islamic" and "of interest" or "from interest" rhyme, and make this a catchy phrase. This idiomatic quality cannot be easily reproduced in English.

3. See note 1. Also, in *hadith*: Abu Juhaifa as saying, "The Prophet forbade the use of the price of blood and the price of a dog, the one who eats usury [and] the one who gives usury, the woman who practices tattooing and the woman who gets herself tattooed" (cited in Sahih Bukhari, Book 77, *Hadith* 5945; Bukhari 1987, 437).

4. His works were quite popular with the staff at the Islamic Bank, who added to my information with copies of the lectures they had attended and documentation they had collected. A number of employees also expressed jealousy at my meeting with these notable gentlemen from the Postal Savings System. In fact, they talked about Dr. Rihan and his teachings in ways that echoed strongly the way young people respond to Amr Khaled, as discussed in chapter 1.

### 8. Branding Islam

1. I would like to thank an anonymous reviewer for this insight. See also Hunter and Malik 2005.

2. http://www.aljazeera.com/programmes/oneonone/2011/04/20114191 15959257764.html.

3. Ibid. See also Mir-Hosseini 1999, Najmabadi 1991, 1998.

4. Baker Ahmad Alserhan. 2010. "On Islamic Branding: Brands as Good Deeds." *Journal of Islamic Marketing* 1 (2):101–06.

# GLOSSARY OF ARABIC TERMS

*Abaya:* A long, black, women's cloak.

*Ahl Al-Salaf:* The early generation of Muslim scholars.

*Ajarid:* A spiritual blessing for doing something good.

*'Aleyhi wa salam:* Peace Be Upon Him.

*Al-Hamdulilah:* Praise God.

*Al-Islam Al-Haqqiqi:* The real Islam.

*Al-kharaji Islami, wa al-dakhali riba'wi:* Lit. "The exterior is Islamic and the interior is of interest"; frequently recited in reference to Islamic banking.

*Al-Urdun:* Jordan.

*Ammani:* A colloquial term for a resident of Amman, Jordan.

*Ansaar:* The residents of Medina who supported the Prophet Mohammed and Muslims during the *hijra,* or migration/flight, from Mecca to Medina in 622 CE or 1 AH.

*3rabeezi / 'Arabeezi:* A word that mixes *'Arabi* and *Ingleezi,* or the Arabic and English languages in a similar fashion to "Spanglish."

*'Araya:* An Islamic contract that allows for the barter of unripened dates against their ripened value.

*Argeelah:* A water pipe used to smoke flavored tobacco; known as *sheesha* in Egypt and the eastern Arab countries, or by its Indian name, *hookah.*

*Asaala:* Lit. "authenticity."

*Ashura:* Tenth day of the month of *Muharram.* For Sunnis, a day of fasting to honor Moses and the Exodus

*'Asriya:* Lit. "modern."

*Athaan:* Call to prayer.

*'Awra:* Nakedness or genitalia that should be covered.

*Aya:* Verse in the Qur'an.

*Bint:* Girl, daughter; a virgin, an unmarried female.

*Bismillah:* Lit. "in the name of God"; used as a standard invocation for Muslims prayers or Qur'anic recitation when part of *Bismillah al-rahman al-rahim,* or "In the name of God, Most Gracious, Most Merciful."

*Da'wa:* Lit. "to call"; the call to convert new Muslims and to proselytize.

*Dawla:* State.

*Dhikr:* A recitation of the ninety-nine names of Allah; also a Sufi ritual.

*Dirham:* Unit of currency, expressed in coins, in the Ottoman Empire and many Persian states.

*Dishdash:* Long, white, single-piece dress worn by Jordanian men on Fridays and daily in the Gulf region.

*Du'aa':* Prescribed prayers recited at specific times of day and in various contexts.

*Duwaar* (pl. *da'irat*): Colloquial term for a traffic circle in Amman.

*'Eid:* Lit. "holiday" or "festival"; typically refers to *'Eid al-Fitr*, the little feast at the end of Ramadan, or *'Eid al-Adha*, the feast of the sacrifice.

*'Eid Al-Fitr:* The "Little Feast" at the end of Ramadan.

*'Eid Al-Hob:* Lit. "holiday of love"; Valentine's Day.

*Fajr:* Just before sunrise: the first call to prayer of the day sounds at this time.

*Fatwa* (pl. *fatawi*): Legal opinion issued by an Islamic jurist or scholar.

*Fi shobha:* In doubt.

*Fiqh:* Islamic rulings and jurisprudence.

*Fitna:* Disorder, chaos. Also used in reference to the first civil wars in Islam. Used colloquially to refer to a seduction of men away from religious practice.

*Fitra:* The innate and natural state of human beings as created by God; used as the natural state that everyone is born into, which is as a Muslim.

*Getayif:* Also colloquially *Qatayef* and *'Atayif*; Ramadan sweet of a small pancake stuffed with walnuts and cinnamon or cheese.

*Gharrar:* Speculation or uncertainty.

*Gheir:* Without.

*Ghotra:* Red-and-white shawl used as a head covering, often associated with men in Saudi Arabia.

*Hadith* (pl. *ahadith*): Traditions and sayings attributed to the Prophet Mohammed; regarded as a source of religious guidance second in importance only to the Qur'an.

*Hadritak:* Lit. "you"; used in very formal settings.

*Hajj:* The pilgrimage to Mecca. One of the five pillars of Islam.

*Halal:* Permissible, legal.

*Halaqa:* Gatherings for giving lessons about Islam.

*Hammam:* Public bath, often of Turkish or North African style; found throughout the Middle East.

*Hanafi:* A school of Sunni law named for Abu Hanifa; prevalent in Central Asia and the Middle East.

*Hanbali:* A school of Sunni law named for Ahmad Hanbal; prevalent in Saudi Arabia.

*Haram:* Forbidden, wrong.

*Hijab:* Women's headscarf; see chapter 4 for an extensive discussion of the meaning.

*Hijra:* The emigration of Mohammed and his earliest followers out of Mecca to Medina; the beginning of the Islamic calendar.

*Hiyal:* Legal ruses used in implementing Shari'a in economic transactions.

*Iftar:* The dusk meal breaking the fast during Ramadan.

*Ihtiram:* Respect.

*Imam:* Leader of a religious community; leader of the daily prayers.

*Isnaad:* Chain of transmission of the *hadith*.

*Israa:* Night journey of Mohammed from Mecca to Jerusalem.

*Jabal:* Rise or hill.

*Jama'iyya* (pl. *jama'iyyat*): Rotating-credit association.

*Jenna:* Heaven, paradise.

*Jihad:* Lit. "struggle."

*Ka'aba:* The black square structure in Mecca around which Muslims pray and circumambulate during Hajj and 'Omrah; the most holy space in Islam.

*Khalas:* That's it; enough.

*Khaliji:* A resident of the Arabian Gulf, colloquial and at times derogatory; also the proposed currency for the G.C.C.

*Khimar:* A veil that covers the face, head, and torso.

*Khutba:* Friday address given by an Imam at a mosque.

*Kiteer:* Lit. "very."

*Laylat Al-Qadr:* The "Night of Power," in which it is believed that the Qur'an was revealed and extra blessings are God-given.

*Madhhab (pl. madhaahib):* School of law in Islamic jurisprudence; the four schools are named after their founders, Maliki, Hanafi, Shafi'i, and Hanbali.

*Maghrib:* Sunset; the fourth call to prayer of the day sounds at this time.

*Mahram:* Close male and unmarriageable kin who include a woman's husband and his father, her father, brother, nephews, and milk-siblings.

*Maliki:* A school of Sunni law named after Malik Anas; prominent in North Africa.

*Maqlubah:* A Palestinian dish of flavored rice with some vegetables, topped with fried almonds and other nuts and chicken or other meats.

*Maqruh:* Unfavorable, disapproved, forbidden according to analogy.

*Misalsalat:* Lit. "serials"; used in reference to Ramadan soap operas.

*Mudaraba:* Venture capital with one financier and one entrepreneur found in Islamic banks; the financial arrangement between the Prophet Mohammed and his first wife Khadija.

*Mudarib:* The financier in *mudaraba* arrangements.

*Muhajaba (pl. muhajabat):* A woman who wears *hijab*.

*Muhajerun:* The earliest Muslims who migrated from Mecca to Medina in the Hijra.

*Muhtasib:* Those tasked with commanding right and forbidding wrong.

*Murabaha:* Cost-plus financial arrangement found in Islamic Banks with spot or deferred repayment.

*Musa'ida:* Helpfulness.

*Musharaka:* Venture capital with both parties financing and working for the entrepreneurial endeavor found in Islamic banks; the financial arrangement between the Muslims from Mecca and the *ansar* of Medina.

*Mutidayin:* Religious.

*Nahda:* Lit. "the revival"; also the name of a political Islamist party in Tunisia.

*Nar:* Hell.

*Niqab:* Black face veil connected from ear-to-ear across the nose that ties in the back and only reveals the eyes.

*'Omrah:* "Mini-*Hajj*" during which the pilgrim visits the sites of a *Hajj* but does not fulfill the fifth pillar of Islam.

*Qamr Ad-Din:* Sweet apricot drink during Ramadan.

*Qard (pl. quruud):* Loans.

*Quraish:* Dominant and powerful tribe in Mecca at the advent of Islam.

*Riba':* Lit. "increase"; used to mean "usury" or "interest."

*Ribah:* Lit. "profit"; allowed in Islam.

*Sadaqa:* Voluntary charitable giving.

*Sahaba:* Companion of the Prophet Mohammed, considered the perfect embodiment of religious authority after the Prophet Mohammed.

*Sahih:* Lit. "correct"; often used with *hadith* to indicate a strong *hadith*.

*Salafi:* A member of an austere, fundamentalist movement that aims to emulate the life and lifestyles of the earliest Muslims or *Salaf;* often considered closely related to *Wahhabis.*

*Salalahu 'Aleyhi wa Salam:* Prayers and Peace Be Upon Him; said after uttering the name of the Prophet Mohammed.

*Sanjak:* Ottoman administrative district for the province.

*Seerah:* The life and times of the Prophet Mohammed.

*Shafi'i:* School of Sunni Law named after Muhammed Idris al-Shafi'i; prominent in East Africa and Southeast Asia.

*Shari'a:* Islamic Law, comprises the Qur'an, *sunna,* and *ahadith,* including legal and ethical norms.

*Sharif:* Descendent of the Prophet Mohammed.

*Sheikh* (pl. *sheyukh*): A religious scholar.

*Siyam:* Fasting.

*Sohour:* Meal before sunrise and the last opportunity to eat before daybreak during Ramadan.

*Sohour Ramadan:* Late-night gatherings during Ramadan during which people eat, drink, smoke *argeelah,* play cards, listen to concerts, and are entertained.

*Subhan Allah:* Praise God.

*Sunna:* The normative example of the Prophet expressed in transmitted reports of his teachings and personal conduct.

*Sunni:* Orthopraxy, but often translated as orthodoxy. Also the largest branch of Islam.

*Suq:* Market.

*Sura:* Chapter in the Qur'an.

*Sura Al-Baqara:* Lit., "Chapter of the Cow"; the second and longest chapter of the Qur'an.

*Ta'alim:* Educated ones, scholars.

*Tafsir:* Explication of Qur'anic verses.

*Tajweed:* Musical, a capella recitation of the Qur'an.

*Tamarhind:* Sweet tamarind drink served during Ramadan.

*Tarawih:* Prayers during Ramadan nights, not required but encouraged.

*Tawarruq:* Also known as "reverse *murabaha*"; a liquidity raising contractual arrangement between three entities for the sale and purchase of specified goods. It is used in the Gulf and Malaysia Islamic banks and forbidden in Jordan.

*Tawhid:* The oneness of God and the coherence of knowledge.

*'Ulama:* Religious scholars, clerics; also the religious establishment.

*Urdun / Urduni:* Arabic rendering of "Jordan" and "Jordanian."

*Waqf* (pl. *awqaaf*): Religious endowments.

*Wazirat al-Awqaaf wa al-Shu'oon al-Islamiya:* Ministry of Religious Endowments and Islamic Affairs.

*Zakat:* Islamic alms and taxes paid on accumulated wealth; one of the five pillars of Islam.

*Zawiyya:* Islamic center that hosts religious events, including Sufi dhiker and other rituals.

# BIBLIOGRAPHY

Abaza, Mona. 2002. *Debates on Islam and Knowledge in Malaysia and Egypt: Shifting Worlds*. London: RoutledgeCurzon.

Abel, Father Michel. 1928. "Chronique: le circuit de Transjordanie." *Revue biblique* 37:590–604.

Abu Dawud Sulayman ibn al-Ash'ath, Al-Sijistani. 1993. *Sunan Abu Dawud*. Edited by Ahmad Hasan. New ed. New Delhi: Kitab Bhavan.

Abu-Dayyeh, Nabil I. 2004. "Persisting Vision: Plans for a Modern Arab Capital, Amman, 1955–2002." *Planning Perspectives* 19 (1): 79–110. doi:10.1080/0266 543042000177922.

Abu-Ghazzeh, Tawfiq M. 2002. "Children's Spatial Behavior in Al-Rawdah Housing Development in Amman, Jordan." *Architectural Science Review* 45:97–115. doi:10.1080/00038628.2002.9697498.

Abu-Lughod, Janet. 1971. *Cairo: 1001 Years of the City Victorious*. Princeton, NJ: Princeton University Press.

———. 1987. "The Islamic City: Historic Myth, Islamic Essence, and Contemporary Relevance." *International Journal of Middle East Studies* 19 (2): 155–76. doi:10.1017/S0020743800031822.

Abu-Lughod, Lila. 2005. *Dramas of Nationhood: The Politics of Television in Egypt*. Chicago: University of Chicago Press.

Adely, Fida. 2004. "The Mixed Effects of Schooling for High School Girls in Jordan: The Case of Tel Yahya." *Comparative Education Review* 48 (4): 353–73. doi:10.1086/423361.

———. 2007a. "Gender Struggles: Nation, Faith and Development in a Jordanian High School for Girls." Ph.D. diss., Columbia University.

———. 2007b. "Is Music 'Haram'? Jordanian Girls Educating Each Other About Nation, Faith and Gender in School." *The Teachers College Record* 109 (7): 1663–81.

———. 2012. *Gendered Paradoxes: Educating Jordanian Women in Nation, Faith, and Progress*. Chicago: University of Chicago Press.

Afshar, Haleh. 1998. *Islam and Feminisms: An Iranian Case-Study*. New York: Macmillan.

Ahmed, Leila. 1992. *Women and Gender in Islam: Historical Roots of a Modern Debate*. New Haven, CT: Yale University Press.

Al-Abdullah, Rania. 2007. "Interview with the Italian Daily *Corriere della Sera*." Interview, February 7. http://www.queenrania.jo/media/interviews/corriere-della-sera.

Al-Asad, Mohammad. 2004. "Cities of the Arab East: Urban Crossroads #5." *Jordan Times*, May 20. http://www.csbe.org/e-publications-resources/urban-crossroads/cities-of-the-arab-east/.

Al-Isfahani, Husayn ibn Muhammad Raghib. 1991. *Mufradat fi Gharib al-Qur'an.* Beirut, Lebanon: Dar El-Ma'refah.

Al-Khazendar, Sami. 1997. *Jordan and the Palestine Question: The Role of Islamic and Left Forces in Foreign Policy-Making.* Reading, U.K.: Ithaca Press.

Al-Razzaz, Mounis. 2002. *Laylat 'Asl [Sweetest Night].* Amman: Al-Mu'assasat Al-Arabiya Lil-Diraasaat wa Al-Nashar [The Arab Foundation for Studies and Publishing].

Alam, Arshad. 2008. "The Enemy Within: Madrasa and Muslim Identity in North India." *Modern Asian Studies* 42 (2/3): 605–27. doi:10.1017/S0026749 X07003113.

Alchaar, Mohamad Nedal, and Abboud Sandra. 2006. *Islamic Finance Qualification.* London: Securities & Investment Institute.

Amawi, Abla M. 1994. "The Consolidation of the Merchant Class in Transjordan During the Second World War." In *Village, Steppe and State: The Social Origins of Modern Jordan,* edited by Eugene L. Rogan and Tariq Moraiwed Tell, 162–86. London: IB Tauris.

An-Na'im, Abdullahi Ahmed. 2009. *Islam and the Secular State: Negotiating the Future of Shari'a.* Cambridge, MA: Harvard University Press.

Anderson, Benedict R. 1991. *Imagined Communities: Reflections on the Origin and Spread of Nationalism.* Revised and Extended Edition. London: Verso.

———. 2006. *Imagined Communities: Reflections on the Origin and Spread of Nationalism.* New Edition. London: Verso.

Anderson, Betty S. 2005. *Nationalist Voices in Jordan: The Street and the State.* Austin: University of Texas Press.

Appadurai, Arjun. 1996. *Modernity at Large: Cultural Dimensions of Globalization.* Vol. 1. Minneapolis: University of Minnesota Press.

Armbrust, Walter. 2000a. "Introduction: Anxieties of Scale." In *Mass Mediations: New Approaches to Popular Culture in the Middle East and Beyond.* Edited by Walter Armbrust. Berkeley: University of California Press.

———. 2000b. *Mass Mediations: New Approaches to Popular Culture in the Middle East and Beyond.* Berkeley: University of California Press.

———. 2002. "The Riddle of Ramadan: Media, Consumer Culture, and the "Christ-masization" of a Muslim Holiday." In *Everyday Life in the Middle East* edited by D. L. and E. A. Early Bowen, 335–48. Bloomington: Indiana University Press.

———. 2006. "10 Synchronizing Watches: The State, the Consumer, and Sacred Time in Ramadan Television." In *Religion, Media, and the Public Sphere*, edited by Birgit Meyer and Annaliese Moors, 207–26. Bloomington: Indiana University Press.

Asad, Talal. 1986. *The Idea of an Anthropology of Islam.* Washington, D.C.: Center for Contemporary Arab Studies, Georgetown University.

———. 1993. "The Construction of Religion as an Anthropological Category." *Genealogies of Religion: Discipline and Reasons of Power in Christianity and Islam.* Baltimore: Johns Hopkins University Press. 27–54.

Ask, Karin, and Marit Tjomsland, eds. 1998. *Women and Islamization: Contemporary Dimensions of Discourse on Gender Relations.* Oxford: Berg.

Atia, Mona. 2012. "'A Way to Paradise': Pious Neoliberalism, Islam, and Faith-Based Development." *Annals of the Association of American Geographers* 102 (4): 808–27. doi:10.1080/00045608.2011.627046.

———. 2013. *Building a House in Heaven: Islamic Charity in Neoliberal Egypt.* Minneapolis: University of Minnesota Press.

Barany, Zoltan. 2013. "Unrest and State Response in Arab Monarchies." *Mediterranean Quarterly* 24 (2): 5–38. doi:10.1215/10474552-2141881.

Baroudi, Sami E. 2002. "The 2002 Arab Human Development Report: Implications for Democracy." *Middle East Policy* 11 (1): 132–41. doi:10.1111/J.1061-1924.2004.00146.X.

Barth, Fredrik. 1993. *Balinese Worlds.* Chicago: University of Chicago Press.

Bayat, Asef. 2007. *Making Islam Democratic: Social Movements and the Post-Islamist Turn.* Stanford, CA: Stanford University Press.

———. 2010. *Life as Politics: How Ordinary People Change the Middle East.* Stanford, CA: Stanford University Press.

Berger, Peter, and Anton C. Zijderveld. 2009. *In Praise of Doubt: How to Have Convictions Without Becoming a Fanatic.* New York: HarperOne.

Berkey, Jonathan Porter. 1992. *The Transmission of Knowledge in Medieval Cairo: A Social History of Islamic Education.* Princeton, NJ: Princeton University Press.

———. 2003. *The Formation of Islam: Religion and Society in the Near East, 600–1800.* Cambridge: Cambridge University Press.

Bonner, Michael. 2008. *Jihad in Islamic History: Doctrines and Practice.* Princeton, NJ: Princeton University Press.

Boulby, Marion. 1999. *The Muslim Brotherhood and the Kings of Jordan, 1945–1993.* Atlanta: Scholars Press.

Bourdieu, Pierre. 1977. *Outline of a Theory of Practice.* Translated by Richard Nice. Cambridge: Cambridge University Press.

———. 2008. "The Forms of Capital." In *Readings in Economic Sociology*, edited by Natalie Woolsey Biggart, 280–91. Malden, MA: Blackwell.

———. 2013. *Distinction: A Social Critique of the Judgement of Taste.* London: Routledge.

Bourgois, Philippe I., and Jeffrey Schonberg. 2009. *Righteous Dopefiend.* Berkeley: University of California Press.

Bowen, John. 2012. *A New Anthropology of Islam.* Cambridge: Cambridge University Press.

Brand, Laurie A. 1994. *Jordan's Inter-Arab Relations: The Political Economy of Alliance Making.* New York: Columbia University Press.

Brown, L. Carl. 2000. *Religion and State: The Muslim Approach to Politics.* New York: Columbia University Press.

Bukhari, Muhammad ibn Ismaʿil. 1987. *Ṣaḥīḥ al-Bukhari.* Edited by Muṣṭafa Dib Bugha. al-Ṭabʿah. 3rd ed. Damascus, Syria: Dar Ibn Kathir.

Byman, Daniel L., Akram Al-Turk, Pavel Baev, Michael S. Doran, Khaled Elgindy, Stephen R. Grand, Shadi Hamid, Bruce Jones, Suzanne Maloney, and Jonathan D. Pollack. 2011. *The Arab Awakening: America and the Transformation of the Middle East.* Washington, D.C.: Brookings Institution Press.

Calder, Norman. 1993. *Studies in Early Muslim Jurisprudence.* Oxford: Clarendon Press.

Charfi, Abdelmajid. 2010. "Islam: The Test of Globalization." *Philosophy & Social Criticism* 36 (3–4): 295–307. doi:10.1177/0191453709358563.

Chen, Nancy N. 2001. *China Urban: Ethnographies of Contemporary Culture.* Durham, N.C.: Duke University Press.

Clark, Janine. 2004. *Islam, Charity, and Activism: Middle-Class Networks and Social Welfare in Egypt, Jordan, and Yemen.* Bloomington: Indiana University Press.

Cole, Debbie. 2010. "Enregistering Diversity: Adequation in Indonesian Poetry Performance." *Journal of Linguistic Anthropology* (20): 1–21. doi:10.1111/j.1548-1395.2010.01045.x.

Comaroff, John L., and Jean Comaroff. 2009. *Ethnicity, Inc.* Chicago: University of Chicago Press.

Cook, Michael. 2000. *Commanding Right and Forbidding Wrong in Islamic Thought.* Cambridge: Cambridge University Press.

Daily, H. 2010. "Accuracy in Genesis." Accessed July 15. http://www.accuracy ingenesis.com.

Davis, Nancy J., and Robert V. Robinson. 2006. "The Egalitarian Face of Islamic Orthodoxy: Support for Islamic Law and Economic Justice in Seven Muslim-Majority Nations." *American Sociological Review* 71 (2): 167–90. doi:10.1177/000312240607100201.

Deeb, Lara. 2006. *An Enchanted Modern: Gender and Public Piety in Shi'i Lebanon.* Princeton, NJ: Princeton University Press.

Denny, Frederick M. 1989a. "Orthopraxy in Islam and Judaism: Convictions and Categories." In *Studies in Islamic and Judaic Traditions*, vol. 2, edited by William M. Brinner and Stephen D. Ricks, 83–95. Atlanta: Scholars Press, 1989.

———. 1989b. "Qur'an Recitation: A Tradition of Oral Performance and Transmission." *Oral Tradition* 4 (1–2): 5–26. http://journal.oraltradition.org/files/articles/4i-ii/2_Denny.pdf.

Droeber, Julia. 2005. *Dreaming of Change: Young Middle-Class Women and Social Transformation in Jordan.* Leiden: Brill.

Eickelman, Dale F. 1974. "Is There an Islamic City? The Making of a Quarter in a Moroccan Town." *International Journal of Middle East Studies* 5 (3): 274–94. doi:10.1017/S0020743800034942.

Eickelman, Dale F., and James P. Piscatori. 1996. *Muslim Politics, Princeton Studies in Muslim Politics.* Princeton, N.J.: Princeton University Press.

El Fadl, Khaled M. Abou. 2001. *And God Knows the Soldiers: The Authoritative and Authoritarian in Islamic Discourses.* Lanham, MD: University Press of America.

El-Gamal, Mahmoud Amin. 2006. *Islamic Finance: Law, Economics, and Practice.* Cambridge: Cambridge University Press.

El Guindi, Fadwa. 1999a. *Veil: Modesty, Privacy and Resistance.* Oxford: Berg Publishers.

———. 1999b. "Veiling Resistance." *Fashion Theory: The Journal of Dress, Body & Culture* 3 (1): 51–80. doi:10.2752/136270499779165626.

El-Nawawy, Mohammed, and Sahar Khamis. 2009. *Islam Dot Com: Contemporary Islamic Discourses in Cyberspace.* New York: Palgrave Macmillan.

El-Zein, Abdul Hamid. 1977. "Beyond Ideology and Theology: The Search for the Anthropology of Islam." *Annual Review of Anthropology* 6:227–54.

Eldem, Edhem. 1999. *French Trade in Istanbul in the Eighteenth Century.* Leiden: Brill Academic.

Eldem, Edhem, Daniel Goffman, and Bruce A. Masters. 1999. *The Ottoman City Between East and West: Aleppo, Izmir, and Istanbul.* Cambridge: Cambridge University Press.

Estruch, Joan A., and Elizabeth L. Glick. 2000. *Saints and Schemers: Opus Dei and Its Paradoxes.* Bridgewater, NJ: Replica Books.

Farrell, Stephen. 2012. "Jordan Protests Suggest Whisper of an Arab Spring " *New York Times*, February 10, 2012. Accessed July 16, 2013. http://www.nytimes.com/2012/02/10/world/middleeast/jordan-protests-whisper-of-an-arab-spring.html?_r=0.

Fernea, Elizabeth Warnock. 2011. *The Arab World*. New York: Knopf Doubleday.

Fernea, Elizabeth Warnock, and Robert A. Fernea. 1997. "Symbolizing Roles: Behind the Veil." *Conformity and Conflict: Readings in Cultural Anthropology*. New York: Longman. 235–42.

Foucault, Michel. 1991. *The Foucault Effect: Studies in Governmentality*. Edited by Colin Gordon, Peter Miller, and Graham Burchell. London: Harvester-Wheatsheaf.

Gallagher, Sally K. 2012. *Making Do in Damascus: Navigating a Generation of Change in Family and Work*. Syracuse: Syracuse University Press.

Gammer, Moshe. 2004. *Community, Identity and the State: Comparing Africa, Eurasia, Latin America and the Middle East*. London: Routledge.

Gandhi, Jennifer, and Ellen Lust-Okar. 2009. "Elections Under Authoritarianism." *Annual Review of Political Science* 12:403–22. doi:10.1146/annurev.polisci.11.060106.095434.

Geertz, Clifford. 1973. "Thick Description." In *The Interpretation of Cultures*, 3–30. New York: Basic Books.

——. 2000. "Introduction." In *The Interpretation of Cultures: Selected Essays*, ix. New York: Basic Books.

Gifford, Lindsay A. 2009. "Nashta: Rotating Credit Associations and Women 'Being Active' in Syria." Ph.D., Anthropology, Boston University.

Gordon, Joel. 2003. "Singing the Pulse of the Egyptian-Arab Street: Shaaban Abd Al-Rahim and the Geo-Pop-Politics of Fast Food." *Popular Music* 22 (1): 73–88. doi:10.1017/S0261143003003052.

Guazzone, Laura, and Daniela Pioppi. 2009. *The Arab State and Neo-Liberal Globalization*. Reading: Garnet Publishing.

Haenni, Patrick. 2005. *L'islam de marché: l'autre révolution conservatrice*. Paris: Seuil.

Haidt, Jonathan. 2001. "The Emotional Dog and Its Rational Tail: A Social Intuitionist Approach to Moral Judgment." *Psychological Review* 108 (4): 814. doi:10.1037//0033-295X.108.4.814.

Ham, Anthony, and Paul Greenway. 2003. *Jordan*. Footscray: Lonely Planet Publications.

Hanssen-Bauer, Jon, Jon Pedersen, and Åge Tiltnes. 1998. *Jordanian Society: Living Conditions in the Hashemite Kingdom of Jordan*. Oslo: Fafo Institute for Applied Social Science.

Hardaker, David. 2006. "Amr Khaled: Islam's Billy Graham." *The Independent* 4. http://www.independent.co.uk/news/world/middle-east/amr-khaled-islams-billy-graham-521561.html.

Hartigan, John. 1999. *Racial Situations: Class Predicaments of Whiteness in Detroit*. Princeton, NJ: Princeton University Press.

Harvey, David. 2005. *A Brief History of Neoliberalism*: Oxford: Oxford University Press.

Hassan, Riaz. 2008. *Inside Muslim Minds*. Carleton, Victoria: Melbourne University Press.

Heck, Gene. W. 2006. *Charlemagne, Muhammad, and the Arab Roots of Capitalism*. Berlin: Walter de Gruyter.

Hefner, Robert W. 1993a. "Islam, State, and Civil Society: ICMI and the Struggle for the Indonesian Middle Class." *Indonesia* 56 (1993): 1–35. doi:10.2307/3351197.

——. 1993b. *The Political Economy of Mountain Java: An Interpretative History*. Berkeley: University of California Press.

——. 1998a. *Market Cultures: Society and Morality in the New Asian Capitalisms*. Boulder: Westview Press.

——. 1998b. "Multiple Modernities: Christianity, Islam, and Hinduism in a Globalizing Age." *Annual Review of Anthropology* 27 (1998): 83–104. doi:10.1146/annurev.anthro.27.1.83.

——. 2000. *Civil Islam: Muslims and Democratization in Indonesia*. Princeton, NJ: Princeton University Press.

——. 2003. "Civic Pluralism Denied? The New Media and Jihadi Violence in Indonesia." In Dale F. Eickelman and Jon W. Anderson, eds. *New Media in the Muslim World: The Emerging Public Sphere*. 158–79. Bloomington: Indiana University Press.

——. 2005. *Remaking Muslim Politics: Pluralism, Contestation, Democratization*. Princeton, NJ: Princeton University Press.

——. 2006a. "Ambivalent Embrace: Islamic Economics and Global Capitalism." Visible Hands: The Changing Nature of Capitalism in Relation to Religious Culture, CURA, Boston University. In *Markets, Morals, & Religion*, edited by Jonathan B. Imber, 141–55. New Brunswick, NJ: Transaction Publishers.

——. 2006b. "Islamic Economics and Global Capitalism." *Society* 44 (1): 16–22. doi:10.1007/BF02690463

——. 2011. *Shari'a Politics: Islamic Law and Society in the Modern World*. Bloomington: Indiana University Press.

Hefner, Robert W., and M. Q. Zaman. 2007. *Schooling Islam: The Culture and Politics of Modern Muslim Education*. Princeton, NJ: Princeton University Press.

Helfont, Samuel, and Tally Helfont. 2012. "Jordan: Between the Arab Spring and the Gulf Cooperation Council." *Orbis* 56 (1): 82–95. http://dx.doi.org/10.1016/j.orbis.2011.10.005.

Henry, Clement M., and Rodney Wilson, eds. 2004. *The Politics of Islamic Finance*. Edinburgh: Edinburgh University Press.

Herrera, Linda. 2001. "Downveiling: Gender and the Contest over Culture in Cairo." *Middle East Report* 219 (Summer): 16–19. doi:10.1177/1043463112440683.

Hirschkind, Charles. 2006. *The Ethical Soundscape: Cassette Sermons and Islamic Counterpublics*. New York: Columbia University Press.

Hobsbawm, Eric, and Terence Ranger, eds. 1983. *The Invention of Tradition*. Cambridge: Cambridge University Press.

Hunter, Shireen T., and Huma Malik. 2005. *Modernization, Democracy, and Islam*. Westport, CT: Greenwood Publishing Group.

Hutchins, Edwin. 1995a. *Cognition in the Wild*. Vol. 262082314: Cambridge, MA: MIT Press.

——. 1995b. "How a Cockpit Remembers Its Speeds." *Cognitive Science* 19 (3): 265–88. doi:10.1207/ s15516709cog1903_1.

Ibn Anas, Malik. 1989. *Al-Muwatta of Imam Malik ibn Anas: The First Formulation of Islamic Law*. Edited by Aisha Abdurrahman Bewley. Islamic Classical Library. London: Kegan Paul International.

Islamic Council of New England Conference proceedings. Boston University, October 17, 2009.

Jacobs, R. M. 2002. *Nirvana for Sale?: Buddhism, Wealth, and Modernity in Contemporary Thailand*. Chicago: Northwestern University Press.

Jameson, Fredric. 1984. "The Politics of Theory: Ideological Positions in the Postmodernism Debate." *New German Critique* (33): 53–65. doi:10.2307/488353.

Jazerah, M. 2008. "Closing of Books@Cafe." 7iber.Com. Accessed July 13. http://www.7iber.com/2008/09/closing-of-bookscafe/.

Jones, Justin. 2011. *Shi'a Islam in Colonial India: Religion, Community and Sectarianism*. Cambridge: Cambridge University Press.

Kaddoura, Huzam, and Siham Malkawi. 2007. "The Character of Amman." In *Ontology of Amman: Soul and Body Study of the Development of the Arab Modern City*, 6–29. Amman: Al-Safir Printing Press.

Kadhim, M. B., and Y. Rajjal. 1988. "Amman." *Cities* 5 (4): 318–25. doi:10.101 6/0264-2751(88)90021-2.

Kahf, Monzer. 2004. "Islamic Banks: The Rise of a New Power Alliance of Wealth and Shari'a Scholarship." *The Politics of Islamic Finance*, edited by Clement M. Henry and Rodney Wilson, 17–36. Edinburgh: Edinburgh University Press.

Kaya, Laura Pearl 2010. "The Criterion of Consistency: Women's Self Presentation at Yarmouk University, Jordan." *American Ethnologist* 37 (3): 526–38. doi:10.1111/j.1548-1425.2010.01270.x.

Khosravi, Mohammad Reza, and Ali Bayat. 2008. "The Confrontation of the Iranian Society and the Muslim Arabs in the First and Second Centuries A.H." *Jostarha-ye Tarikhi (Farhang)* 21 (3): 117–55.

Kimmelman, Michael. 2010. "D.I.Y. Culture." *New York Times*, April 18. http://www.nytimes.com/2010/04/18/arts/18abroad.html.

Kondo, Dorinne K. 1990. *Crafting Selves: Power, Gender, and Discourses of Identity in a Japanese Workplace*. Chicago: University of Chicago Press.

Kuran, Timur. 1997a. "Islam and Underdevelopment: An Old Puzzle Revisited." *Journal of Institutional and Theoretical Economics (JITE)* 153 (1): 41.

———. 1997b. "The Genesis of Islamic Economics: A Chapter in the Politics of Muslim Identity." *Social Research* 64 (2): 301–38.

———. 2004. *Islam and Mammon: The Economic Predicaments of Islamism*. Princeton, NJ: Princeton University Press.

———. 2011. *The Long Divergence*. Princeton, NJ: Princeton University Press.

Lawrence, T. E. 1997. *Seven Pillars of Wisdom*. Hertfordshire: Wordsworth Editions Ltd. Originally published in 1922.

Lings, Martin. 1994. *Muhammad: His Life Based on the Earliest Sources*. Jakarta: Penerbit Serambi.

Loewenstein, George F., Elke U. Weber, Christopher K. Hsee, and Ned Welch. 2001. "Risk as Feelings." *Psychological Bulletin* 127 (2): 267. doi:10.10371/0033-2909.127.2.267.

Lust-Okar, Ellen. 2009. "Reinforcing Informal Institutions through Authoritarian Elections: Insights from Jordan." *Middle East Law and Governance* 1 (1): 3–37. doi:10.1163/187633708X339444.

Lynch, Marc. 2012. "Jordan, Forever on the Brink " *Foreign Policy*. http://www.foreignpolicy.com/posts/2012/05/07/jordan_forever_at_the_brink.

Mackenzie, Donald. 2008. *Material Markets: How Economic Agents Are Constructed.* Oxford: Oxford University Press.

Macleod, Arlene. 1993. *Accommodating Protest: Working Women, the New Veiling, and Change in Cairo.* New York: Columbia University Press.

Mahmood, Saba. 2005. *Politics of Piety : The Islamic Revival and the Feminist Subject.* Princeton, NJ: Princeton University Press.

Malley, Mohammed. 2004. "Jordan: A Case Study of the Relationship between Islamic Finance and Islamist Politics." In *The Politics of Islamic Finance*, edited by Clement M. Henry and Rodney Wilson, 191–215. Edinburgh: Edinburgh University Press.

Marçais, Georges. 1957. "L'urbanisme Musulman." In *Melanges d'histoire dt d'archeologie de l'occident Musulman, Tome I, Articles et conferences de Georges Marcais*, 219–31. Algiers: Impr. officielle.

Marçais, William. 1928. "L'islamisme et la vie urbaine." *Comptes-rendus des séances de l'académie des inscriptions et belles-lettres* 72 (1):86–100. http://www.persee.fr/web/revues/home/prescript/article/crai_0065-0536_1928_num_72_1_75567. doi:10.3406/crai.1928.75567.

Masters, Bruce. 1988. *The Origins of Western Economic Dominance in the Middle East: Mercantilism and the Islamic Economy in Aleppo, 1600–1750.* New York: New York University Press.

——. 2004. *Christians and Jews in the Ottoman Arab World: The Roots of Sectarianism.* Cambridge: Cambridge University Press.

Maurer, Bill. 2005. *Mutual Life, Limited: Islamic Banking, Alternative Currencies, Lateral Reason.* Princeton, NJ: Princeton University Press.

Mawdudi, Sayyid Abul Ala. 2009. *First Principles of Islamic Economics.* Markfield, UK: The Islamic Foundation.

McDermott, Nicole. 2010. "Modernization of the Hijab in Amman, Jordan: A Symbol of Islam and Modernity." ISP Collection, S.I.T. http://digitalcollections.sit.edu/isp_collection/832.

Mernissi, Fatima. 1987 (1991). *Women and Islam: An Historical and Theological Enquiry*, Trans. Mary Jo Lakeland. Oxford: Blackwell.

Messick, Brinkley M. 1993. *The Calligraphic State: Textual Domination and History in a Muslim Society.* Berkeley: University of California Press.

Metcalf, Barbara Daly. 1982. *Islamic Revival in British India: Deoband, 1860–1900.* Princeton, NJ: Princeton University Press.

Mir-Hosseini, Ziba. 1999. *Islam and Gender: The Religious Debate in Contemporary Iran.* Princeton, NJ: Princeton University Press.

Mitchell, Timothy. 2002. *Rule of Experts: Egypt, Techno-Politics, Modernity.* Berkeley: University of California Press.

Moaddel, Mansoor. 2002. *Jordanian Exceptionalism: A Comparative Analysis of State-Religion Relationships in Egypt, Iran, Jordan, and Syria.* New York: Palgrave Macmillan.

Moll, Yasmin. 2010. "Islamic Televangelism: Religion, Media and Visuality in Contemporary Egypt." *Arab Media & Society* 10:1–27. http://www.arabmediasociety.com/?article=732.

Monin, Benoît, David A. Pizarro, and Jennifer S. Beer. 2007. "Deciding versus Reacting: Conceptions of Moral Judgment and the Reason-Affect Debate." *Review of General Psychology* 11 (2): 99. doi:10.1037/1089-2680.11.2.99.

Muslim ibn al-Ḥajjaj, al-Qushayri. 2000. *Sahih Muslim: Being Traditions of the Say-ings and Doings of the Prophet Muhammad as Narrated by His Companions and Compiled Under The Title Al-Jamī us Sahih*. Edited by Abdul Hameed Siddiqui. New Delhi: Kitab Bhava.

Najmabadi, Afsaneh. 1991. "Hazards of Modernity and Morality: Women, State and Ideology in Contemporary Iran." In *Women, Islam and the State*, edited by D. Kandiyoti, 48–76. Philadelphia: Temple University Press.

———. 1998. *The Story of the Daughters of Quchan: Gender and National Memory in Iranian History*. Syracuse, NY: Syracuse University Press.

Nasr, Seyyed Hossein. 1979. "Reflections on Islam and Modern Thought." In *Is-lamika II*, edited by Lutfi Ibrahim, 97–113. Kuala Lampour: Sarjana.

———. 1980. "Reflections on Islam and Modern Life." *Al-Islam*. Accessed July 29. http://Al-Islam.org/Al-Serat/Reflect-Nasr.htm.

———. 1983. "Reflections on Islam and Modern Thought." *Studies in Comparative Re-ligion* 15 (3 and 4). http://www.studiesincomparativereligion.com/uploads/articlepdfs/384.pdf.

Nasr, Vali. 2009. *Forces of Fortune: The Rise of the New Muslim Middle Class and What It Will Mean for Our World*. New York: Free Press.

Norton, Augustus R. 1995. *Civil Society in the Middle East*. Vol. 1. Leiden: Brill.

———. 2001. *Civil Society in the Middle East*. Vol. 2. Leiden: Brill.

Ong, Aihwa. 1990. "State versus Islam: Malay Families, Women's Bodies, and the Body Politic in Malaysia." *American Ethnologist* 17 (2): 258–76. doi:10.2307/645079.

———. 2006. *Neoliberalism as Exception: Mutations in Citizenship and Sovereignty*. Ra-leigh, NC: Duke University Press.

Orlove, Benjamin S., and Henry J. Rutz. 1989. "Thinking About Consumption: A Social Economy Approach." In *The Social Economy of Consumption*, edited by Henry J. Rutz and Benjamin S. Orlove, 1–58. Lanham, MD: University Press of America.

Oueslati-Porter, Claire Therese. 2011. "The Maghreb Maquiladora: Gender, Labor, and Socio-Economic Power in a Tunisian Export Processing Zone." Univer-sity of South Florida. http://scholarcommons.usf.edu/etd/3737/.

Peterson, Mark Allen. 2011. *Connected in Cairo: Growing Up Cosmopolitan in the Mod-ern Middle East*. Bloomington: Indiana University Press.

Pizarro, David A., and Paul Bloom. 2003. "The Intelligence of the Moral Intuitions: A Comment on Haidt (2001)." *Psychological Review* 110 (1): 193–96. doi:10.1037/0033-295X.110.1.193.

Potter, Robert B., Khadija Darmame, Nasim Barham, and Stephen Nortcliff. 2009. "Ever-Growing Amman, Jordan: Urban Expansion, Social Polarisation and Contemporary Urban Planning Issues." *Habitat International* 33. http://arlt-lectures.de/jordan-amman.pdf.

Quna, Saleem Ayoub. 2008. *Downtown Amman: A Social Tapestry*. Amman: B2BE.

Qureshi, Regula Burckhardt. 1986. *Sufi Music of India and Pakistan: Sound, Context, and Meaning in Qawwali*. Cambridge: Cambridge University Press.

———. 2006. "Islam and Music." In *Sacred Sound: Experiencing Music in World Religions*, edited by Guy L. Beck, 89–111. Waterloo, ON: Wilfrid Laurier University Press.

Racy, Ali Jihad. 2003. *Making Music in the Arab World: The Culture and Artistry of Tarab*. Cambridge: Cambridge University Press.

"Ramadan: The Holy Month of Prayers and Reflection—80 Years of Fasting." 2008. *Sayidaty* (September): 101.

Ramady, Mohamed A. 2012. *The GCC Economies: Stepping up to Future Challenges.* New York: Springer.

Robins, Philip. 2004. *A History of Jordan.* Cambridge: Cambridge University Press.

Robinson, Glenn E. 1997. "Can Islamists Be Democrats? The Case of Jordan." *The Middle East Journal* 51 (3): 373–87. http://www.jstor.org/stable/4329086.

Rock, Aaron. 2010. "Amr Khaled: From Da 'Wa to Political and Religious Leadership." *British Journal of Middle Eastern Studies* 37 (1): 15–37. doi:10.1080/13530191003661104.

Rodinson, M. 1978. *Islam and Capitalism.* Austin: University of Texas Press.

Rogan, Eugene L. 1994. "Bringing the State Back: The Limits of Ottoman Rule in Transjordan 1840–1910." In *Village, Steppe and State: The Social Origins of Modern Jordan,* edited by Eugene L. Rogan and Tariq Moraiwed Tell, 32–57. London: IB Tauris.

———. 1999. *Frontiers of the State in the Late Ottoman Empire: Transjordan, 1850–1921.* Cambridge: Cambridge University Press.

Roy, Oliver, and Carol Volk. 1996. *The Failure of Political Islam.* Cambridge, MA: Harvard University Press.

Rudnyckyj, Daromir. 2010. *Spiritual Economies: Islam, Globalization, and the Afterlife of Development.* Ithaca, NY: Cornell University Press.

Rueschemeyer, Dietrich, Evelyne Huber Stephens, and John D. Stephens. 1992. *Capitalist Development and Democracy.* Cambridge, UK: Polity Press.

Rutz, Henry J., and Benjamin S. Orlove. 1989. *The Social Economy of Consumption.* Lanham, MD: University Press of America.

Sadiki, Larbi 2012. "Jordan's Arab Spring: To 'Spring' or Not To 'Spring'?" *Ammon News.* Accessed July 16, 2012. http://en.ammonnews.net/article.aspx?articleNO=15741#.VXsEUmDfATM.

Salam, Monem. 2009. "Investing in the Stock Market in a Halal Way." Paper presented October 17 at the Islamic Council of New England 24th Annual Conference, Boston.

Salamandra, Christa. 2004. *A New Old Damascus: Authenticity and Distinction in Urban Syria.* Bloomington: Indiana University Press.

Salibi, Kamal S. 2006. *The Modern History of Jordan.* London: IB Tauris.

Savignac, Raphaël. 1925. "Chronique: excursion en Transjordanie et au KH. Es-Samrâ." *Revue biblique* 34:110–31.

Schielke, Samuli, and Liza Debevec. 2012. *Ordinary Lives and Grand Schemes: An Anthropology of Everyday Religion.* Vol. 18. New York: Berghahn Books.

Schuon, Frithjof. 1998. *Understanding Islam.* Bloomington, IN: World Wisdom.

Schwedler, Jillian. 2006. *Faith in Moderation: Islamist Parties in Jordan and Yemen.* Cambridge, UK: Cambridge University Press.

———. 2007. "Democratization, Inclusion and the Moderation of Islamist Parties." *Development* 50 (1): 56–61.

———. 2010. "Amman Cosmopolitan: Spaces and Practices of Aspiration and Consumption." *Comparative Studies of South Asia, Africa and the Middle East* 30 (3): 547–62. doi:10.1057/palgrave.development.1100324.

Scott, Rachelle M. 2009. *Nirvana for Sale?: Buddhism, Wealth, and the Dhamma Temple in Contemporary Thailand.* Albany: State University of New York Press.

Seeley, Nicholas. 2012. "Jordan's Arab Spring Continues to Disappoint." Wag-ing Nonviolence: People-Powered News & Analysis, Last Modified No-vember 30, 2012. Accessed July 16. http://wagingnonviolence.org/feature/jordans-arab-spring-continues-to-disappoint/.

Seligman, Adam B., Robert P. Weller, Michael J. Puett, and Bennett Simon. 2008. *Ritual and Its Consequences: An Essay On the Limits of Sincerity*. Oxford: Oxford University Press.

Shannon, Jonathan H. 2003. "Emotion, Performance, and Temporality in Arab Music: Reflections on Tarab." *Cultural Anthropology* 18 (1): 72–98. doi:10.1525/can.2003.18.1.72.

Sharp, Jeremy. M. 2005." US Foreign Assistance to the Middle East: Historical Back-ground, Recent Trends, and the FY2006 Request." Congressional Research Service, Library of Congress. http://fpc.state.gov/documents/organization/50383.pdf.

———. 2010. "US Foreign Assistance to the Middle East: Historical Background, Recent Trends, and the FY2011 Request." DTIC document. http://www.fas.org/sgp/crs/mideast/RL32260.pdf.

Shirazi, Faegheh. 2001. *The Veil Unveiled: The Hijab in Modern Culture*. Gainesville: University Press of Florida.

Shryock, Andrew. 1997. *Nationalism And the Genealogical Imagination: Oral History and Textual Authority in Tribal Jordan*. Berkeley: University of California Press.

Sloane-White, Patricia. 2011. "Working in the Islamic Economy: Sharia-Ization and the Malaysian Workplace." *Sojourn: Journal of Social Issues in Southeast Asia* 26 (2): 304–34. doi:10.1353/soj.2011.0011.

Smith, Wilfred Cantwell. 1957. *Islam in Modern History*. Princeton, NJ: Princeton University Press.

Smith-Hefner, Nancy J. 2007. "Javanese Women and the Veil in Post-Soeharto In-donesia." *The Journal of Asian Studies* 66 (2): 389–420. doi:10.1017/S0021911 807000575.

Stadler, Nurit. 2009. *Yeshiva Fundamentalism: Piety, Gender, and Resistance in the Ultra-Orthodox World*. New York: New York University Press.

Starrett, Gregory. 1998. *Putting Islam to Work: Education, Politics, and Religious Transfor-mation in Egypt*. Berkeley: University of California Press.

Stern, Gustaf. 1931. *Meaning and Change of Meaning, with Special Reference to the English Language*. Bloomington: Indiana University Press. https://archive.org/details/meaningchangeofm00ster.

Stoller, Paul. 2010. *Money Has No Smell: The Africanization of New York City*. Chi-cago: University of Chicago Press.

Stowasser, Barbara Freyer. 1994. *Women in the Qur'an, Traditions, and Interpretation*. New York: Oxford University Press.

Strathern, Marilyn. 2000. *Audit Cultures: Anthropological Studies in Accountability, Ethics and the Academy*. London: Routledge.

Stratton, Allegra. 2006. *Muhajababes*. Melbourne: Melbourne University Publishing.

Tal, Lawrence. 1995. "Dealing with Radical Islam: The Case of Jordan." *Survival* 37 (3): 139–56. doi:10.1080/00396339508442807.

Tarlo, Emma. 2010. *Visibly Muslim: Fashion, Politics, Faith*. Oxford: Berg.

Tawarneh, Neseem. 2005. "The Force of Imagination." *JO Magazine* (September): 40–43.

Teller, Matthew. 2002. *Rough Guide to Jordan*. London: Rough Guides Limited.

Tobin, Sarah A. 2009. "Islamic Banking In the Global Financial Crisis: The Value of Banking Rightly." *Anthropology News* 50 (7): 13–14. doi:10.1111/j.1556-3502.2009.50713.x.

———. 2012. "Jordan's Arab Spring: The Middle Class and Anti-Revolution." *Middle East Policy* 19 (1): 96–109. doi:10.1111/j.1475-4967.2012.00526.x.

———. 2013. "Ramadan Blues: Debates in Pop Music and Popular Islam in Amman, Jordan." *Digest of Middle East Studies* 22 (2): 306–30. doi:10.1111/dome.12025.

Trevor-Roper, Hugh. 2010. *History and the Enlightenment*. New Haven, CT: Yale University Press.

Tripp, Charles. 2006. *Islam and the Moral Economy*. Cambridge: Cambridge University Press.

Tyser, C. R., D. G. Demtriades, and Ismail Haqqi Effendi. 1967. *The Mejelle: Being An English Translation of Majallahel-Ahkam-I-Adliya and a Complete Code on Islamic Civil Law*. Lahore: All Pakistan Legal Decisions. Reprint of 1901 edition.

Vikør, Knut. S. 2005. *Between God and the Sultan: A History of Islamic Law*. London: C. Hurst.

Vogel, Frank E., and Samuel L. Hayes. 1998. *Islamic Law and Finance: Religion, Risk, and Return*. Cambridge: Kluwer Law International.

Vohs, Kathleen D., Roy F. Baumeister, and George Loewenstein. 2007. *Do Emotions Help or Hurt Decision Making?: A Hedgefoxian Perspective*. New York: Russell Sage Foundation.

Warde, Ibrahim. 2001. "The Prophet and the Profits: Islamic Finance." *Le Monde*. September 9. http://mondediplo.com/2001/09/09islamicbanking.

———. 2004. "Global Politics, Islamic Finance, and Islamist Politics Before and After 11 September 2001." In *The Politics of Islamic Finance*, edited by Clement M. Henry and Rodney Wilson, 37–62. Edinburgh: Edinburgh University Press.

———. 2009. "The Relevance of Contemporary Islamic Finance." *Berkeley Journal of Middle Eastern & Islamic Law* 2:159.

———. 2010. *Islamic Finance in the Global Economy*. Edinburgh: Edinburgh University Press.

White, Jenny B. 1999. "Islamic Chic." In *Istanbul Between the Global and the Local*, edited by Caglar Keyder. Boulder: Rowman and Littlefield.

———. 2002. "The Islamist Paradox." In *Fragments of Culture: The Everyday of Modern Turkey*, edited by D. Kandiyoti, 191–217. London: I.B. Tauris.

———. 2003. *Islamist Mobilization in Turkey: A Study in Vernacular Politics*. Seattle: University of Washington Press.

Wickham, Carrie R. 2002. *Mobilizing Islam: Religion, Activism, and Political Change in Egypt*. New York: Columbia University Press.

Wiktorowicz, Quintan. 2001. *The Management of Islamic Activism: Salafis, the Muslim Brotherhood, and State Power in Jordan*. Albany: State University of New York Press.

Wilkins, Charles L. 2009. *Forging Urban Solidarities: Ottoman Aleppo 1640–1700*. Leiden: Brill Academic.

Wilson, Rodney. 1987. "Islamic Banking in Jordan. Islamic Banking: The Jordanian Experience." *Arab Law Quarterly* 2 (3): 207–29.

———. 1991. "Islamic Banking: The Jordanian Experience." In *Politics and the Economy in Jordan*, edited by Rodney Wilson, 115. New York: Routledge.

Yom, Sean L. 2009. "Jordan: Ten More Years of Autocracy." *Journal of Democracy* 20 (4): 151–66.

Zaman, Muhammad Qasim. 2002. *The Ulama in Contemporary Islam: Custodians of Change*. Princeton, NJ: Princeton University Press.

Zhang, Li. 2002. "Spatiality and Urban Citizenship in Late Socialist China." *Public Culture* 14 (2): 311–34. doi:10.1215/08992363-14-2-311.

Zubaida, Sami. 1989. *Islam, The People and the State: Essays on Political Ideas and Movements in the Middle East*. London: Routledge.

———. 2003. *Law and Power in the Islamic World*. Library of Modern Middle East Studies. London: I.B. Tauris.

# INDEX

activism, 17–18, 110, 187
adequation, 103–10, 121, 124, 127–29, 132, 154
advanced capitalism, 16, 26, 109, 114
advertisements, 62–64, 125
aesthetics
  middle-class, 7–9, 84
  modern, 17–18, 67, 90, 127
  of the *hijab*, 76, 92–94
affective responses, 62, 156–61, 168, 175, 182
alcohol, 13, 40, 75, 86, 112
  and Islamic banking, 140–41, 145, 154, 175
  in nine investment "screens," 120–22
  during Ramadan, 48, 51–55, 58–59, 73, 75
Allah, 30, 105, 109
  and economic practice, 119, 128, 135–36, 146–50, 155, 162–76
  and the *hijab*, 78–80, 88–89, 93, 193
  and Ramadan, 46–51, 60–61, 66, 69–70
  women's perspectives on, 10
  *See also* adequation
almsgiving, 13, 40, 75, 115. *See also* charity
Amman
  and Christian history, 29–34
  Islamic Revival in, 34–37
  link to ancient Islam, 28–30
  modern middle-class, 37–45
  the "unrecognizable," 22–25
  urban development in, 26–28
amplification of the individual, 160, 182
amplification of the self, 108
ancient Islam, 28–30
anxiety about Islam, 3, 6
Arabian Gulf, 14, 17, 94–95, 99
Arab Spring, 18, 21, 184–86, 188, 189
arranged marriage, 17, 40, 91
authentic Islam
  competing visions for, 181, 190
  and economic practice, 115, 122, 155–57, 170

  in public piety, 21, 47
  and Ramadan, 68
  "too religious" for, 147
  and women's clothing, 80, 95–97, 101–02
  *See also* "real" Islam
authenticity and modernity, 9–11, 22, 132
'awra, 93–94

banking and finance. *See* Islamic banking
bank interest
  debates about, 152–55, 159, 162, 166–67
  Hanafi interpretation of, 112
  prohibitions against, 115–20, 138
  in risk management, 132–34 (*see also* debt and repayment)
  versus *ribah* (profit), 119–20
bank policy, 103, 132
Battle of Badr, 49–50
beards, 18, 36, 92, 146, 149–50
being "Islamic enough," 98, 137, 144, 183
Books@Cafe, 52–54
branding Islam, 193–94

calculative agency
  in economizing Islamic practice, 5–7, 59, 63, 147, 188, 192–93
  and the *hijab*, 77–78, 89, 96–98, 102
  in Islamizing economic practice, 5, 63, 157
capitalism, 16, 26, 114, 117, 193
capitalist, 5, 48, 109, 111, 116
charity, 2, 51, 115, 172, 174, 177. *See also* almsgiving
choice, 11, 17, 20–21, 30–32, 40, 54–55, 69, 70–72, 76, 86–91, 100, 146, 156, 162, 171–72, 175
Christians and Christianity, 194
  family names, 39, 192
  in history of Amman, 29–32, 34, 37

normative ethics
  and the *hijab*, 74–102
  in Islamic banking, 124, 150, 155–58,
    163–68, 191
  during Ramadan, 55–59
  *See also* ethics
normativity, 13, 40, 55, 132, 160

Orientalism, 24, 26. *See also* Western World
orthodoxy, 11–12, 191
  analytic separation of, 150
  in evaluating the Islamic bank, 157,
    162–64, 182
  and the *hijab*, 72, 76, 102
  in Islamic bank employment, 144–45, 147–48
orthopraxy, 11–13, 115, 191
  and the *hijab*, 75, 77, 80, 90, 102
  in the Islamic bank, 132, 144, 148,
    150–58, 161–72, 182
  during Ramadan, 56, 58, 60, 63, 72
  "too much," 147

Palestine, 29, 33, 39
Palestine Liberation Organization, 122
Palestinian-Israeli conflict, 17
Palestinians
  in history of Amman, 31, 34, 36, 39
  in political Islam, 186–87
  refugees, 4, 8, 33, 45, 184–85
  seen as ethnic majority, 7
  women, 16, 83, 90, 170
personal piety, 3, 19, 47, 61–63, 71–72,
  77–80, 150–54
piety. *See* family: role in public piety;
  Islamic piety; neoliberal piety;
  personal piety
pillars of Islam, 13, 50, 56
pornography, 37, 120
post-Islamism, 19–20, 186–88
Postal Savings System, 179–80
prayer, 2, 15–16, 30, 147
  in economic practice, 135–36
  in Islamic banks, 159, 169
  in public piety, 13, 26, 36
  during Ramadan, 51, 54, 61, 69, 73
  Shari'a interpretations of, 111
  in urban life, 26, 36
preachers, 17–18, 20, 36, 193
privacy, 76, 111, 126, 159, 171, 176
profit
  evaluations of, 5
  in Islamic banking, 138, 140–41, 154,
    172, 177–78, 180

prohibition of, 116–19, 120
striving toward, 6, 66
Prophet Mohammed
  in educational curriculum, 15
  and *hijab* ethics, 93–94
  and history of Amman, 29, 31, 32, 35
  invoked in authenticity debates, 9–10,
    16, 30
  and origins of Islamic banking, 110–11,
    113, 117–19, 128, 135–36
  and Ramadan, 46, 69
  as source of "sixth pillar," 56
propriety and impropriety, 47, 145, 156,
  169–70
public life, 36, 45, 55
public norms, 12, 47–48, 55, 56–62, 109
punishment. *See* reward and punishment

Queen Rania, 101
Quraish, 10, 49–50, 72
Qur'an, 2, 13, 15, 85, 190–91
  calculative principles in, 6, 190
  debated on the radio, 16
  and the *hijab*, 93, 96, 101
  and individual responsibility, 11
  and Ramadan, 49–50, 68–70
  revelations to Mohammed, 10
  role in Islamic banking, 110–20, 128,
    135–36, 146, 155, 174, 178
  stories located in Jordan, 29–30
Qur'anic injunctions, 112–13, 116, 122,
  156, 175
Qur'anic recitation, 12, 17, 40, 75, 87, 127

radio, 16–17, 47, 142. *See also* mass media;
  television
Ramadan, 5, 40, 75, 99, 146, 161
  and Books@Cafe, 52–54
  commanding right and forbidding wrong,
    56, 58, 61–62, 72
  commercialization of, 48, 62–68, 72
  competitive pieties in, 72–73
  consumption during, 60–69, 192
  fasting, 3, 12–13, 17–19, 46–63, 51–56
  history of, 49–51
  *iftar*, 59–61, 63–71
  legislation of, 47, 51, 55, 57–58, 62–63
  marketization of, 62–68
  minority experiences of, 56–60
  Night of Power, 49, 68–72
  orthopraxy in, 58, 60–63, 72
  public norms of, 36, 47–48, 55, 56–62
  weddings during, 49, 68–72